THE CHURCH UNDER THATCHER

THE CHURCH UNDER THATCHER

Henry Clark

First published in Great Britain 1993
Society for Promoting Christian Knowledge
Holy Trinity Church
Marylebone Road
London NW1 4DU

British Library Cataloguing-in-Publication Data

A catalogue record for this book is available from the British Library

ISBN   0-281-04658-1

Typesetting by David Mackinder, using *Nota Bene* software
Printed in Great Britain by MacKays of Chatham plc

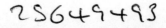

Contents

Preface

I hope that this book will serve two distinct purposes with two different audiences. I hope, first of all, that it will be read by a sizable group of lay persons who have in the past paid relatively little attention to Church social witness – and who will be convinced by this account that paying heed to what the Church has to say on political and economic issues is very much worth their effort. In addition, I hope that the social action leadership of many religious groups, in Britain and elsewhere, will be able to learn something from this study about how to be *effective* in articulating and carrying out the social witness of their denomination. If these two audiences can profit in these ways, I shall feel amply repaid for the five years work I put into researching and writing the book.

I have attempted to avoid sexist language, but I have also eschewed the repetition of clumsy constructions such as 'he or she' and 'his or her.' Instead, I sometimes use the masculine pronoun, while at other times I use the female.

There is no way for me to mention all of the people and institutions which have helped me carry out this project, or to thank them as much as they deserve. The most important thing to be said in this connection is that dozens of persons, most of them involved in one way or another with the social action leadership of the Church of England, were exceedingly generous with their time and their counsel – and I find their generosity and their kindness all the more remarkable in view of the fact that I was to almost all of them a stranger from another country, a visitor who really had no claim on them and nothing tangible to give in return. Their helpfulness and graciousness made my work a pleasure as well as a challenge. Special thanks are due to Chris Beales and Graham Howes: the former provided me with an office in Church House and access to the files of the Industrial and Economic Affairs Committee of the Board for Social Responsibility; the latter gave me invaluable bibliographical guidance and did a meticulous reading of the first draft of the manuscript. Others who were particularly helpful in telling me what to read, whom to see and how to make sense of the data were Ronald Preston, John Atherton, Paul Brett, Peter Sedgwick, Giles Ecclestone, Tony Dyson, Pat Dearnley, Margaret Jeffrey, John Gladwin, David Skidmore, Alan Suggate, Mike Atkinson, Kenneth Leech, Charles Elliott, Digby Anderson, John Habgood and Eric James, Paul Abrecht, George Moyser and Richard O'Brien. I am also grateful to the University of Southern California for the sabbatical leave and travel funds which made it possible for me to spend seven months in Britain in 1988, and to make two return trips in 1990 and 1991 to gather additional information and interview important contacts there.

Henry Clark
Los Angeles, 1992

1

'Open Acrimony':
The Established Church vs Thatcherism

During the nineteenth and twentieth centuries a new form of 'social Christianity' arose in Europe and North America. Its concept of the ends towards which church people should strive expanded to include a much more detailed and complete notion of human welfare and fulfilment in this life, here and now, and its concept of appropriate means expanded to include a much greater emphasis on secular institutions – particularly on 'the positive role of the state.' To lay exclusive stress upon personal salvation in the world to come was now seen as a tragic distortion of the meaning of the faith. In the past, the social outreach of the Church had been expressed in various charitable services to the poor, the sick, the bereaved and all who were in some sense 'needy.' Now this traditional *pastoral* ministry was supplemented by a *prophetic* ministry which was expressed in organized attempts to influence social policy in the dominant institutions of society. In the words of a famous book by Walter Rauschenbusch, the greatest American exponent of the social gospel, the challenge to which Christians in the modern era should address themselves was said to be that of 'Christianizing the social order.' To call this new social witness of the Church 'prophetic' was to emphasize its affinity with the ethical critique of the powers that be which Jesus and the social prophets of the Old Testament had proclaimed.

The Church of England has played an extremely significant role in the rise of social Christianity; indeed, a prominent official of the World Council of Churches, Paul Abrecht, has declared that the two most effective ecclesiastical social action groups operating in the world today are the Roman Catholic bishops of the USA and the Board for Social Responsibility of the Church of England (hereafter, BSR).[1] But this proud heritage has been challenged in the past decade and a half by the rise of Thatcherism. The challenge has been recognized and articulated by Giles Ecclestone, who served for ten years as the General Secretary of the BSR. In 1985, commenting on the notion of the established Church as 'the conscience of the nation,' Ecclestone wrote:

> I do not think that the Churches as institutions in any significant sense lead moral thinking in society. It is however unduly simplified to say that they are merely tagging along behind. I believe that what happens is that the Churches participate in shifts of thinking and feeling, contributing, for those influenced by religious categories, their own formulations in terms of Scripture and tradition of the issues and the choices, while pursuing in the main the same specific and finite objectives as those uninfluenced by the Churches. . . . The question which is of more than academic interest is whether, in a colder social climate, increasingly influenced by moral conservatism and a punitive attitude to social failures of all

kinds (including the unemployed), the Churches will reflect this latest shift in their attitudes and policies.[2]

Ecclestone's question is all the more sobering in the context of Abrecht's tribute, for he seems to be asking whether or not the Church of England will remain faithful to the teachings which it has put forth during the past 150 years. Now that Thatcherism and the New Right have created a two-nations policy and a moral climate in which a large percentage of the population feels gleefully *right* about its acquisitive individualism, will the Church retreat from the political fray or muffle its prophetic voice?

This book provides an answer to that question, for it is an examination of what the Church of England said and did on issues of economic justice during the Thatcher era. It tells the story of the dramatic clash between the government and an established Church which until recently was often referred to (rather derisively) as 'the Tory Party at prayer.' It explains how the rise of social Christianity manifested itself in Anglican thought and practice, changing the Church of England from a relatively docile supporter of the established order to a resolute foe of injustice. It documents the contribution of religious thinkers to the celebrated 'post-war consensus' in social philosophy which led to the establishment of the welfare state in Britain, and it describes the role of the Church in defending the values represented in this consensus against the assaults of Thatcherism.

There was a time, of course, when the Tories were directed by what is often referred to as its 'Christian patrician' wing; indeed, both Harold Macmillan and Edward Heath were men of this stripe. But the Tory insurgents represented by Margaret Thatcher turned their backs on this ingredient of *noblesse oblige* in the history of the Conservative Party, attempting to replace it with 'conviction politics' that featured excessive reliance on monetarism and a one-sided glorification of 'enterprise culture.' It was inevitable, then, that the relationship between the Church of England and the new Tory leadership would be marked by 'open acrimony'[3] – and this was all the more true because of the fact that Mrs Thatcher took religion very seriously and was motivated by a specifically religious concept of her mission as prime minister.

The Rise of the Welfare State

Scholars agree that the welfare state came into being as a result of three main developments. The first was the result of advances in social science (particularly Keynesianism, most especially Keynesian doctrine as assimilated into the thinking of a new generation of political leaders such as Beveridge and Macmillan). The second was the appearance of a new social philosophy which stressed individual rights and denounced the extremes of class stratification and economic inequality which had been more or less accepted for centuries in most European countries before the nineteenth century. The third was the historical experience of the British people in the twentieth century, particularly the hardships of the Great Depression and the frightening but exhilarating challenges of the Second World War.

The importance of the first factor is obvious; it created an expectation – in terms of which all governments in the industrial world are measured – that nation states are no longer in the grip of a pitiless *fortuna* which dooms them to the deprivations and dislocations of boom-and-bust economic cycles, but can manage their economic affairs in such a way as to maximize achievement of national goals. The second factor will be discussed at some length in the first part of the following chapter, for it

was absolutely crucial in defining the concept of Christian social witness in contemporary Anglicanism. What I want to emphasize here is the third factor; namely,
the psycho-social impact of 'the long weekend between the wars' and of the rigours
of British life during the Second World War.

Working-class people experienced the Great Depression as being almost as savage
and heartless as the trench warfare of the Great War.[4] On the eve of the war with
Nazi Germany, millions of Britons were filled with resentment about the sufferings
they were being forced to endure as a result of unemployment and class inequity,
and very much in the mood to demand substantial reforms. Thus the wartime experience between 1939 and 1945 was critical. The anguish of seeing themselves as a
beleaguered nation which just barely escaped defeat and occupation made an
indelible impression upon the mind and spirit of the British people. Because of the
war, 'a new sense of national community and interdependence was experienced, and
this fellowship and mutual care in the light of a common purpose was found to be
good.'[5] Disillusionment with capitalism was accompanied by a new conviction that a
warfare state capable of mobilizing a people's resources for military activities could
also be a welfare state 'capable of acting on behalf of the whole community, and
[thus] the whole understanding of the scope of government was enlarged along with
a conviction of the beneficence of state action.'[6] This widely held belief that 'the
state is an effective guardian of the common good and should be the principal
provider of welfare'[7] was instrumental in the election of a Labour government just
after the war, and in its rapid installation of a host of measures designed to implement the Beveridge Plan and transform Britain into a modern welfare state.

The war was also responsible for an infusion of new blood into the aristocratic
elites who traditionally assumed the responsibilities of governance. When the new
economic doctrines of John Maynard Keynes first appeared in the 1920s and 1930s,
they attracted immediate support from a number of aspiring young statesmen who
began to popularize the doctrines and mobilize support for social policies based upon
them. Not the least among these was Harold Macmillan, whose *The Next Five Years*
(1935) and *The Middle Way* (1938) exerted considerable influence on the thinking of
ordinary citizens (and even gave a name – 'middle opinion') to those who gathered
under the Keynesian banner. The Second World War thrust many of these men into
government service, where they had an opportunity to implement their ideas in public policy: 'A whole series of younger economists and academics [which included
Beveridge and Macmillan as well as Keynes] scattered throughout wartime
Whitehall, bringing with them what Keith Middlemas calls "the sedimentary
intellectual deposits" laid down in the pre-war debates.'[8]

Moreover, the support of working people was crucial, and it was obtained on the
basis of an intra-class social contract which Beveridge made explicit in a speech
given to a union audience as early as 1940. He declared: 'If our movement and our
class rise with all their energy now and save the people of this country from disaster,
the country will always turn to the people that saved them.'[9] As Nicholas Deakin
comments, 'A bargain had been struck; the unions had been asked to play a full part
in the war effort and they were entitled to their share of the rewards of victory.'[10] In
sum:

> The bridge that linked all these separate positions [being articulated by politi-
> cal spokespersons during the last years of the war] was the concept of the Welfare
> State, accepted by the victorious end of the war at every level of society as
> expressing 'something greater than a simple description of the activities of
> government in respect of one area of its activities. It expressed the desire for a

more socially just, more materially equal, more truly democratic society, in short, everything that prewar society had not been.'[11]

The Decline of the Welfare State

But the welfare state began to run into grave difficulties soon after it was established, and the consensus on values which legitimated it began to crumble. The three most important elements in its decline are these: (1) the decline of the British economy occasioned by deindustrialization, (2) the emergence of the 'New Right' and (3) the dominance of the Thatcherite wing of the Conservative Party.

Deindustrialization

The consequences of deindustrialization are revealed in a glance at the statistics concerning relative growth and per capita wealth in the period from 1950 to 1973. In the 1950s, for example, Britain averaged only 2.5% increase in GNP while the corresponding figure for the industrialized world was 4%, and for West Germany, 5%. The pattern in the 1960s was similar (Britain 3.75% vs 5.5% for the industrialized world), and over the whole long boom period from 1950 to 1973 it was 3% for Britain vs 9.7% for Japan, 6% for Germany and 5.1% for France. Peter Jenkins sums up his survey of 'steep relative decline' by observing that there is no record in recent history of 'any other power falling behind at such startling speed,' and by pointing out that after 1973 Britain lost even her own domestic markets to foreign competition: 'By 1983 Britain, once the proverbial workshop of the world, had become for the first time since the Industrial Revolution a net importer of manufactured goods.'[12] Even worse, he argues, is the decline in 'underlying economic performance' as measured by productivity (output per head) and 'the lag in *new* manufacturing investment: in the 1970s, Japan and Germany invested about twice what Britain did, and other industrial nations invested substantially more.' The same is true of 'the factors which affect future performance – investment, research and development, applications of technology, education and training, management science, and so on.'[13]

The psychological shock of deindustrialization was felt with special ferocity by those who were particularly proud of the welfare state and its underlying moral consensus. As the section on 'Historical Factors' of a BSR publication on *Power-Sharing in Industry* observes:

> There was no counterpart to the 'New Deal' of America, which achieved so much and which convinced Americans that those in authority both cared and were capable of initiating policies that set the wheels of industry in motion after the traumatic effects of the Great Depression.
>
> Not till Ernest Bevin as Minister of Labour in the wartime coalition spearheaded thought about post-war problems did a blue-print emerge that was enshrined in the Beveridge report. Thus at a time when we were financially crippled and when the whole of British industry was in desperate need of modernisation the available resources were diverted to the equally essential need for social change. The result has been to produce a health system that has no parallel in the world, a social security system that is beyond the dreams of planners between the wars. But it has been achieved at a price and it may be that virtual

destruction of German and Japanese industry masked the price tag for too long. It is only now as the country faces the severest crisis since the war with many industries uncompetitive in the international market that stark reality . . . is being unfolded. The shock could be the greater because the social system developed since the war has given the possibly ill-founded impression of greater security.[14]

The facts about industrial decline are more certain than the psycho-cultural reasons sometimes advanced to explain it. But surely some attention must be given to Martin J. Wiener's provocative (although not universally accepted) theory regarding the ambivalence of upper-class Victorian opinion towards technology and trade. In *English Culture and the Decline of the Industrial Spirit 1850–1980*, Wiener assembles numerous quotations from writers such as Carlyle, Ruskin and Arnold in support of his thesis that the 'creeping deindustrialization' which gradually destroyed the technological and economic well-being of what was once the mightiest industrial power on earth was caused, to a large extent, by the foolishness of the culture-bearers.[15] The notion of 'Englishness' and the image of 'the British gentleman' propagated among the intelligentsia in the nineteenth century (and disseminated through the public schools and universities under their control) contributed mightily to the unfortunate 'gentrification of the industrialist,' which discouraged the brightest youth from undertaking careers in industry, and made those who did so feel woefully inferior and apologetic about their choice and the work in which they were immersed.[16] Corelli Barnett contends that the stereotyped 'cult of chivalry' propounded in the poetry of Tennyson, the art of the Pre-Raphaelites, and the imperial notion of 'the white man's burden' produced a disdain for money (and, more pervasively, for *winning*) which

> supplied a key element in the character of the twentieth-century British Establishment as a whole; and, in the form of upper-middle-class politicians and intelligentsia motivated by a wish to come to the help of those less fortunate than themselves, it was especially strong in the 'enlightened' wing of that Establishment.[17]

I believe it is important to be aware of these alleged cultural roots of deindustrialization, for surely (as the analysis of Thatcherism later in this chapter tends to confirm) resentment against the presumed disdain of the intellectuals is one powerful ingredient in the emotional intensity of the challenge to the post-war consensus mounted by the New Right. Neoconservatives feel justified in denouncing proponents of the welfare state for two egregious errors: for having been irresponsibly extravagant in their distribution of economic benefits (beyond the nation's capacity to provide), and for having paid far too little attention to the importance of the creation of wealth (indeed, for having demeaned the character and belittled the efforts of those who busied themselves in this essential undertaking). Thus New Right conservatives may understandably feel a sense of righteous indignation towards their opponents, and they may find themselves easily persuaded by the superficially plausible and psychologically attractive arguments of those who proclaim that self-reliant hard work in an unshackled free market which rewards merit and punishes sloth is the *only* path to renewed prosperity and self-respect for the British populace.

The New Right

The New Right is a social philosophy which attempts to explain why certain economic policies are necessary and right, and Thatcherism is a political movement – an 'authoritarian populism,'[18] – within a major political party. The two entities are not identical, and the Conservative Party of Britain is not synonymous with either. But they all feed on each other, and they are all a part of the challenge to Christian social thought and praxis which has arisen in the Thatcher era. As religious leaders have learned during the past decade, they must be able to respond to New Right attacks with fresh arguments if they are to obtain a fair hearing for the Church's social message. Church leaders have found, for example, that traditional appeals to 'compassion' or 'justice' can be discounted in the light of certain New Right dicta which give new definitions to many familiar words or concepts and transvalue many cherished ideals. The following summary of the tenets of New Right thinking gives a number of salient examples:[19]

1. Poverty must be measured in absolute quantitative terms, not at all in psychological terms which venture into 'subjective' notions such as 'relative deprivation.' (When this argument is accompanied by continual redefinitions of the poverty line – a numerical figure which has been redefined some *twenty-three* [23!] times during the Thatcher administration, it is easy to create the impression that very few people are really poor.)

2. Freedom is *the* supreme human and social value, and it is misleading to say that lack of money constitutes lack of freedom. (A poor person in a politically free society is just a free person who has not yet used his freedom to win the economic well-being he can attain if he thinks and works hard enough.)

3. The laws of the market are analogous to the laws of physics; they cannot be contravened by human action, and the attempt to do so is misguided and bound to be futile. (Thus policy-makers in industry cannot be held accountable for their decisions; the contention that 'economic rationality made me do it' cannot be questioned, let alone refuted.)

4. There is no *injustice* without malicious intent on the part of some evildoer. (Thus people who end up at the bottom of the pile because of the inexorable workings of the market may be regarded as 'unfortunate,' but they cannot be regarded as 'victims of injustice.')

5. Those who exhibit extraordinary merit rise to the top, and they deserve the handsome rewards they get. (It *is* unjust to deny them these rewards in full measure, and those who endeavour to make laws which accomplish this wicked purpose are motivated by resentment and ill-will.)

6. It is appropriate that those who are losers in the market game should be stigmatized by public disapproval, for only if driven to desperation will the best of them do whatever they must to become winners. (The Church, and individual Christians, should not be unduly rigorous in dispensing charitable benefits which alleviate misery and override stigma – but it is important that society's 'official' posture be one of stern disapproval. To dispense charitable relief indiscriminately, or to let it be known ahead of time that the bite of stigma is less cruel than its bark, is 'the kindness that kills.')

Thatcherism

Of course, the school of thought known as political economy achieved remarkable heights of virulence in the nineteenth century, and Hayek has been around for almost fifty years (Friedman for about twenty-five). What is decisive for Britain is not the resurgence of the nineteenth-century ideology in a slightly new form with a new tag, but rather the arrival of Margaret Thatcher and the triumph of her wing of the Conservative Party.

There are four aspects of what Peter Jenkins calls 'Mrs Thatcher's Revolution' which are particularly important: its 'fatal impacts' on distributive justice in the economic realm; its political implications; its attack upon the counter-culture of the 1960s; and its aspirations to be a *religious crusade*.

Economic Implications

The heart of Thatcherism is its determination to undermine the welfare state by reverting to a nineteenth-century reliance upon *laissez-faire* economic policies. Now, it must be admitted that Thatcherism took off somewhat more slowly and cautiously than the notion of 'the politics of conviction' might suggest. This is probably a function of the political necessities of the early months: the victorious Thatcher wing of the Conservative Party had to show that 'there really wasn't anything for Heathites and Thatcherites to disagree about.' It may also be related to the fact that the British public still believes in the crucial welfare state services and is willing to be taxed to support them:

> The majority remained in favour of the Welfare State. Consistently more people opted for more social spending than for cuts in their taxes, not – we may suspect – on strictly instrumental grounds or because they did not want their taxes cut, but because it seemed the decent thing to say, a way of casting a vote of confidence in an aspect of their society in which they felt pride, or had done and wanted to.

Given this sort of sentiment as registered in opinion polls, it is not surprising that 'Parliament flinched' on dismantling the welfare state in the early 1980s.[20]

Even so, the first goal of Thatcherism's two-pronged attack upon previous thought and practice is its aggressive assault on the institutional policies and programmes of social democracy. The implications of the slogan 'free market, strong government' were soon made clear, for a number of state-owned enterprises were privatized, and there was a virtual crusade against trade unions and other structures, laws or habitual administrative practices which were construed as exerting a serious restraint on private investment in profitable enterprise.[21] What is sometimes less obvious is the systematic attempt made by Mrs Thatcher's government to eliminate effective centres of power and political initiative which might interfere with its plans.

Political Implications

Opponents of the Thatcher government contend that there is now a hardline attitude on the part of law enforcement officials which views violations of civil liberties as a small price to pay for the preservation of order. *Rights*, the journal of the National Council for Civil Liberties, has charged that 'hundreds of peaceful processions were banned in [the early months of the decade of the 1980s]' and it contends that 'freedom of assembly is now at the mercy of the Home Secretary.'

This trend is reinforced by what most informed citizens regard as extremely sympathetic and/or cleverly manipulated mass media:

By 1985 the media had been sucked into reflecting government propaganda rather than facts, so much so that the BBC reversed film which had been taken when mounted police attacked miners at Orgreave during the miners' strike, in order to make the victims appear guilty of the first offence. Gareth Pierce, writing in the *Guardian* on 12 August 1985, drew a stark parallel between the capacity for revulsion at state violence in the past, when violence was more commonplace, and the attitude of the media in the present day. . . . Not surprisingly it was revealed in 1985 that the BBC had been engaged in secret vetting of the political opinions and affiliations of its journalists and producers, in conjunction with MI5.[22]

Much controversy has also attended the launching of the National Security Law. It makes government secrecy and partisan cover-ups alarmingly easy by banning the so-called 'public interest defence.' Nothing which can be construed *by the government* as affecting national security can be revealed or criticized in public, and anyone who dares to do so will not be allowed to argue that his actions were taken in order to protect the public against something improper or damaging being done by a government agency or government officials.[23]

Most devastating of all, in the minds of those who believe in grass-roots democracy, is the Thatcher government's attack on local governments (which are often, not coincidentally, composed of officials elected by strong Labour constituencies). By means of a series of administrative decisions, the central government has abolished certain structures of local government and emasculated others by putting restrictions on their ability to levy local taxes according to their understanding of local capacities and needs. The effect is to cripple their ability to provide many services. Yet it is the local council which gets the blame for declining services or for new taxes designed to fill the gap left by withdrawal of national funds.[24] The authors of a book entitled *Democracy in Crisis: The Town Halls Respond* summarize the attack in these words:

> Central government was restricting local public services and their contribution to economic and social life in those parts of Britain which were 'underdeveloping,' in much the same way as the International Monetary Fund and the world financial community have constantly demanded reductions in essential investment in 'underdeveloped' countries.
>
> Chaos followed this use of financial power for political ends, in one case at the international level, in the other nationally. The only people who really gained were the banks and the financial interests, free to recoup profit from future interest paid on the money lent to councils, thus adding to the long-term burden on people in areas least able to pay. . . . Those councils which cut and trimmed, accepting the mantle of 'responsible good housekeepers' which the government placed on them, were politically responsible for helping to create a climate in which national policy was less likely to change as worsening services discredited collective provision.[25]

*   *   *

We may summarize our discussion of these first two criticisms of Thatcherism by emphasizing two especially important points. The first has to do with the financial aspects of government policy; the second, with the political implications of the Thatcher revolution.

There is widespread agreement among expert analysts that budgetary pressures are *not* sufficiently grave to make the continuing operation of the welfare state in Britain impossible. The financial crisis which initially fuelled the neoconservative assault on the welfare state has eased considerably, and 'present demographic and economic trends [make it clear that] the cost of providing benefits and services at the level of the mid-1980s is unlikely to go beyond the country's capacity to afford.'[26]

It is hardly surprising, then, that many old-style Tories are absolutely horrified at the way in which hard-core Thatcherites have abandoned the sense of *noblesse oblige* once characteristic of upper-class Christians and of many Conservatives, religious or nonreligious.[27] Many sources speak of the racism, the 'naked class warfare' and the 'incipient fascism' of the Thatcherites. As a prominent British economist has observed:

To argue for ever greater cuts in welfare (always other people's, of course) and for greater tax concessions to the well-paid (including oneself) may have a crazy market rationale. But it is also selfishness masquerading as truth. The society it would create is a profoundly immoral one, built on greed and inequality, on suffering and deprivation. Selfish people can invest abroad. The North-East can be turned into an industrial wasteland. Inaction can be covered by platitude and rhetoric. The poor can be blamed for their own poverty. The desperate can be taught patience by those too powerful to have to wait. But the bankruptcy of the philosophy which underpins all that cannot be denied.[28]

In the words of an experienced civil servant who is now a highly regarded BSR consultant:

I do not believe that Mrs Thatcher wants to be a dictator, nor do I believe that the people around her are planning some kind of totalitarian conspiracy which they seek to impose upon our unsuspecting democracy. But if the people currently in power *were* of that sort, and if they really *did* want to install a facist regime, they would do exactly what they have been doing ever since they got control of the reins of government![29]

Attack on the Counter-Culture

The third part of the Thatcherite agenda has to do with cultural counter-revolution. From the very beginning, Margaret Thatcher's claim to be a politician of conviction meant that she was determined to *change the cultural ethos* of the nation. As early as 1977, the Conservative Party's unpublished position paper called 'Stepping Stones' spoke of the New Right's conviction that it was crucial to bring about 'a change in public attitudes.'[30]

Another logical implication of this fundamental stance was its abhorrence of, and subsequent attack upon, the values of the counter-culture, especially its romantic view of revolution. In the words of Stuart Hall, the counter-culture came to be seen as

a moral conspiracy against the State; no longer simply getting and spending, clothes and records, fun and games – but drugs, crime, the withdrawal from work, rampant sex, promiscuity, perversion, pornography, anarchy, libertinism and violence. It became a source of moral-political pollution, spreading its infection in its every form; the conspiracy to rebel. In a profound sense, the dominant culture – face to face with this spectacle – felt itself out of control.[31]

And this, of course, is why what Britain needed (in Mrs Thatcher's view), was nothing less than a *new religion*! Since this was an era of new hopes,

> A new religion was necessary, for one hope can only be knocked on the head by another. The money religion offered a means of social redemption provided people could be persuaded that the laws of economics were written in heaven and not the Treasury. . . . And so the Thatcher Government promised more by promising less. Expectations must be lowered, the satisfaction of wants post-poned, hope contained. Yet a hundred years of decline was to be arrested and reversed! How? By a cultural counter-revolution, a transformation of attitudes, Decline, it seems, *was* at heart a moral issue.[32]

Thatcherism as a Religious Crusade

The religious dimension of Thatcherism deserves careful analysis. Its point of depar-ture is a recognition of the fact that Margaret Thatcher really *cares* about religion, and *reads and thinks* about it! This means that her highly publicized 'Sermon on the Mound' in May 1988, at the convocation of the Church of Scotland in Edinburgh, is worthy of special attention – and it also means that the thinking of the conservative faction of the Church of England which tends to agree with Mrs Thatcher on many important points, and to welcome her policy initiatives, must be attended to with special care.

Disagreement between the established Church and the Thatcher government began to manifest itself as soon as she took office. This conflict broke out in an especially dramatic way at the time of the Falklands Memorial Service in 1982, when the Prime Minister was grievously offended by the Church's refusal to baptize the nation's military action in an unqualified manner and to make the service a tri-umphant victory celebration. (See Chapter 5.) But the conflict arose most often in regard to economic issues, and the most bellicose Tories endeavoured to dismiss whatever the Church of England said on these matters as Marxist rubbish (which was doubly infuriating to Thatcherites because, in their eyes, it constituted a betrayal of religion's proper message concerning law, order and personal morality; that is, a betrayal of the Church's proper role as a force for social cohesion which legitimates what the state does and what the society is).

The new antagonism between Church and state had a special edge because, ironi-cally, Margaret Thatcher takes religion more seriously than most political leaders, and she *studies* religion (e.g., through reading the Old Testament from beginning to end during her term at Number 10 Downing Street!). As Hugo Young, one of her most authoritative biographers, puts it, the relationship between her government and the Church of England 'engaged the personal attention of Mrs Thatcher more closely than that of any of her predecessors, [for] she thought about religious questions more than most prime ministers have publicly admitted doing.'[33]

The trouble is (from the standpoint of today's ecclesiastical vanguard), her understanding of Christianity is that of a *highly* individualistic evangelical Meth-odism in which the sum and substance of religion is seen as personal salvation and energetic self-discipline leading to self-reliance and, ideally, to self-sufficiency. She loves to quote the hymn 'I Vow to Thee, My Country,' which says, 'Soul by soul and silently her shining bounds increase, and her ways are ways of gentleness and all her paths are peace.' Her inference ('triumphantly insisted,' according to Young!) is this: 'There is the message – soul by soul.'[34] As early as 1976 she gave voice to this emphasis on individual striving in a speech to the Greater London Young Conservatives which extolled the moral importance of freedom. Claiming that 'welfarism and moral decay go hand in hand' because reliance on the state tends to deny a person's nature as 'a moral being . . . who exercises his own judgment in choice on matters great and small,' she exalts 'responsibility to self, family, firm, community, country, God. She would put it in that order of ascent, for self-regard was the fount of all virtue; what else could have been meant by the injunction, "Love thy neighbor as *thyself*"?'[35] As journalist Peter Jenkins wryly observed, 'Her moral agenda [in this speech] could have been written on a sampler.'[36]

Mrs Thatcher's interpretation of Christianity as an earnest cultivation of the bourgeois virtues was reaffirmed and made even more explicit in the aforementioned May 1988 speech in Edinburgh which was immediately dubbed 'The Sermon on the Mound.' As a remarkable assessment of this talk by Jonathan Raban points out, its real target was the bishops of the Church of England, for 'never since the English Revolution had there been such open acrimony between the government and the established church.'[37] It asserts that 'Christianity is about spiritual redemption, not social reform' and it contrasts what Mrs Thatcher sees as the conventional work-and-family values of the common people with the 'airy-fairy concepts' of idealistic do-gooders (e.g., concepts such as 'society,' which Mrs Thatcher regards as a meaningless abstraction). Raban interprets the speech's use of terms such as 'mercy' and 'succour' as an indication of the Prime Minister's 'minimal terms' conception of the welfare 'safety net' for those in desperate economic straits, and he finds in her remarks on 'tolerance' a severely conditioned willingness to share England's turf only with those outsiders who will become assimilated to the accustomed British life-style and fit in with its existing requirements of utility and respectability. He concludes: 'It is an audacious piece of work. This is the language of power, of parliamentary majority translated into unimpeded action and unimpeded words; a language bereft of concessions, as it is bereft of all the usual strategies of persuasive argument.'[38]

The Sermon on the Mound was of a piece with her vehement rejection of the recent social witness of the Anglican Church and her truly fervent dislike of the bishops who 'command the headlines with utterances running wholly against the new political orthodoxy, not to mention old and, as most Tories thought, eternal theological truths.'[39] And when these same bishops (notably David Jenkins, the Bishop of Durham) have the gall to accuse her government of 'not caring' about poverty and unemployment, or to call for unilateral nuclear disarmament, or to reject her concept of Christianity as 'a disgraceful travesty of the gospel,'[40] it is easy for the Prime Minister to feel not only right but *righteous* about her conclusion that 'whether on the cities or the Bomb, the Archbishop [of Canterbury] and his friends were entirely unreliable acolytes.'[41]

Needless to say, the conflict between the recent leadership of the Church and the government has tended to generate a crisis of confidence within the Church. More traditional elements of the Anglican communion which are not especially happy about the rise of social Christianity have taken the occasion to voice their protests and their demand for a return to doctrinal or liturgical purity, and to express their right to a stronger voice in shaping the policies of the ecclesiastical institution. The current middle-of-the-road 'liberal' leadership is faced, then, with a challenge to its wisdom and authority, a challenge to which it must respond by articulating a more convincing argument for the positions it has taken and the actions it has pursued. Edward Norman accuses the mainstream leadership of the Church of having sold out to a bland middle-class secularism which betrays the true nature of biblical faith.[42] The sociologist David Martin echoes this complaint, contending that there is no distinguishable difference, now, between the staff personnel of the Church of England and any other interest-group bureaucracy striving for essentially narrow organizational ends.[43] And Gareth Bennett, the writer of a controversial preface to *Crockford's* directory of clergy, who took his own life in the wake of the furore caused by his essay, bemoans what he calls the 'liberal ascendancy' which controls the ecclesiastical hierarchy and perpetuates itself through an incestuous process of selecting new bishops. For Bennett, the General Synod is 'an essentially reactive body' which leaves the real power in the hands of the Church House bureaucracy. The liberal ascendancy is actually engaged in a sort of conspiracy to override both tradition and the feelings of most ordinary Anglican parishioners.[44] Says Bennett: 'Deep in the liberal mind is a conviction that with a little procrastination and an application of pastoral "sensitivity" the changes which they propose can be forced through.'[45]

This book is an investigation of one aspect of this fascinating story. It chronicles the efforts made by the social action leadership of the Church of England to carry out a faithful and effective social witness on issues of economic justice, and to formulate a rationale for this witness which increases comprehension and support within the household of faith, and which also earns greater respect and acceptance for the Church's stance on the issues in the nation as a whole. This study will be of particular interest to church people throughout the modern world, most particularly church leaders, but it should also be of compelling interest to reflective citizens of any philosophical or religious persuasion who care about building a decent society. I believe – and hope – that everyone who reads this book will come away with a new respect for the social witness of the Church of England, and a new conviction that what it has to say about social problems is worthy of being studied and pondered seriously.

The Analytical Categories and the Thrust of the Argument

It is important at the outset to define the scope of this study and the principal categories of analysis to be employed in it. The crucial aspects of such a statement can be covered in a single sentence, the italicized words of which will then be explained: 'This book is a study of efforts made *during the Thatcher era* by *the Church of England* to *influence social policy at the national level* on issues of *economic justice*.'[46]

Now, as to the meaning of each specific item in the sentence:

1. The Thatcher era is the period from 1975 to 1990. We begin a little earlier than the actual date of Mrs Thatcher's succession to the office of Prime Minister, but that actually has two advantages: first, the Thatcher faction was already achieving control of the Conservative Party well before 1979, and the ideas on which it fed were already coming into vogue; moreover, some of the most important church documents on economic affairs were published during the second half of the decade of the 1970s.

2. As noted above, the Church of England is by no means a monolithic organization. The factionalism to which we have referred results from the 'great diversity of belief in all churches,'[47] especially the 'diversity of fundamental Christian worldviews within [the Anglican communion].'[48] Furthermore, 'the contemporary Church of England is pluralist in its approaches to ethics and to social and political issues.'[49] Even so, by citing documents published by official church agencies reporting on official proceedings, this study serves to highlight what is said and done by

the mainstream leadership of the denomination. From time to time, criticisms or alternative points of view articulated by representatives of dissenting Anglican opinion will be reported – but it should be clear that when we speak of 'the social witness of the Church of England on economic issues,' we shall be speaking for the most part about the position taken by the reigning General Synod, its Board for Social Responsibility (BSR), the bishops and their appointees in local churches and diocesan agencies, and/or to the writings of theologians and social scientists to whom this leadership looks for information and advice. Also included are writings published in the name of Industrial Mission, a movement which is to some extent ecumenical in reality as well as in theory, but one which is very heavily Anglican in numbers, financial support and theological inspiration.[50] To phrase it in the terms which will be explained and utilized in Chapter 5, we shall attempt to describe and assess three principal types of activity carried out by the Church of England: the 'ordinary' social witness which is generated by the routinized (regularized) operations of the BSR, the 'extraordinary' initiatives taken by the bishops, and the 'specialized' work of Industrial Mission. The term 'social action leadership' is used throughout to refer to the staff persons, clergy, academic professionals and lay activists who are charged with the special responsibility of articulating the Church's social witness and communicating it to Anglicans and the British people. (Readers who are completely unfamiliar with the Board for Social Responsibility and Industrial Mission may want to scan the description of their activities in Chapter 5 before reading about their output in Chapters 3 and 4.)

3. As the very first paragraph of the book points out, its focus is on *prophetic* social witness; i.e., the Church of England's endeavours to work through political channels to influence what policy-makers in government, industry and other major institutions decide to strive to accomplish in the organizational instruments under their control. This is not to disparage the more traditional pastoral ministry of the Church, which performs praiseworthy acts of charity in binding up the wounds of the economically disadvantaged. But our *main* interest is not in *relief* or *revolution*, but in *reform* of the way that 'business as usual' is carried out in secular institutions. In this connection, some attention is also given to *rehabilitation* and church *renewal* as indirect or instrumental reform activities. (This typology is explained in Chapter 5.)

Another important implication of the focus on national policy is that the bulk of the discussion in Chapter 3 will be centred on the Church of England's stance regarding the social market economy and the welfare state.

4. The major focus of this study is on pronouncements and programmes initiated by national leaders in national structures. If, however, the work being undertaken in a metropolitan area, or at the diocesan level, constitutes a particularly noteworthy implementation of national denominational intent, it will of course be described and analysed in some detail.

5. Since practically every social problem has an economic dimension, it is somewhat artificial to exclude a number of high visibility issues from consideration. But if this is to be a useful commentary on questions of productivity, distributive justice, unemployment and the role of mega-institutions such as government and business in the delivery of welfare services to the poor and the disadvantaged, it cannot attempt to deal with all of the political, sociological, psychological and theological concerns which are relevant. Environmental protection will be included because not to do so would be to perpetuate a serious shortcoming of all too many religious statements on economic issues throughout most of the past six decades – and it is now apparent

that policies on economic growth and productivity simply cannot be responsibly analysed without reference to ecological factors such as sustainability and environmental damage. Moreover, the study will also cover another concern which previous studies have tended to treat as an 'externality,' namely, the global dimensions of economic justice.

2

The Conviction Politics of the Church

The historical emergence of social Christianity in the Church of England is a fascinating story in itself. In order to understand the clash between the Church and Thatcherism, one must understand both the legacy of Anglican social thought which has developed in the past 150 years and the most important theories concerning exactly how the Church ought to speak out on social issues. After examining these aspects of the Church of England's conviction politics, this chapter will conclude with a statement of the author's point of view on the proper rationale for Christian social witness and on the goals which it ought to pursue.

Developments in Social Philosophy

The founding of the welfare state in Great Britain owed a great deal to social science and its theories regarding the *means* which might be used to construct a good society (e.g., Keynesianism). But the post-war consensus underlying its array of social programmes could not have been forged without new currents of thought in social philosophy which called for new *ends*. Many of the ideas incorporated into the consensus were theological ideas emerging from nineteenth- and twentieth-century Anglican social thought; some were the fruit of a quasi-religious 'ethical socialist' tradition which began as early as the sixteenth century. Present-day pronouncements of the Church of England owe a great deal to both schools of thought and to the kinds of political activity they inspired.

English Ethical Socialism

What A. H. Halsey and Norman Dennis call 'English ethical socialism' begins with More's *Utopia* and extends through the Christian moralizing of William Cobbett (1763–1835), the Aristotelian idealism of L. T. Hobhouse (1864–1929), the eccentric vision of George Orwell (1903–1950), the sociological doctrine of T. H. Marshall (1893–1981) to the Christian humanism of R. H. Tawney (who is an important figure in the development of both socialist and religious ideas). This school of thought is important for our purposes because of its resolute stress on *character* and *community* (or, to use the terms most typically employed by these thinkers of the pre-feminist era, 'fraternity' or 'fellowship').

The emphasis given to high moral character in one's view of the Good Society is striking. This was in part a ratification of the humanistic ideal of self-development; in part, also, it was an insistence on defining happiness and well-being in terms that were wisely limited by a common-sense notion of *enough*: for Cobbett, this meant that true independence was 'freedom from submission to one's own greed or socially defined standards of well-being beyond those necessary for a fully creative life';[1] for

Hobhouse, it meant that (following Ruskin) wealth could be like a heavy sack of gold which, tied to the body of the passenger of a ship, would merely drag him down to destruction.;[2] for Tawney, it was a view of *decency* as 'a proper concern for one's personal interests,' which yet insisted that 'when important issues are at stake everyone realizes that decent people do not stand for their price.'[3]

Tawney regarded fellowship as the *sine qua non* of a just society, and he once commented that England did not deserve to win the Great War unless 'fellowship replaced acquisitiveness as the rationale of the social order.'[4] Justice was emphasized in almost everything he ever said or wrote, and its link to character was expressed in his conviction 'that those who render service faithfully should be honourably paid, and those who render no service should not be paid at all.'[5] The emphasis on fellowship is in contrast to 'competitive struggle for individual self-advancement at the expense of others,' and it postulates 'a capacity to enjoy sociable relationships' as one of the essential traits of a fully-developed personality.[6]

Anglican Social Thought

The contemporary social witness of the Church of England owes a great deal to Anglican social thought in the nineteenth and earlier twentieth century. This book, dealing with a particular set of issues over a limited span of time, is not the place to attempt a comprehensive account of the Church of England's moral theology during the past 150 years – but it is important to comment on the importance of certain especially noteworthy trends and highlights. Chief among these will be Christian socialism, the seminal contribution of Tawney and Temple, the influence of Protestant ecumenical ethics since the 1930s, and the rise of Industrial Mission.

Christian Socialism

Almost everything written on economic issues by present-day historians of Christian social thought pays tribute to 'Christian socialism,' a school of thought which arose in the mid-nineteenth century under the impetus of illustrious thinkers such as Charles Kingsley, F. D. Maurice and John Ludlow. The significance of the movement must be seen in the light of the advance it represents over the moribund state of the established Church in the previous two centuries. According to Reckitt, 'the social tradition of the Church had been utterly lost' during the period between 1650 and 1850, and 'the arid latitudinarianism and political sycophancy of eighteenth century religion' led only to a preoccupation 'either with individual spirituality or with doctrinal orthodoxy' based on the assumption that 'the fruits thereof in personal benevolence would be sufficient for the alleviation of human suffering.'[7] The class stratification of society was mirrored in the 'caste system of opulent, comfortable and needy' within the ministry, with curates having to subsist on a standard salary of eighty pounds a year. It was a time when a famous man of letters (Trollope) could describe a 'likeable clergyman' in these words: 'He had known the Bishop of Elmham intimately for a dozen years and had never heard from the Bishop's mouth – except when in the pulpit – a single word concerning religious teaching.' As Reckitt says, 'Such tactful restraint in princes of the Church is hardly likely to inspire a Christian challenge to the dominant forces of their age.'[8]

So the adumbration of social Christianity which occurred in the so-called Christian socialism of the nineteenth century must be recognized as a wholesome step forward. But it must be admitted that the term is apt to be somewhat misleading today, for the morally concerned upper-class citizens who founded this school were never advocates of a serious and systematic move towards collective ownership and management of the means of production. The Christian socialists of a century and half ago were moved by a rather class-bound, paternalistic benevolence for the poor and downtrodden, and their energies were directed primarily towards the goal of moral uplift (through education) for the lower classes.[9] In the words of Marx in the *Communist Manifesto*, 'Christian Socialism is but the holy-water with which the priest consecrates the heart-burnings of the aristocrat.'

It was, in fact, a rather finicky aristocratic paternalism which was often politically reactionary, and which was filled with distaste for the unwashed masses, whom it wanted to protect and educate from the vantage point of a superior wisdom, status and moral authority.[10] Its religious sentimentality made it devoid of the kind of political savvy which is necessary to achieve specific reforms,[11] and the movement was associated with an explicit abhorrence of revolution (i.e., a determination *not* to see in Britain a repetition of the events of 1848 in France).[12] Despite their good intentions, they achieved very little, for they thought nothing mattered but 'the authority of Jesus and the moral beauty of his teachings,' and 'they were politically naive enough to think that no other appeal was necessary.'[13] In sum, the benevolent concern of the nineteenth-century Christian socialists for the rights of workers was often undercut by their opposition to political reforms which threatened to disrupt public order or undermine genteel decorum. Some of them were evidently confused by a typically aristocratic disdain for the lower classes, and a strong distaste for mingling with them any more than was absolutely necessary in taking up the righteous burden of educating them (as George Bernard Shaw noted!) to standards of middle-class morality.

Even William Temple's often-quoted remark concerning the fateful choice between socialism and heresy was little more than an attempt to make two specific points: to redeem socialism from the charge that it was inevitably atheistic, and to counter the widespread charge that 'the aims of the Labour movement are outside the sphere of Christianity as such [and] cannot be supported by the authority of the gospels.'[14]

Tawney and Temple

Far more important than the patricians who are usually labelled Christian socialists are two monumental figures who are much more appropriately described as religious exponents of democratic socialism, R. H. Tawney and William Temple. Tawney was especially important as a social philosopher who continuously proclaimed the need to strive for a society characterized by equality and fellowship instead of individualistic acquisitiveness; Temple, as a Christian Platonist whose importance for this study lies primarily in his conceptualization of the Church's proper social witness and his administrative abilities.

Tawney is a seminal figure, a 'political and moral *guru* to several generations of radicals,'[15] whose authorship of the Church of England's celebrated *Fifth Report* in 1919 'set the tone for most post-war Anglican thinking.'[16] Although Tawney was himself a product of Rugby, this item in his personal history did not keep him from becoming an uncompromising opponent of what he called 'the ideology of wealth' and the privileges – such as private education – which perpetuated inequality in Britain. He wrote:

What is wrong with the modern world is that having ceased to believe in the greatness of God, . . . it has to invent distinctions among *men*. It does not say 'I have said, "Ye are gods!"' Nor does it say 'all flesh is grass'. . . . What it does say is that *some* men are gods, and that some flesh is grass, and that the former should live off the latter (combined with pate de foie gras and champagne), and this is false.[17]

Since equality of opportunity is a 'Tadpole Philosophy' which merely consoles the disadvantaged by assuring them that 'exceptional individuals can succeed in evading [social evils],' the task of those who desire justice is 'to diminish inequality with all deliberate speed in order to permit human individuality, freedom and fellowship to flower.'[18]

Archbishop William Temple is a staunch advocate of these same values. In *Christianity and Social Order*, he maintains that 'the natural law of production is that it exists for consumption,' and that 'if a system of production is regulated by private profit rather than by common need, certain consequences will "naturally" follow, including an everwidening gap between rich and poor.'[19] Yet Temple was anything but a simple-minded idealist. His excellence as an administrator was due in no small measure to his appreciation for the importance of technical expertise, and he was very much aware of the gap between Christian ideals and 'the real world.' He was unremittingly staunch in his conviction that 'to deny the reality of moral purpose is wanton,'[20] but he realized that ideals had to be translated into principles which could be made applicable to social policy:

> Temple increasingly distinguished ideals from principles. The way of principles, he claimed in 1923, was a *via media*. It was idealist in that it went beyond the mere remedying of admitted evils and suggested positive relationships to be established; but it was realist in that it was always concerned with the application of principles to what is, rather than with dreams of what might be. [And] the principles he enunciates at this time are four: respect for personality; fellowship; the duty of service; the power of sacrifice.[21]

In addition, he saw the need 'to work out Christian social principles into more specific recommendations, widely known as middle axioms.'[22] (This concept – which originated in the thinking of J. H. Oldham – will be discussed in greater detail in the next section of this chapter.) Suffice it to say at this point that a middle axiom stands between metaphysical or moral principles, on the one hand, and concrete policy options on the other. It is a fairly general guideline for policy which can be commended to politicians and to politically concerned citizens as an indication of the end towards which the details of certain specific policies should be aimed. Temple thought, for example, that since unemployment compromises three of the principles he deemed essential in a healthy society – personality, community and service – *full employment* can be identified as a middle axiom which deserves to be endorsed in Christian social witness.[23]

What is decisive here is the fact that Temple insists on leaving it up to policy-makers and concerned citizens to work out the details of valid policy and to see to its implementation. Although he is a passionate advocate of 'the right of the Church to interfere in the social order' (rejecting out of hand 'the supposition of completely separate spheres of religion and politics, economics and so on [as] a modern aberration'), he is equally convinced of the limits of the Church's competence:

> The Church must announce Christian principles and point out where the existing social order at any time is in conflict with them, [but] it must then pass on to Christian citizens, acting in their civic capacity, the task of re-shaping the exist-

ing social order in closer conformity to their principles, for at this point technical knowledge may be required, and judgments of practical expediency are always required.[24]

Temple's recognition of the importance of empirical data, and of technical expertise in the interpretation of that data, made him a powerful advocate of the rule that every church pronouncement on a social issue should grow out of a study process in which prestigious scholars in the relevant fields were included.[25] This insight was in part a function of another important feature of his thinking, namely, his faith in what various writers refer to as 'corporatism' or 'club government'[26] – by which I mean the historically grounded confidence of British elites (up to 1950 or so) that social order was best left to the co-operative planning of a relatively small number of well-connected economic, political and cultural leaders. It is hardly surprising that Temple followed most of his immediate predecessors at the summit of ecclesiastical leadership in believing quite sincerely that Britain was a society in which relatively wise and benevolent men (sic!) could (under the influence of Christian faith) rise above narrow partisan interests and enter into compromise agreements which would redound to the benefit of all. 'There is one welfare of England which includes the welfare of all classes,' he declared, so 'he viewed with alarm the rapid growth of militant class consciousness' and asserted (without argument) that national loyalty is 'morally superior to class loyalty.' Temple believed that

> when social conflicts arise ecclesiastical leaders may contribute to a solution by urging 'the spirit and method of conciliation' and by admonishing the parties in a conflict to return to proposals made by Royal Commissions and other supposedly impartial bodies. The assumption throughout is that there are no basic conflicts of interest and that with a bit of good sense and Christian charity adjustments can be made which will satisfy all parties.[27]

It should be emphasized that the efficacy of Christian spirituality is decisive in this model of enlightened corporatism. If the Church is doing its job, it will 'inculcate Christian principles and the power of the Christian spirit' in the body politic and in respectable statesmen. 'While Christianity cannot supply the answers to concrete political problems, it can lift the parties to a level of thought and feeling at which the problem disappears.'[28] The first General Secretary of the BSR, Edwin Barker, shared Temple's optimism regarding corporatism, for it was said that his concept of social witness centred on the telephone: when 'the conscience of the nation' needed to be heard on some matter of pressing public concern, Barker would often pick up the phone and have a congenial but pointed conversation with the policy-maker who most needed to hear it.

Temple's indisputable contributions to Anglican social thought may be summarized as follows. First, he developed a very clear rationale for the Church's right (and obligation) to speak out on social issues and to seek to shape public policy. Second, he formulated a theory about the logic of moving from theology to moral principles to 'guidelines or objectives for government' which is still evident in a continuing debate among British ethicists about 'middle axioms.' Third, he was an able administrator and ecclesiastical entrepreneur who was strikingly successful in organizing special conferences or study projects which directed the attention of both Church and nation to particular social problems.[29]

Subsequent Developments

A full consideration of the significance of recently articulated religious ideas would have to include an account of several items which can only be mentioned here. Among them are British contributions to Protestant ecumenical ethics and the distinctive British approach to industrial mission.

Ecumenical Ethics

One of the most dramatic developments in world Christianity during the twentieth century has been the establishment of the World Council of Churches (WCC), which serves to promote ecumenical dialogue and co-operation among most of the earth's non-Roman Catholic churches. Anglicans have played a prominent role in creating, staffing, funding and carrying out the programmes of the WCC. Temple and Oldham were both quite active in ecumenical circles, the latter being credited with being not only the first exponent of middle axioms but also the chief architect of the 1937 Oxford Conference, which was decisively important in leading to the establishment of the WCC just after the Second World War. Also important in this connection are Denys Munby and R. H. Preston, to mention only two of the British thinkers who have served on a number of the study commissions of the Division of Church and Society of the WCC.

Denys Munby's two books on *Christianity and Economic Problems* (1956) and *God and the Rich Society* (1961) are milestones in the articulation of ecumenical ethics since the founding of the WCC. In the first place, he is important for his declaration that issues in the area of economic justice were absolutely crucial to the church social witness in the twentieth century. He praised Oldham for his work in the Christian Frontier Council, which 'has kept alive a serious and detailed concern for everyday problems among Christian laymen,' but he complained that 'the economic field is one where [its] contribution has been most inadequate and ineffective.'[30] As a case in point, he cites a report on 'Prices, Productivity and Incomes' put out by the Cohen Council during the 1950s: this statement by 'three wise men' was utter rubbish, says Munby, but it was hailed as a noteworthy pronouncement by Anglican bishops.[31] For Munby, this deplorable record of inattention and incompetency stands in stark contrast to the Church's *capability* of producing (and thus *obligation* to produce) 'public statements at the highest levels on matters of public importance':

> The mere fact that we live in a most complicated world, each of us in his own very different compartment, makes it more necessary that we should have guidance about matters that are not within our immediate purview. It may be that the guidance will take the form of a definite statement of policy; it may be that it will be a matter of putting forward several points of view, each of which it is possible for Christians to adopt. It may be that all that is needed is to point out how limited are the moral and human issues involved in a particular matter.[32]

Munby was a dedicated supporter of the BSR and of what its establishment meant for the Church of England; he contrasted its publications and the processes by means of which they were created with 'the work of a few devoted enthusiasts' at the Malvern Conference and in subsequent reports of the Church Assembly.[33]

As for Ronald Preston, his importance – and that of his principal disciple, John Atherton – will be apparent in the account of the Church of England's activities and stance which follows in subsequent chapters. Suffice it to say here that Preston, who deserves more than anyone else on the current scene to be called the doyen of Christian social ethics in Britain, has been revered by at least two generations of those who comprise the social action leadership of the Church of England – and that, along with a number of British Christian social ethicists (including some future bishops) such as John Habgood, David Jenkins and David Gosling, he has done much of the work which has made the World Council of Churches a major voice for Third World concerns and for intelligent social policy in Europe.

Industrial Mission

As a self-conscious movement, Industrial Mission (IM) seems to have arisen in the thinking and the administrative practice of Bishop Leslie Hunter. But if the acknowledged patron is Bishop Leslie Hunter, it is E. R. Wickham who is revered as the founder and guiding spirit of Industrial Mission in Britain. Hunter installed Wickham as head of the Sheffield Industrial Mission in 1944.[34]

Wickham and the other IM pioneers were motivated by a deep concern for the large numbers of working people who were so deeply alienated from the Church (especially the Church of England). IM was seen as a way of bridging the gap between workers and the Church, and also the gap between the Church and industry. It was also intended to mitigate the bias against commerce and industry which existed in the minds of intellectuals and 'gentlefolk' of various kinds, including church leaders. The most compelling criteria of IM were from the beginning these four: stress on the positive good of wealth creation; selection of the 'principalities and powers' at all levels of national life as targets to be contacted and influenced; belief in the ministry of the laity; and stress on human fulfilment in work (and *through* work).

IM may have been inspired to some degree by the worker-priest movement in France, but there are several key differences.[35] In the first place, industrial chaplains are visitors on the industrial scene who are paid by the Church to do a special ministry with people in industry. Second, worker-priests are full-fledged jobholders whose ordination is, in regard to the jobs they hold, beside the point. They are fully subject to the whims of employers who disapprove of their performance, or dislike the effects of their 'Christian presence' in the industrial setting.

At the time of the establishment of the Sheffield Industrial Mission, there were only a few other similar undertakings, notably the Iona Community in Scotland and the evangelical academies in Germany. The Sheffield IM maintained contact with all of these operations, and when the first meeting of the Assembly of European Churches took place in 1959 (under the leadership of men such as Hunter and Dibelius), E. R. Wickham addressed the gathering on the subject of IM. The WCC soon created an office on Urban Industrial Mission, and the Industrial Mission Association was founded in the late 1950s, to be followed shortly thereafter by the official and self-consciously ecumenical organization known as the Church Consortium on Industrial Mission.

The wave of popularity which lifted IM into prominence in the late 1950s may have been a mixed blessing, for it led to a watering down of the movement. Half-time and part-time industrial chaplaincies became common, and they were often terribly unrepresentative and ineffective (thus damaging IM's reputation in the eyes of many people). The vogue of non-stipendiary ministries led to a further scattering and diluting of energy that was even more lamentable than half- and part-time chaplaincies.

. . . [As] more ground was covered, . . . dilution of work took place, and a kind of Gresham's law operated in what was an intractable field of mission, where, it could be argued, work that was less than the highest in quality and objective was hardly worth doing. It 'showed the flag'; it might show the Church's interest and concern and be genuinely welcomed. But such visitation was less than serious mission.[36]

Today, most knowledgeable observers of the IM scene would agree that a new vitality is evident in the movement. The soul-searching which brought IM to its 'fourth generation' of activity, with its new emphasis on area development programmes, is described in Chapter 5.

The Debate about Appropriate Social Witness

What scholars designate 'social Christianity' is no more monolithic than the Church of England. Just as there are several parties within the Church which are based on, and seek to express, differing notions of Christian faith and discipleship, there are a number of different concepts of social witness vying for attention and allegiance. They lie along a continuum of distinctive positions which range from non-involvement in politics to a conviction that religious groups have a duty as well as a right to speak out vigorously in favour of (or in opposition to) specific policy options. These different concepts of appropriate social witness can most fruitfully be analysed under three principal headings: minimalist positions, 'the conventional wisdom,' and what I would like to call the Niebuhrian model.

Minimalist Positions

The first two concepts actually stand in opposition to social Christianity as it has been elaborated in the twentieth century, but they must be briefly described because of their importance in the thinking of those who denounce the current social action leadership of the Church of England.

The Church Should Stay Out of Politics!

The fundamental conviction here is that Christianity is a salvation religion which goes astray when it attempts to promote a social gospel instead of concentrating on its central mission, i.e., to save souls. Its most prominent spokesperson is Edward R. Norman, a church historian whose ferociously polemical 1978 Reith Lectures asserted that

> a reading of the Gospels less indebted to present values will reveal the true Christ of history in the spiritual depiction of a man who directed others to turn away from the preoccupations of human society. At his baptism in the River Jordan, Jesus initiated a ministry that was characterized by a call to personal redemption, to the renunciation of sin, and a departure from the world's values. It was also a rejection of the politicized official religion of his day. Time was short: eternity pressed near.[37]

Lest anyone misunderstand his position, Norman emphatically proclaims his conviction that the religion of Christ is a religion which concerns itself almost exclusively with the private realm:

To contend, as I am doing, for the separation of individual Christian action from the corporate witness of the Church, and to regard Christianity as being by nature concerned primarily with the relationship of the soul to eternity, is these days denounced within Christian opinion as a 'privatization' of religion. I think that is exactly what it is.[38]

In advancing this opinion, of course, Norman is aligning himself with a long tradition of Christian thinkers whom Richard Niebuhr classified as exponents of a 'Christ Against Culture' point of view that is typical of certain fathers of the early Church, monastics of various centuries, and latter-day advocates of spiritual purity such as Tolstoy. Dean Inge, that enormously popular twentieth-century preacher, may also belong in the same camp, because he contended that 'the Gospel is a message of moral and spiritual regeneration, not of social reform.' Among secular apologists for this doctrine are Edmund Burke, who once observed that 'No sound ought to be heard in the Church but the healing voice of Christian charity,' and E. Coppleston, who argued (in 1819) that those who opposed the extreme economic individualism of classical Political Economy were victims of intellectual confusion, namely, 'the confusion of moral duty with the task of legislation.' The basic flaw here is said to be that of 'destroying the essence not only of benevolence but of all virtue by making it compulsory.'[39]

It is hardly surprising, then, that Norman is not alone among contemporary adherents of the Church of England in advocating a 'hands off' posture vis-à-vis the world. Writing in *Crucible*, the BSR journal, an Anglican civil servant named Alexander Grey maintains that

> the right approach for the Church [in regard to the fiercely contested miners' strike of 1978–79] is to get *above* the conflict by stating clearly the Christian standards and ideals to be followed, and *below* it by personal example in helping to relieve the distress and hardship caused to individual miners and their families. The stuff in the middle – the wheeling and dealing that has to be part of government – should be avoided.[40]

This dictum is in line with his conviction that 'the source of the Church's moral authority . . . is in faith and belief rather than in rational analysis.' On the basis of this criterion, he condemns Bishop Jenkins' recent reinterpretation of Christian doctrine concerning the virgin birth and resurrection, calling it an 'essentially intellectual approach . . . which undermine[s] the authority [of Church leaders] and [is] too precious to help people understand and develop their faith.'[41]

Make Pronouncements Only on 'Moral Issues'

A second fundamental perspective on the Church's social witness declares that its pronouncements should not be concerned with 'politics,' but should be made only in that special *area* of collective life which has to do with morality. The Church should speak only in regard to issues which can be rightly understood as 'moral issues.' This point of view was nicely articulated by no less a personage than Prince Albert, who gave the following advice to Samuel Wilberforce upon the latter's installation as Bishop of Oxford in 1845:

> A Bishop ought to abstain completely from mixing himself up with the politics of the day, and beyond giving a general support to the Queen's government, and occasionally voting for it, should take no part in the discussion of State affairs

(for instance Corn Laws, Game Laws, Trade or Financial questions); but he should come forward whenever the interests of humanity are at stake, and give boldly and manfully his advice to the House and country. (I mean questions like Negro emancipation, education of the people, improvement of the health of towns, recreation of the poor, against cruelty to animals, for regulating factory labour, etc.)[42]

This distinction between moral and political issues is paralleled by the distinction sometimes made between 'issues of principle' and 'technical issues,' and by the distinction between 'political' and 'moral-pastoral' matters.[43]

The logic of this position seems to hinge on two considerations: competence, and the avoidance of idolatry. The argument from competence asserts that religious leaders ought to confine themselves to giving counsel on moral issues in public life because that is the only area where they can be presumed to know what they are talking about. They are seen as 'men of the cloth' whose background, experience and learning are somewhat sheltered from the wicked ways of the world, so they do not understand politics (or economics, or modern psychology or whatever aspects of human life you do not want them to comment on); on the other hand, though, they are supposed to be 'specialists' or 'experts' on religious and moral matters, and it is appropriate for them to give advice on topics so classified.

The argument concerning idolatry is that no secular cause, programme, party or person is good enough to be baptized as (fully or perfectly) 'Christian.' To appear to urge church people to support some partisan endeavour, then, is to proclaim a religious duty where none can rightly be said to exist (or where no church leader is wise enough, good enough or authoritative enough to assign obligation to members of the household of faith). A former Anglican bishop makes this point by quoting the papal encyclical, *Gaudium et spes*, which warns against confusing the Church with any political system or binding her to any such system; moreover, he goes on to say that identifying the Church with a political party 'suggests that party has the straight route to the Kingdom of Heaven on earth,' and that 'once the Christian cause is identified with any particular party, its message is relativized and the force of the Gospel diminished.'[44] John Selwyn Gummer, a high-ranking Thatcherite who is also a member of the General Synod of the Church of England, and who often presumes to express his opinions regarding the Church and social issues, complains (with Norman) that partisan pronouncements constitute a betrayal of the authentic gospel of Christianity, a *substitution* of a one-sided secular message for the true message of biblical faith.[45]

The Conventional Wisdom

Needless to say, however, the mainstream leadership of the Church of England does not believe in restricting social witness to a minimalist approach. It explains its concept of appropriate church pronouncements by postulating a distinction between *directions* and *directives*, or by elaborating the concept of *middle axioms*. A similar approach is echoed in the notion of *fruitfulness* recently advanced by James M. Gustafson, the doyen of Christian ethics in America.

'Directions,' Not 'Directives'

The distinction between directions and directives was introduced into the contemporary debate concerning Christian ethics by Paul Ramsey, whose bellicose critique of the WCC's 1966 Geneva Conference was published under the title *Who Speaks for the Church?* Arguing that the churches should concentrate on 'cultivating the political ethos of a nation and informing the conscience of the statesman [*sic*],' he rejected the notion that churches should presume to venture policy recommendations. To do so would be to impugn the conscience of 'the magistrates' (i.e., those whose position in government makes them responsible for formulating policy and making decisions about implementing it), for 'policy formation . . . is the awesome responsibility of magistrates.'[46] Says Ramsey:

> It is not the church's business to recommend but only to clarify the grounds upon which the statesman must put forth his own particular decree. Christian political ethics cannot say what should or must be done but only what may be done. . . . The religious communities as such should be concerned with *perspectives* upon politics, with political doctrine, with the direction and structures of the common life, not with specific directives. They should seek to clarify and keep wide open the legitimate options for choice, and thus nurture the moral and political ethos of the nation.[47]

Ramsey's theoretical position is based in part upon his scepticism concerning the *capability* of church leaders – or, more specifically, the 'social action *curia*' (professional staff in denominational agencies with the social responsibility portfolio) – to understand the complexities of social, political and economic life well enough to recommend policy in these areas. For Ramsey, 'the notion that laymen who are experts . . . can enable the church to speak a relevant Christian word to today's world and at the same time to point out the particular policy to be followed is simply an illusion.'[48] He comments:

> Can it really be believed that a popery of the expert, whose particular voice shortly becomes the church's recommendation, no matter how expert he is, would be the way to improve the present popery of committees and conferences? This might add some merit to the church's policy-making exercises, but it would be no improvement in the church speaking.[49]

Thus he concludes, 'It is *deliberation* upon the social and ethical implications of the Christian faith that is most lacking today, not particular recommendations. . . . Not even church-sponsored social action is the issue, but before that *proper* deliberation!'[50] Vatican II is a better model than conferences like Geneva as a mechanism for carrying out proper deliberation.[51] Vatican II consisted of '*several* sessions . . . over a period of years' (my italics) and it provided both time to study 'the work prepared beforehand by experts' and time during the sessions for official participants 'to hear and question the experts, to discuss with them the meaning of draft statements in process of being prepared for adoption.' Moreover, there was time *between* sessions 'for substantive theological-ethical work to be done on the drafting.' Only in this way can there be 'ample debate on the floor, and [adequate] revision and re-revision of any statement that is finally promulgated.'[52]

Ramsey's point of view is cited in a recent BSR publication as an explanation of the rationale underlying all of the agency's pronouncements on policy issues. It begins by citing his contention that 'the purpose of the address of the Church to the world . . . ought to be the broadening and deepening of public debate on urgent issues,' and his further belief that the result of the Church's public statements 'ought not to be to stop or narrow down this debate or polarise the debate that is going on by finding in favour of a specific policy behind which we are seeking merely to mobilise public opinion.'[53] It ends by raising a number of important questions:

> Resounding resolutions are good but not good enough: the problem remains how to make effective what is known and believed through a process of continuing theological reflection. Here we come up against some basic questions. How much and to what degree does religious faith mandate choice of strategy and tactics? How does the Church find the right balance between describing or prescribing, indicating and specifying? Having confessed one's faith is one compelled to campaign?[54]

The task force which produced *Peacemaking* believes that the process which it entered into in order to address the Church and the nation on war/peace issues is a paradigm of the 'proper deliberation' which Paul Ramsey calls for. In order to arrive at conclusions which could be 'offered back to the Church for debate,' the task force 'came together to study the issues, to examine both ethical and political dimensions.' The aim is not to *dictate* to church members or citizens exactly what they should do; it is to present certain findings in the form of resolutions which can 'help church people think their way through the serious issues' involved '*with the expectation that* the whole church [will] use these resolutions as a basis for action.'[55] The discussion of this point ends by asserting that 'The elected body may have the responsibility of producing the text; the entire body must then use the text as a guide to its own thinking and exploration.'

Middle Axioms

British and American Christian social ethicists have tried to move a little beyond mere directions towards directives by elaborating the concept of the middle axiom. As noted above, in the discussion of William Temple, a middle axiom is a guideline for policy which is rather more specific than a moral principle such as 'distributive justice' yet considerably less specific and detailed than a legislative proposal or an organizational programme. One can, for example, favour a progressive income tax as a way of implementing distributive justice without saying what percentage of a given level of income ought to be taken. This presumably enables theologians and ethicists to argue that Christians ought to support progressive taxation without insisting that every churchgoer who does not support a particular tax measure proposed by a particular political leader (or party) is a fraud. Those who believe that the Church should beware of proclaiming a partisan political or economic position as a *casus confessionis* (as writers such as Duchrow have recently urged the Lutheran Church to do[56]) believe that restricting church pronouncements to middle axioms is a wise rule of thumb to follow. It will save the Church from both arrogance and error, not to mention the embarrassment that would go along with baptizing too enthusiastically a specific law or programme which turned out to have serious flaws.

The term originated with J. H. Oldham, a leading Anglican theologian of the first half of the century, and it was appealed to by William Temple at the Malvern Conference in 1941 even before he made use of the concept in *Christianity and the Social Order* in 1942. In this book he deduced from fundamental Christian principles such as freedom, fellowship and service a set of six broad policy criteria on which he 'believes all Christians should be able to agree with him.'[57] But he made a point of relegating his recommendations regarding specific policies and programmes to an appendix, for which he claimed no special authority.

Most subsequent Anglican writers have accepted what they evidently regard as the wholesome discipline of middle axioms. One of the best statements concerning the significance of the middle axioms approach comes from R. H. Preston:

> The aim of corporate investigation into a problem of social ethics is to come to an understanding of the main facts and trends in a situation, assess their significance and indicate the general direction in which it is desirable that change may be fostered. This is a middle level between general principles (like liberty, equality and fraternity) and detailed policies. It is unlikely that a consensus will get as far as these. In such a case all that can be achieved is to establish, if possible, an agreed analysis, and then list the questions that Christians who advocate one type of policy wish to ask those who advocate a different one, and urge each group to take seriously the questions posed to them by fellow Christians who disagree with them, and not lose their common togetherness in Christ because of tensions caused by their differences. This has happened in the case of those Christians who take a pacifist position which abjures all violence in principle, and those who do not rule it out in all circumstances (e.g., the WCC study on 'Violence, Non-violence and the Struggle for Social Justice').
>   When it comes to detailed policies for action it is possible that Christians who agree on the middle ground . . . may disagree on these in so far as the decision depends on an estimate of the likely consequence of following each of the options for action which are available; no one can be certain of future consequences.[58]

Hugh Montefiore, former Bishop of Birmingham and episcopal head of the BSR, points out that middle axioms 'require knowledge of the empirical situation' and emerge from 'the *praxis* and experience drawn from . . . living out the faith.' In this connection, he cites one of the six examples of middle axioms advanced by Temple:

> Every child should find itself a member of a family housed with decency and dignity, so that it may grow up a member of that basic community in a happy fellowship unspoilt by underfeeding or overcrowding, by dirty and drab surroundings or by mechanical monotony of environment.[59]

Of course, individuals will inevitably find it difficult to agree on exactly what sort of commentary constitutes a middle axiom, and even when they reach agreement on this they may disagree on the amount of *detail* which ought to be included in a middle axiom concerning a particular area of social policy. (Some of the details implied in Temple's pronouncement given above might be questioned today – as well as the wisdom of packing so many elements into one middle axiom!)

Fruitfulness

Some analysts of church social witness address themselves to the question of what kinds of pronouncements are likely to be most helpful to policy-makers (or most likely to be heard and pondered by thoughtful citizens). One of the wisest and most conscientious commentators of this stripe is James Gustafson, whose recent assessment of the ethical writings of the Church and Society Division of the World Council of Churches deserves serious attention. After dividing the writings in question into four categories, ranging from (1) prophetic utterances which indict social evils and project utopian visions of What Ought To Be through (2) narrative accounts which reinforce the moral identity of the household of faith to (3) 'scientific' examination of moral discourse and (4) 'policy analysis,' Gustafson declares that 'by being in focus on the root of the evil, [prophetic discourse] cannot inform incremental choices made by persons and institutions where good and bad are commingled, and where trade-offs have to be defended.'[60] Moreover, the prophetic focus on 'an ideal future . . . often has little to say about means to shorter range ends in view.'

A somewhat less austere point of view is offered by John A. Williams, who shares Gustafson's concern about fruitfulness. In an article entitled 'A Bishop Should Speak Out – But What Can He Say?' Williams suggests that church leaders are hamstrung by a kind of 'Catch 22': anything they say which smacks of 'traditional religion' will be dismissed as an irrelevant cliche, whereas anything which is not in accordance with the prevailing canons of establishment idealism may be attacked as impertinent, subversive or heretical. To appeal to God or to 'British values' is almost certain to induce boredom in millions of readers; however, a 'vestigial Christianity' (what some sociologists would refer to as 'secular Anglicanism') is still operative in the thinking of a significant percentage of the public.[61] What normally occurs, says Williams, is something like this: if church leaders are commenting, say, on an industrial dispute, they are apt to 'call for the recognition of the "spiritual dimension," or talk about the need for "reconciliation," without making clear what these abstractions have to do with the express aims and objectives of either labour or management institutions.'[62]

In order to escape from the vacuity of such utterances, some bishops resort to what C. Wright Mills called 'liberal practicality': they 'give up trying to enunciate general principles in favour of getting down to social action [on concrete problems and issues]'; that is, they advocate piecemeal incremental reforms 'without ever doing the hard thinking that would lead to a cogent critique of the underlying structural causes.' Williams avers that this is just the kind of error which plays into the hands of right-wing critics, and he proposes the following resolution for the dilemma he has chosen to dissect:

> It is one thing for the Church to set up projects to help the unemployed, but another to produce a theological critique of, say, the equation of 'work' with 'paid employment', or the hiring out of labour in return for rationally calculated remunerations, which the present system takes for granted. Where churchmen have radical things to say, these must be seen to arise out of thorough engagement with the social realities of the secularised middle ground, for in no other way can the vital link be made in the consciousness of the man in the street between that ill-defined, loose collections of beliefs that are his private religion, and the remote and formalised abstractions . . . he sees dramatised in the rituals of Church and State.[63]

A Critique and a Modest Proposal

The normative assumptions regarding appropriate social witness which inform this study are somewhat different from any of the positions outlined thus far. As Chapter 7 will make clear, I find it very difficult to have any sympathy for the minimalist positions (even though I respect a number of their particular arguments on specific issues). And although I respect the conventional wisdom, and agree with many of its tenets, I believe that Christian social action must go beyond (mere!) directions and middle axioms – and I end this chapter with a critique of all these positions and a modest proposal for a more audacious option.

Those who believe in social Christianity find it difficult to grant much credibility to either of the minimalist approaches, each of which strikes them as a sadly one-sided understanding of authentic Christian faith. They see the 'Stay Out of Politics!' view as a wrong-headed 'pseudotransformationism' which can easily be dismissed as hopelessly unrealistic;[64] indeed, they have to struggle very hard to avoid perceiving it as the rationalization of a highly partisan reactionary posture, especially when (as is often the case) it is set forth with 'the implied assumption that to be a supporter of the Conservative Party is not to be "politically active."'[65] If a relatively impartial observer sets aside her commitment to keep an open mind regarding adversary viewpoints, her intuition tells her that most of the people who adopt this posture are disturbed (as the authors of *Believing Bishops* say of Margaret Thatcher) not by the fact that the Church of England is speaking out on social issues, but by *what it says* on these issues.[66]

It is equally difficult to credit the legitimacy of the desire to limit church pronouncements to 'moral issues.' It may well be true, as Moyser and Medhurst report, that Britons do in fact expect their established Church to steer clear of involvement in political affairs, and to restrict itself to concern for and involvement in '*moral-pastoral* matters.'[67] But this bit of evidence regarding the persistence of stereotyped thinking in the general public has no normative standing, and the fact is that any attempt to classify a special set of issues as 'moral issues' is bound to prove unworkable. Mrs Thatcher's tendency to equate Christianity with thoroughgoing individualism was attacked by a Church of Scotland commentator, who responded to the Sermon on the Mound by maintaining that the one-sidedness of her point of view was in a fact a *theological* matter: he contended that her attempt to portray individualism as the heart of Christian faith was a theological *error*.[68]

The conventional wisdom represents a much more credible option than either version of the minimalist position. A better rationale for the Church's social witness is to be found in both Ramsey's doctrine concerning 'directions, not directives' and in the BSR's emphasis on middle axioms. The notion that a church's contribution should be focused on the *grounds* for choosing one policy option in preference to others, not in prescribing *exactly what ought to be done*, has great appeal to anyone who fears idolatrous preoccupation with any proposed solution to a complex social problem, or any idolatrous allegiance to a given party or leader. And anyone who shares this culture's belief in the importance of individual rights and individual freedom of mind and speech can appreciate a position which advocates reliance upon the consciences of individuals as the final arbiter of choice and action. But Ramsey's insistence that the consciences of the magistrates should be so fully respected seems to go a bit further than the BSR position does in restricting the role of the churches; indeed, it seems to require what Hinchliff dubs a 'civil servant' role, in which the churches remain *subservient* to the state, and thus unable to criticize it openly. Hinchliff accuses Margaret Thatcher herself of buying into this assumption when she remarks that 'if the churches took sides on practical issues' they would fail in their obligation to 'help the thinking of all political parties.' He goes on to observe, 'This seems to be saying that the churches can be very influential as long as they do not actually try and influence anything.'[69]

I find encouragement in the fact that both Hinchliff and Duncan Forrester (whose *Beliefs, Values and Policies* is the finest single statement I have seen on the theory of church social witness) agree with me in thinking that church pronouncements must go beyond directions and middle axioms. Forrester concedes that the middle axioms approach may have worked tolerably well 'while Britain was a much more outwardly Christian country than it is today,' but he points out its failure to 'enable leading churchmen to see through the Munich Agreement or . . . to denounce area bombing and massive direct attacks on the German civilian population.' He applauds the fact that 'the two most important and influential Church of England reports in recent years – *The Church and the Bomb* and *Faith in the City* – both advisedly set aside the middle axiom logic and make specific policy proposals.'[70] Hinchliff asserts that 'moral outrage' is certainly not enough, and even though he is wary of attempting to formulate detailed plans for implementation, he affirms that is it certainly possible to be *concrete* in criticizing a particular policy, party or person without being 'partisan,' and that it is certainly an obligation of the churches to do so:

> This model of political neutrality, where what is thought to matter is not the moral quality of the government's policies nor the integrity of the methods used to put them into practice, but that one should never be *seen* to be taking sides under any circumstances whatsoever, is an unfortunate one for the churches to be expected to adopt. . . . To criticize or even condemn the policies of one party is not the same thing as being partisan. It is perfectly possible to argue that the government's programme is unjust, without necessarily implying that the opposition's programme is perfect. Even in very practical and detailed criticisms, such as Mrs Thatcher was referring to, one can be completely neutral in the sense that one can be reserving the right to be equally critical of programmes of other subsequent administrations.[71]

He concludes that it is a mistake to do nothing more than carry out 'an even-handed review of the possible options, pointing out the pros and cons of each,' for this 'civil service model of neutrality, [which] the churches have all too often adopted, saying, on the one hand, this about capitalism and, on the other, that about the welfare state, . . . merely makes them seem bland and ineffective.'[72]

As for the emphasis put upon the concept of fruitfulness by Gustafson and Williams, many readers will not accept their compartmentalization of prophetic assertion, nor will they agree that it cannot be useful in helping policy-makers to make *better* assessments of trade-offs and devise more imaginative means to desired societal ends. They will argue that Gustafson himself admits the critical need for prophetic influence on the thinking of policy-makers when he says that policy discourse 'works within limited visions, limited frames of reference, [accepting] conditions which from prophetic and ethical perspectives might be judged to be morally wrong, or at least inadequate.' When he declares that 'the ethical informs but does not determine the choices of the policy-maker in most circumstances,' he admits the possibility and the desirability for merging prophetic discourse and policy analysis – and he undercuts the validity of his subsequent remark to the effect that prophetic discourse 'is not of much help to Christians in positions of policy responsibility in public or private sectors.'[73]

A Niebuhrian Model[74]

The most basic presupposition, however, is this: the social witness of a church ought to be what the commentary of *any* person or agency is, namely, an analysis of issues *from the standpoint of the speaker* which ends with tentative recommendations about the *kinds* of policies which are needed to achieve the values to which the speaker is committed (and which are identified, or even defended and advocated) in the commentary being announced. This means, in common-sense terms, that a church pronouncement will side with whichever party deserves to be sided with on the merits of the case under discussion, and it will urge action aimed at combating policies deemed undesirable and/or at promoting policies deemed wise, constructive and worthy of support. If it happens that the line of analysis taken, and the policy recommendations arrived at, run parallel to the analysis being made or the policy recommendations being set forth by some other group (secular or otherwise), that is coincidental – and it would be foolish, gutless and both morally and theologically despicable to *refrain* from making the kind of pronouncement required by the situation just to avoid being criticized for agreeing with Marxists, Labourites, neoconservatives or anyone else who just happens to be saying something similar on an issue! Some observers contend that churches have erred in allowing the complex nature of many social issues, and the specialization of knowledge required, to persuade them to seek out expert contributions and to adopt, where relevant, the language of social scientists. But what is so dangerous about this? Should expert opinion be *excluded*, and should the rhetoric employed be purged of all similarities with 'the language of specialists'? The avoidance of social-science jargon would of course be a consummation devoutly to be wished, and the same may be said about theological jargon – but reliance upon appropriate expertise is a *strength*, not a shortcoming, and the use of such expertise is not *intrinsically* or *inevitably* a capitulation to amoral professionalism. It may be perfectly true that arguing from Christian assumptions carries no weight in specialized technical debate, and arguing from purely technical assumptions makes no distinctive Christian contribution – but the social witness of the churches *never* argues *purely* from technical assumptions, and it is a *non sequitur* to maintain that a social-policy analysis which *combines* theological and technical wisdom in a pronouncement that concerns both morality and politics is devoid of distinctively Christian prophecy.

But this appraisal of the situation needs to be chastened and guided by Duncan Forrester's qualms about 'the reign of the experts' (which is linked in his mind to dissatisfaction with William Temple's excessive individualism). Forrester praises Oldham's influence on 'doing social theology,' especially his insistence on getting secular experts to supply their knowledge to the theologians (whose theological wisdom was not sufficient in itself). He points out, however, that 'the whole approach from Oldham to recent times has an inbuilt *elitist* tendency: it is the *experts*, the articulate and skilled ones with relevant experience, who are brought together and allowed to share in shaping social theology.' He grants that this 'may be far preferable to leaving the issues exclusively in the hands of the ecclesiastics or theologians' – but he warns against two perils: forgetting the social location (and the attendant bias) of the experts themselves, and the tendency (of late) for theologians and ethicists to become little more than impresarios who bring the experts together and moderate *their* discussion (so that the theologian 'gets the right people on stage at the right time, while he himself stays in the wings').[75] Forrester grants that 'there is something genuinely attractive and Christian in the idea of the theologian as having a servant-role: the modest and self-effacing theologian, more given to listening than to talking, [who] sees himself as a catalyst and an enabler' – but he argues that the pendulum has swung too far away from the days when church leaders presumed to know *everything* and do *all* the talking. Forrester satirizes the 'philosopher' who is nothing more than a linguistic analyst, contending that theologians who are nothing more than impresarios make the same mistake. He clinches his argument by citing R. H. Preston's disdain for the 'swing from refusing to recognise the proper autonomy of secular disciplines to an uncritical and adulatory reliance on them.'[76]

Furthermore, to express an opinion which is intended to be a stimulus to reflection and (one hopes) appropriate action is *by no means* to violate the conscience of anyone (whether she is a fellow Christian or not) – but even if it were, that would be better than attributing too much wisdom or good will to magistrates, scholars, linguistic analysts or any other group whose good opinion one might understandably desire to have. The BSR is to be commended for avoiding the astonishing lack of realism in the position taken by both Ramsey and Gustafson.[77] The former seems to believe that magistrates are not political animals with all kinds of private or agency agendas which typically produce a drastic amount of goal-displacement in their supposed pursuit of the national interest or the common good (especially the common good of the entire human family, as opposed to the interests of the people in one country, or certain classes in that country, or certain elites who control most of the power in that country). The latter seems to believe that sweet reason will convince any social analyst or any political operative, and that it is somehow unseemly to employ any other means to influence their thinking or shape their behaviour.

The implications of this position are clear: as the authors of *Believing Bishops* (along with many other observers of various religious and political persuasions) declare, church leaders should be *expected* to speak out on behalf of the poor, and to be a sort of 'loyal opposition' to any government, particularly one which seems to be pursuing policies that constitute a violation of the 'bias to the poor' which so many contemporary theologians discern as a pronounced motif in biblical faith.

The most audacious statement regarding the Church's social witness made during the period under consideration is found in *Living Faith in the City*, a progress report on follow-up activities which was published five years after the appearance of the original manifesto. It dares to 'reiterate the *Faith in the City* recommendation that the Church of England should continue to question the morality of economic policies in the light of their effects,' proceeding to observe that doing so 'is clearly an ongoing task for the General Synod's Board for Social Responsibility.' Then comes the following declaration: 'We would like to see the Church of England making a moral input into the Government's economic decision-making on a par with representations made annually by bodies such as the Confederation of British Industry, the Trades Union Congress, etc.'[78] This position is echoed in *Living Faith in the City*'s recommendations to the BSR regarding its 'heavy load as the Church's agent for pursuing at national level the majority of the social and economic issues raised by *Faith in the City*,' for the BSR is urged to articulate a critique of the *underlying assumptions* of government policy as well as its consequences: the social action leadership is enjoined to 'continue to examine the principles which govern the structure of the benefit system, with special reference to the needs of people in UPAs.'[79] The fullest single statement on this point is one of the 'Conclusions' advanced at the end of *Living Faith in the City*'s chapter on 'Poverty and Unemployment':

> Over the next five years those who take poverty in our society seriously will find themselves involved in much more than a statistical debate about gainers and losers. They will need to talk about the *principles* behind the welfare state and income support and to recognise the impact of the philosophical shift behind the move from universal benefits to 'targetted,' means-tested benefits.[80]

Among the specifics alluded to in this connection are the issues of *participation* and 'the great need to promote a more informed understanding of *the respective roles of charity and justice.*' On the first of these issues, the 1990 report contends that

> the lack of consultation, and the speed with which legislation has been enacted [during the Thatcher era], have meant that those who are poorly organised and largely disenfranchised have not been able to make their interest count, . . . [and] if the goal of social policy [since 1979] is individual freedom rather than social

cohesion and mutual responsibility, then it is not surprising that the new social vision is excluding so many from the new-found affluence.[81]

On the second, noting that 'a key factor in the present government's economic strategy is the promotion of private charity in place of public expenditure,' the report maintains that

> levels of private giving, whether by individuals or companies, bear no comparison with the reductions in taxation which reduced public expenditure has made possible. The amount of money given to charitable causes, even if massively increased, would still pale into insignificance beside the billions required to support unemployed people or house the homeless. To deal with these issues effectively requires, in the CBI's telling phrase, 'initiatives beyond charity.'[82]

Moreover, a vigorous social witness is *necessary* as well as appropriate: as the writers of the widely applauded *Kairos Document* from South Africa proclaim, the Church must go beyond vague admonitions to benevolence, for

> reliance on 'individual conversions' . . . has not worked and it will never work. The present crisis with all its cruelty, brutality and callousness is ample proof of the ineffectiveness of years and years of Christian 'moralising' about the need for love. The problem we are dealing with here in South Africa is not merely a problem of personal guilt: it is a problem of structural injustice.[83]

Since 'changing the structure of society is fundamentally a matter of politics [which] requires a political strategy based upon a clear social and political analysis,' a purely spiritual approach is worse than ineffective, for it becomes an disingenuous dodge that comforts church people with the *illusion* that are engaging in prophetic action that will serve the interests of the dispossessed. But it is precisely

> the *political* situation that the Church has to address, . . . [and] it is into this political situation that the Church has to bring the gospel. Not as an alternative solution to our problems, as if the gospel provided us with a non-political solution to political problems. There is no specifically Christian solution[, but] there will be a Christian way of approaching political solutions, a Christian spirit and motivation and attitude. But there is no way of bypassing politics and political strategies.[84]

3

The Church of England's Stance on Economic Issues

In searching for an understanding of the Church of England's social witness during the Thatcher era, it is necessary always to bear in mind that this witness is articulated in the context of a cultural environment which is hostile to the heritage of Anglican social thought that was summarized in the previous chapter. Thus much of what is written and said on economic issues is intended to clarify the Church's stance on both the welfare state and the market economy. Assuming that Giles Ecclestone was correct in saying that the typical ecclesiastical leader is 'a mixed economy man,' exactly what does this mean in the light of Thatcherism's rather one-sided emphasis on the enterprise culture and the autonomy of the market? Given the fact that the welfare state must be revamped, which aspects of its overall programme are worthy of refinement and continuation? And which specific programmes and service-delivery systems should be abandoned altogether or changed?

The Social Market Economy†

In carrying out its mandate to 'promote and coordinate the thought and action of the Church in all matters affecting the life of men and women in society,' the BSR keeps its constituency aware of important developments pertaining to Britain's participation in world capitalism, especially the mixed economy capitalism of Europe. It has studied conglomerate mergers, Sunday trading, global economic development, the operations and the societal impact of transnational corporations, the possible ramifications of the Eurotunnel and the implications of British membership in the Single European Market. In addition, it has accepted money from both government and business to participate in job-training programmes and area development, and reports filed by church participants in such activities reveal a distinctive point of view on the strengths and weaknesses of such initiatives.[1]

To be sure, the Church of England's efforts to legitimate and play a role in worthwhile private-sector activities is anything but uncritical. It is ever-vigilant in pointing out dubious aspects of particular free enterprise initiatives, and always quick to condemn any tendencies towards unbridled individualism and ruthless acquisitiveness in Thatcherite hype of the enterprise culture. Many of its publications testify, for example, to the importance of non-economic criteria such as environmental protection, the rights of workers, appropriate technology, democratic education

---

† The adjective 'social' is intended to convey the presence of concern for issues of human well-being that goes beyond unvarnished economic rationality in a mixed economy. It follows that a social market economy *allows* welfare state programmes but does not *require* them: as a matter of fact, both Thatcherism and Reaganism have tried to make the *voluntary* sector responsible for providing many goods and services not afforded by the market which a welfare state puts into the hands of the public sector.

and racial justice. One of the BSR's most recent studies, *The Ethics of Acquisition*, explores the human consequences of corporate takeovers and spells out the moral guidelines which ought to govern such frequently counter-productive manoeuvrings. And *Faith in the City* is filled with implied (or explicit) criticism of a host of 'normal business practices'; indeed, its audacious challenges to the perpetuation of class inequity in private education and the tax deduction for mortgage interest created shock waves in Establishment circles.[2]

But a sizable number of documents are informed by a desire to show that the Church of England should not be accused of ignoring the benefits of the free market system or of exemplifying the indefensible prejudice against commerce and industry highlighted by scholars such as Wiener and Barnett. Especially important in this connection are the series of booklets which were published in 1975-6, the programme named 'Industry Year 1986,' and a 1986 consultation on the social market economy.

The Importance of Wealth Creation

There are several reasons for attributing special significance to the set of five studies outlining crucial aspects of Britain's economic difficulties which appeared in 1975-6. They were commissioned, first of all, at a time when it was becoming increasingly evident that the nation was in serious trouble economically, and that the attendant dislocations in such matters as employment, inflation, and Britain's standing in international commerce and finance were having dramatic repercussions in both politics and culture. Second, the working groups which produced these statements included some of the finest minds which the Church of England could call together, men such as E. R. Wickham (the founder of Industrial Mission in Britain), Kenneth Adam (long-time head of the Industrial Christian Fellowship, and the chief organizer and guiding spirit of Industry Year 1986), Roger Clarke (later to be a key figure at the William Temple Foundation), Michael Atkinson and Giles Ecclestone of the BSR, and a goodly number of leaders from church, business, organized labour and government. Thus the booklets represented the collective wisdom of the Church's social action leadership at a moment of crisis in the life of the nation; indeed, it was intended to offer (using the title and the subtitle of the final booklet in the series) an assessment of *The State of the Nation* which would provide 'A Christian Approach to Britain's Economic Crisis.' They dealt with a set of issues that ranged from inflation, economic growth, industrial democracy, work and business ethics to the theological assumptions about social solidarity and co-operation which ought to guide the nation's efforts to find the path ahead.

Perhaps the best of these publications is the one on *Growth and Inflation* written by E. R. Wickham. In addition to its clarification of the nature and causes of inflation, the booklet is noteworthy because of its reliance upon the corporatist assumptions which were current at the time when Wickham pioneered the establishment of Industrial Mission in Britain. Its affirmation of the Church's prophetic role in constructive social criticism is matched by a list of 'the marks of the "good society" [which] can be understood as the "fruits of the Spirit" expressed in social terms, to be realised in the institutions of society and in its social and economic organisation,' and the author declares that these 'criteria and standards' can logically be translated into 'objectives and goals' which 'have international, global implications for those who believe – as Christians should – in the unity of the human family.'[3] The importance – and the moral legitimacy, the *goodness* – of wealth creation is boldly asserted, and the rising expectations of consumers in modern society are presented as a wholesome expression of the ordinary person's response to welcome progress in technology, industry and commerce.[4] But 'among the complex causes of inflation, probably the most potent and irresistible is the *excessive* demand that public expectation makes on technological capacity for increasing affluence,' so readers are warned of the necessity for restraint and patience as the measures of severity which will be necessary to curb inflation make it necessary for the populace to tighten its collective belt for a while. The challenge is to find a way to 'increase national wealth by securing, maintaining and increasing economic growth' without succumbing to inflation, and all citizens should be willing to undergo 'reduced levels of personal consumption.' However, Wickham enters a tremendously significant two-pronged moral proviso: the case for growth depends on paying attention to 'the social objectives, and morally-convincing objectives that growth must serve in a good society'; moreover, when it comes to increased consumption, 'social policy should give priority to underprivileged groups of society and the needs of those economically weaker groups who are most damaged by inflation.' So the pronounced emphasis on a 'bias to the poor' which is so familiar to readers of church pronouncements in the 1980s is already present in this statement of the Church of England in 1975.

The remedy is to be sought in a reversal of a regrettable set of circumstances which have contributed to the magnitude of the problem: just as inflation 'can be seen as the climactic by-product of a relaxed society, [one] without commanding social objectives, without the sense that there might be a common will about the kind of society we should be,' the cure is to be found in 'some kind of social contract' in which efficiency and growth are 'publicly subjected to some kind of social audit.' These are the societal instrumentalities which are needed to generate 'creative management and enterprise, raw material conservancy and innovation, dynamic industrial relations . . . and enlightened manpower policies,' and attainment of these enlightened organizational practices will 'require good leadership at all levels of industry, in management and unions, considerable governmental intervention and the closest relationship of government, industry and trade unions' – in fact, it will require 'their mutual inter-dependence [*sic*]' in 'overall economic planning,' for 'this is what a "social contract" should be about.'[5] In view of the fact that 'in the short term it now appears that standards of living in our country must fall,' the author realizes that it must not be taken for granted that Britons 'can have the corporate will required in the struggle to surmount our economic problems,' but he holds out the possibility that a nation which is vitally in touch with its Christian roots can do what must be done 'in a good spirit, without falling apart, . . . with graciousness and without ugliness.'[6]

The interest in creative management and enlightened manpower policies voiced in Wickham's booklet is elaborated in a second publication, entitled *Power-Sharing in Industry*. It applauds the fact that the 'essential need for social change' called for in the Beveridge Report received widespread recognition, but it laments the public's failure to see British industry's 'desperate need for modernisation' as equally important. It also reflects the faith in corporatism which was so prominent in *Growth and Inflation*, for it rejects the radical option of a 'root and branch restructuring of the basic political and economic frameworks' of the nation and advocates instead 'the development of imaginative and pragmatic initiatives which enjoy the support of all the powerful interests – government, management, unions, shareholders, employees and the community in general.'[7] The desired power-sharing which will 'enable the individual to achieve greater satisfaction from his job'[8] can only be brought about 'if there is a real shift in management attitudes and styles which can be reflected in but not initiated by employees.'[9]

The third publication in the series is much less substantial than the others, being less than half their average length and consisting of little more than a summary of the highlights of a report issued by the Company Affairs Committee of the Confederation of British Industry (CBI). *Ethical Choice and Business Responsibilities* urges business to adopt 'guidelines or a code of conduct to express how companies are expected to behave within the society in which they are working.' The obligations identified in such a code 'obviously should not . . . impose on the company a duty of general benevolence at the shareholders' expense,' nor should it 'authorise an incursion into fields of social welfare unconnected with the company's business such as are the province of central and local government, [for] the obligations that are to be recognised are limited to those that arise in the pursuit of the company's main objectives.' What, then, should it do? Presumably it should make it clear that 'any company which regards its word as good as its bond, which gives a fair deal and is a good neighbour, has gone most of the way.'[10]

The fourth booklet, *Work or What?*, will be discussed in the second half of this chapter. As for the fifth and climactic volume, *The State of the Nation*, it reiterates many of the themes already touched upon, notably those of wealth creation – which is described as 'a moral duty' – and greater social harmony. In calling for more social interaction between persons of different social classes, it says that 'it would have been better for everyone if the frustrations of the working class had been recognised more effectively before they exploded into the strikes of 1972' – but it also urges the working class 'to be less fixed in the memories of the 1920s, and less censorious about the creators of wealth.'[11] It deplores class hostility, asserting that

> whether the workers' representatives [called for by the ideal of power-sharing] are to have places on supervisory boards or are to be non-executive directors, and whether or not they are to have parity with shareholders in deciding the crucial issues, they will have to be guided by a bigger interest than the battle for wages.[12]

Industry Year 1986

The content and purposes of Industry Year 1986 were explained by the Director of the project, Sir Geoffrey Chandler, CBE, in the press release announcing the project. Following the argument regarding anti-business prejudice articulated by Barnett and Wiener, Chandler alleges that Britain

> now finds [itself] almost at the bottom of the major industrial league by every relevant economic and industrial measure, from training and investment to standard of living, [because of] an inherited culture . . . of attitudes which put industrial activity at the bottom of the social pecking order and of an education which, by ignoring or denigrating it, obscures the connection between quality of life and industrial success.

No wonder, he concludes, that 'our brightest students choose the professions first and industry last.'

The goals of Industry Year 1986 are described as both general and specific: (1) it can help to improve awareness of industry's pervasive contribution to the community and of the fact that it provides a service in which the participants should be able to take a pride, no less than any other walk of life; (2) it can 'cross the deep divides between education and industry' by promoting 'links between schools and companies, the broadening of teacher training, [and] modification of the curriculum'; (3) it 'can encourage industry itself to articulate its role more clearly,' and (4) it can drive home the point that 'the lack of any industrial "Hippocratic Oath" is a positive deterrent to a critical and idealistic student population.'

The service of worship at St Paul's Cathedral which launched Industry Year 1986 featured a sermon delivered by the Archbishop of Canterbury. The Archbishop proclaimed that 'our well-being as a nation largely depends on our manufacturing achievements,' and that 'What Britain makes, makes Britain.' Considerable stress was placed upon the mutually supportive relationship between work and worship; God was portrayed as 'at once the author of all natural gifts, as well as the judge of the use we make of them.' The rather adulatory stance towards industry reflected in all of the materials published in connection with this campaign carried forward into the follow-up programme entitled 'Industry Matters,' which began in 1987. Its hopes for, and faith in, company codes of conduct is expressed in its statement concerning the value of such codes:

> Business and industry are not automatically accorded the social relevance and value accorded to medicine, nursing and teaching. They therefore have to make a positive effort to gain the same moral ground. . . . It is dismaying how often one comes across a popular presumption that dishonesty – or at least a sliding scale of values – is an inevitable part of business success, and that profitability and humanity are in conflict. It is therefore important that the beliefs and principles underlying a business should be made explicit in order to obtain consistent behaviour within a company and to tell the world outside what they are.[13]

The Theory of the Social Market Economy

When *Faith in the City* first appeared, it was 'rubbished' by several Tory spokespersons who denounced it as being more Marxist than Christian.[14] In order to be able to give a carefully considered refutation of this charge – and in response to friendly critics (most notably, Raymond Plant) who warned that the Church's familiar arguments about compassion for the needy would not satisfy politicians and ordinary people who had been seduced by New Right thinking – the Industrial and Economic Affairs Committee of the BSR arranged to devote one of its 1986 residential meetings to a full-scale debate on the question, 'Can a Christian Support a Social Market Economy?' Lord Harris of High Cross, a staunch Anglican and a professional economist, delivered a paper expressing almost unqualified praise for the market; John Atherton responded with a balanced critique which took into account the benefits of the market without overlooking its defects and shortcomings.

Harris began by reciting the familiar New Right litany concerning the evils of too much government intervention in the economy. He conceded the state's essential role in providing income support for the poor ('in cash rather than in kind'), but he deplored 'the massive expansion of government this century [which] has not been guided (or justified) by intellectual analysis or the "public interest" but by electoral expediency driven by political competition for votes and power.'[15] He attacked 'the resultant growth in government taxation, regulation and spending' as disastrously counter-productive, alleging that it 'has not removed (but rather inflamed) the grievances that were its original justification.'[16] In addition, he contended that the market has *political* as well as economic advantages (since competitive markets 'limit the evil bad men can do'), and he pointed out that 'disillusion with overblown government has provoked a world-wide reaction towards the freeing of individual enterprise, even by socialists in countries as different as Australia, New Zealand, Hungary and China.'[17]

Like many New Right thinkers, Harris attacked the naïveté of bishops and clerics who espouse a simple-minded notion of Christianity's 'bias to the poor,' and he chastised religious observers who denounce the motivation of business people; indeed, he rebuked all leftist would-be do-gooders because of their lack of understanding of the pervasiveness of sin, including the ambiguity of all human motives. Quoting the philosopher William Barrett on the tendency of the socialist tradition to overlook the limitations imposed upon life by 'the human condition itself,' and quoting Hayek and Friedman on the virtues of free enterprise, he opined that 'The merit of the market is that it harnesses individual effort, economy and thrift to maximise present and future social output, *not* by the narrow incentive of self-interest, but by the widest opportunity for everyone to pursue his own *self-chosen purposes*.'[18] He concluded that Christians should have a special reason for supporting a market economy; namely, their appreciation of the power of sin and their knowledge that the market is a better check on sin than the state can be.

Atherton concedes the 'appropriateness for advanced western First World societies' of six key features of the free enterprise system (the market mechanism, its scope for individualism - defined as 'the protection and promotion of the particular person,' its harnessing of self-interest, its use of incentives, the legitimacy of profit and its place for competition). What he regards as unacceptable is the degree of poverty and inequality in all market societies, and what he fears especially (and assails) is the *ideological* mind-set of so many market enthusiasts (i.e., their habit of believing uncritically in *laissez-faire* and their tendency to claim that their faith in it is a *science* 'rather than a mixture of fact and value').[19] He concludes the paper for the 1986 consultation with a discussion of the principal features of a social market economy, and the main advantages it offers.

What is a 'social market economy'? Atherton may err in his understanding of the concept in seeming to equate it with 'democratic capitalism' as explained by American spokespersons such as Novak, Benne and Wogaman - but he is correct in saying that it is 'found classically in the UK, the SDP of West Germany, Sweden and France.' Its essence is neatly summed up in the Godesberg programme of 1957, which speaks of 'as much competition as possible, as much planning as necessary.' Its principal features are these: (1) there are many private centres of economic power; (2) the private sector is strong, 'although ultimately responsible to Government'; (3) there are numerous checks and balances, not a unified political elite; (4) there are many incentives 'to harness self-interest to the common good,' and there is a high degree of 'liberty of economic initiative in labour and enterprise'; (5) it is a mixed economy in which equality of opportunity, fair and competitive markets and democratic decision-making prevail, but one in which the operations of the market are limited and guided by a strong government, and supplemented by 'an affordable Welfare State.'[20]

What are the major advantages of the social market economy? To a significant degree, the features listed above are also justifications, because a society characterized by dynamic wealth creation, freedom of choice and movement, democratic decision-making and a pragmatic mentality which eschews the illusory comforts of 'hard sectarian ideologies' (right or left) is in these respects a very good society. The chief advantages of a social market economy - and this is why it is called a *social* market economy - stem from an awareness (which Christians ought to be especially alert to) that, as Reinhold Niebuhr declares, 'If the doctrine of original sin stresses the imperfection of politics, that of original righteousness indicates its necessity and possibilities.' This translates into two crucial corollaries: as (even?!) Brian Griffiths has said, the state *has* to intervene on the side of the poor, and 'morality stretches very significantly beyond the market, which is indeed dependent on the values which pre-date it, and on the contributions of people to the social fabric, including that made through intermediate associations.'[21]

But in keeping with the second part of the ecumenical formula referred to above, John Atherton declared that pure *laissez-faire* is unacceptable for the following four reasons: (1) it is usually advanced in conjunction with a 'hard determinist ideology claiming [spurious] scientific objectivity'; (2) it 'over-values the determining power of free market and economics, and under-values politics in general and democratic politics in particular'; (3) it causes (or perpetuates) 'grave inequalities, poverty and unemployment'; (4) it tends to 'promote private and public selfishness because of its imbalanced concentration on the motives of self-interest and fear.'[22]

The BSR's Reply to 'The Sermon on the Mound'

The indictment of selfishness contained in Atherton's fourth complaint against *laissez-faire* ideology is echoed in virtually everything on the topic of economic justice put forth by the Church of England. The issue has been joined in sermons or other public statements in which a number of bishops (notably David Jenkins) have denounced the Thatcher administration for fostering a cultural atmosphere of heedless self-regard. Particularly significant in this connection is an open letter from the General Secretary of the BSR and the bishop who heads it, attacking the Prime Minister's highly publicized 'Sermon on the Mound.'

As noted in Chapter 1, the Sermon on the Mound was a significant statement of the Prime Minister's social philosophy. It is an affirmation of faith in religious individualism which ignores everything that has been discerned and proclaimed by social Christianity in the past 120 years, and fits very nicely with Mrs Thatcher's notorious statement to the effect that 'there is no such thing as society, only individuals and families.' Interestingly enough, this speech echoes Clement of Alexandria's famous treatise on 'Who is the Rich Man That is Being Saved?' in its spiritualization of the doctrine of radical stewardship which was typical of most of the early church fathers, for it declares that 'it is not the creation of wealth that is wrong, but love of money for its own sake.'[23]

On 27 May 1988, the Chairman of the BSR, the Rt Rev. John Yates, Bishop of Gloucester, joined John Gladwin, General Secretary of the Board, in submitting a rejoinder to Mrs Thatcher's speech. It lauded 'your stress on personal responsibility,' agreeing that 'all serious social policy should be aimed at enabling people to carry out their obligations more responsibly.' But it went on to assert that personal responsibility cannot be properly understood 'without stressing also the essentially social character of human life,' and it pointed out that 'Governments, therefore, have clear social and moral obligations, [namely] . . . to pursue policies which create and encourage that sense of community and mutuality which are the hallmarks of a complete human life.' The letter explains:

> This is why the churches have persistently seemed a nuisance in societies which seem to be casual in their attitude to the poor and distressed. Deep divisions and injustices in society threaten our sense of common life. . . . The question is, do governments accept on behalf of us all in society, a responsibility to play – and to be seen as playing – a crucial and inescapable part in the fight against these

enemies of the human, namely poverty, unemployment, victimisation and distress? These matters are not just about what individuals do but also about what governments do or do not do.

On the subject of wealth creation *per se*, which it says must *not* be described as 'neutral, as though the only moral questions are those concerning what individuals do with this wealth,' the letter from Yates and Gladwin makes three fundamental points. (1) We must ask 'searching questions about how wealth is gained,' because 'wealth gained regardless of the welfare of the rest of the community is difficult to justify.' (2) We must be ever wary of the spiritual dangers of wealth, because great disparities of wealth and poverty tend to produce despair as well as deprivation in the poor and an idolatrous sense of 'total self reliance and independence' in the rich. (3) Since it is

> not realistic to think that the needs of the poor can be met in our sort of world by individual charity alone, . . . it cannot be the case that we should encourage generosity by individuals at one and the same time as government works on a policy of giving only the barest minimum.[24]

Continuing Support for the Welfare State

Most important of all, though, is the Church of England's consistent defence of redistributive revenue policies and welfare state programmes put under attack during the Thatcher years. Proposed cuts in social security, the long-established 'Social Wage' (an unemployment relief measure dating back to the early part of the century), public housing and the National Health Service have been stoutly resisted by BSR spokespersons, and by members of the House of Lords whose speeches are informed (and in some cases drafted) by BSR staff persons.

Key Documents

The Church of England's resolute advocacy of the need for ambitious welfare state programmes at an adequate level of funding which only the state can provide has been repeatedly and consistently declared in high-profile publications such as *Not Just for the Poor*, which emerged from a three-year long inquiry into 'The Future of the Welfare State', and *Faith in the City*, a report on Urban Priority Areas which was issued by an ecclesiastical version of a Royal Commission and has resulted in an extraordinary follow-up programme.

NOT JUST FOR THE POOR

Not Just for the Poor is a 146-page book which appeared in 1986. Significant not only because of its length but also for its content, it represents a substantial leap forward from the group of rather unimaginative publications produced by a different BSR leadership in the mid-1970s.[25] *Not Just for the Poor* offers a useful summary of the continuing need for state provision of welfare entitlements while at the same time facing up to some of the fiscal inadequacies and bureaucratic shortcomings of the British welfare state in practice. It contains a theological section which does a good job of reiterating some of the principal reasons for the Church's role in establishing the welfare state, and it reminds its readers of the extent of continuing public support for health and welfare services, including what opinion polls reveal about the public's willingness 'to pay more in taxes in order to finance some of the public services more generously.'[26] Its defence of the success of certain elements of the welfare state since the Second World War is less elaborate than the defence of New Deal/Great Society programmes in John Schwarz's admirably persuasive *America's Hidden Success*, and it admits that there is no clear path ahead in terms of the *means* through which the aims of the welfare state can be achieved – but it leaves no doubt about the ends towards which policy should be directed. In the words of David Donnison, chairman of the former Supplementary Benefits Commission (and author of a first-rate book on *The Politics of Poverty*):

> To keep out of poverty, people must have an income which enables them to parti-
> cipate in the life of the community. They must be able, for example, to keep
> themselves reasonably fed, and well enough dressed to maintain their self-respect
> and to attend interviews for jobs with confidence. Their homes must be
> reasonably warm; their children should not feel shamed by the quality of their
> clothing; the family must be able to visit relatives, and to give them something on
> their birthdays and at Christmas time; they must be able to read newspapers and
> retain their television sets and their membership in trade unions and churches.
> And they must be able to live in a way which ensures, in so far as possible, that
> public officials, doctors, teachers, landlords and others treat them with the
> courtesy due to every member of the community.[27]

Not Just for the Poor begins with a collection of vignettes describing persons and families whose lives are touched by some aspect of the welfare state. This intro-ductory focus is in keeping with the publication's announced intention to draw atten-tion to 'the small, personal and local,' its stress on *interdependence*, its 'determina-tion not to leave things to the experts', and its attempt to express a hopeful point of view on the problems in question. It goes on to a matter-of-fact examination of the trends affecting the welfare state today, and concludes by offering an assessment of its strengths and weaknesses in the light of very general 'common culture' (common-sense) criteria and in the light of theological presuppositions which it dares to spell out.

The discussion of trends provides certain basic facts about the breakdown of the welfare state consensus[28] and about the rise of the assortment of subsidies, tax bene-fits and infrastructure provisions which have come to be referred to as 'the private welfare state';[29] that is, the ironic situation in which the state very frequently bes-tows greater benefits on the middle-class and the rich than it provides for the poor. Thus the significance of the book's title is given a special twist – but the title is also intended to make the extremely serious and significant point that the welfare state is genuinely conceived of as a societal arrangement which promotes the *common* good of all classes and groups of citizens.

The analysis of benefits and liabilities is rather curious, for the one great achieve-ment of the British welfare state in its nearly forty years of existence is said to be its establishment of the *principle* of certain benefits as *rights*. The major liabilities listed are: (1) the inadequacy of the financial resources allocated for welfare benefits (especially after double-digit inflation in the 1970s); (2) the adoption of ill-conceived patchwork measures (especially, for example, the policies regarding supplementary benefits); (3) the flaws in the social security programme; (4) the regressive effect of the benefits structure; (5) the creation of dependency (and, of course, the resent-ments, confusion and depression which often accompany it); and (6) the rigidities and inelasticities which made it impossible for services and benefits to keep up with changing social conditions (e.g., *long-term* unemployment and the need for conciliation services).[30] In addition, certain 'ideological' criticisms made from such perspectives as feminism, Marxism, New Right and 'localism' are also touched upon. These indictments seem to boil down to two main charges: inadequate delivery of services, and the problem of dependency/demoralization in the alleged beneficiaries of the welfare state.

Among the conceptual questions highlighted are these: (1) What are the true purposes of the welfare state? (e.g., is it intended primarily to furnish a 'safety net' for the least advantaged – or does it seek serious redistribution of economic resources and social cohesion?).[31] (2) What level of benefits and services could be called sufficient? (3) What significance can be found in the attitudes of the populace towards these concerns, and – especially – what are we to make of the fact that most people say they are more than willing to be taxed to pay for welfare state programmes?

But considering the clarity of the descriptive analysis, the normative conclusions are rather lame.[32] Of the five possible policy approaches deemed worthy of consideration, only two are viewed as morally and politically viable: after ruling out 'laissez-faire plus charity' (the position of the New Right), a minimal safety net and thoroughgoing collectivism in which the state provides *everything*, the only two remaining options are (1) the state as funder and setter of standards and (2) the state as provider of essential benefits not provided by the market and the voluntary sector. Six 'areas of choice' are identified, and the following tentative conclusions are advanced: the family cannot do much more than it is now doing; the public sector is in principle just as dignified and effective as the private sector (indeed, it sometimes works *better* – e.g., more *efficiently* – than the private sector); tax and benefits policies should be formulated in tandem and seen as mutually supportive instead of contradictory; and an open mind is recommended on issues such as the role of the voluntary sector, the question of whether benefits should be universal or selective, and the issue regarding the trade-offs pertaining to participation vs flexibility and prompt response to need (which professionals and establishment organizations are often better at than voluntary groups which stress participation).

FAITH IN THE CITY

Faith in the City is a formidable document. It merits careful study for several reasons, not the least of which is the fact that it received extraordinary attention in the press, was bought by almost fifty thousand consumers and read, perhaps, by as many as five or six times that many citizens. Furthermore, the *quality* of the document is first-rate: it represents the thinking of a 'blue ribbon committee' of experts who spent almost two years visiting inner-city areas and gathering data for the report, and its catalogue of needs and policy recommendations is worthy of serious study. What deserves emphasis here are these two aspects of the publication:

1. It reiterates the firmly established Christian notion of the mutual responsibility linking all citizens in a network of covenant obligations. The theologizing of the report may be open to the criticism which it has received, but the central thrust of the moral argument is unimpeachable: all of God's children are enjoined to care about and care for one another. Effective fulfilment of this elemental moral duty requires into use of the powers of the state, which is appropriately called upon to carry out its ordained task of protecting the least advantaged and ensuring a decent standard of living for its citizenry.

2. The policy recommendations of *Faith in the City* are advanced in the context of implicit acceptance of the welfare state. Most of the specific imperatives of the report call for more money to be spent on providing for well-established needs: pub-

lic housing, health care, education, employment training and unemployment relief, etc. Its contribution to the discussion of salient welfare state programmes is covered in the next section of this chapter.

Salient Programmes

Three welfare state programmes have been consistently supported by the Church of England. Its social witness in these important areas of life merits special attention.

Social Security

One of the government initiatives to which the BSR responded was its proposed reform of social security. In addition to offering testimony on this topic to the Department of Health and Social Security in August 1984, the Social Policy Committee of the BSR also submitted a commentary on the government's Green Paper in early 1985 and generated a discussion of the issues concerned in General Synod in August 1985. In keeping with established precedent, the response to the Green Paper did not attempt a detailed critique of the recommendations, but endeavoured instead to 'reflect on the underlying principles and to consider them in the light of [the following questions]':[33]

(a) What are the implications for the poorest and most vulnerable members of our society?
(b) In the allocation of resources available, will the proposals achieve a just and fair distribution?
(c) Are the proposals likely to increase the divisions in our society?

In addition, the Social Policy Committee of the BSR also issued a briefing paper on the Social Fund set up by Social Security reforms which raised many decisive questions about the implications of this highly problematic innovation. It attacked certain features of the new plan, in particular its redefinition of the concept of need and its practical requirement that 'the basic needs of more people will be made in future from charitable funds.' Likening this feature to the infamous Poor Law of bygone days, the briefing paper declared that 'Even if they wanted to comply, it is difficult to see how agencies could make the financial commitment necessary to meet the likely level of need.'[34]

Housing

Since housing is such a crucial aspect of basic economic needs, the Church of England has consistently been involved in striving to see that adequate housing is available to all citizens.[35] Its two most important single statements on this topic are to be found in a booklet on *Housing and Homelessness*, which was published by the BSR in 1982, and in Chapter 10 of *Faith in the City*, which devotes thirty-five pages to a discussion of housing needs in Urban Priority Areas. In addition, of course, the Church has for many decades been involved in helping to raise money for the voluntary housing associations which are so essential as a source of mortgage funds in Britain, and it has made a consistent attempt to influence public policy through responses to government white papers and speeches in Parliament (especially through statements by bishops in the House of Lords).

Housing and Homelessness appeared at a time when the plight of the homeless was receiving a good deal of public attention, and eight of its fourteen pages deal with the desperate problems of this rapidly growing segment of the population. In theory, the homeless are protected by a 1977 Act of Parliament which stipulates that local authorities 'must provide permanent housing to anyone who is homeless and in priority need, where homelessness is intentional.' But in view of the fact that 'priority need' and 'intentional homelessness' are subject to widely varying interpretations (that are often a function of the financial condition of local councils which are being squeezed by the national government), the reality is that more and more unfortunates either have no place to stay at all, or are forced to live in exceedingly unsatisfactory conditions. The situation is severely aggravated by the startling shortage of rental housing in Britain: whereas nine-tenths of all housing accommodations in Britain were rentals in 1914, 'currently the rental sector forms only one-tenth of all tenures.'[36] The crisis is summed up in the following words:

> The structure of the housing market throws the problem of housing into sharp relief. There is an increasing shortage of private rented accommodation, local authority housing is not available for certain groups within the population, owner occupation is beyond the financial means of many and housing associations have been able to touch only the edges of the problem.[37]

Interestingly enough, the 1982 booklet, which closes with no fewer than eleven recommendations for action by concerned Christians, has nothing to say about specific remedies for homelessness *per se*, and *Faith in the City* merely calls for an extension of the Homeless Persons Act to cover all who are homeless, and for some choice of accommodations to be offered to the homeless.[38] Both of the key documents concentrate instead upon the broader aspects of public policy on housing.

Housing and Homelessness, which is directed primarily to members of the Anglican communion, begins by calling for certain changes in attitude which are seen as a prerequisite for any type of constructive action. It urges church people to 'awaken individual and community consciences to the deteriorating housing situation in this country,' and asks parishes 'to receive and welcome into the community those currently inappropriately accommodated in hospitals and hostels, especially mentally handicapped and elderly people.' In addition to its admonitions to individuals ('to contribute to a property purchasing trust' and to 'consider whether or not to rent rooms or provide board and lodging or convert one's own property into flats'), it asks church groups and parish councils to disseminate relevant information, to 'cooperate with Social Service Departments and child care organisations, . . . with agencies such as MIND' (which seeks 'sympathetic landlords/landladies for ex-psychiatric patients') and 'with agencies such as . . . the Probation Service in finding accommodation for ex-offenders.' In short, it endeavours to persuade Anglicans to become fully informed about the housing situation in the nation and in their own area, to investigate the possibilities of allocating church resources to housing and/or support for agencies (such as voluntary housing associations) engaged in promoting housing opportunities, and to help provide better accommodations and friendlier treatment for those whose housing situation is unsatisfactory.[39]

Faith in the City, which is directed to the world as well as the Church, is somewhat more political in its recommendations. It favours heavier investment in this crucial area of need (for 'an expanded public housing programme of new building and improvement, . . . particularly in the UPAs, to ensure a substantial supply of good quality rented accommodation for all who need it, including single people'), administrative changes (such as the keeping of ethnic records 'as a step towards eliminating direct and indirect discrimination in housing allocations' and 'further moves towards the decentralisation of local authority housing services'), and legislative reforms, such as extension of the Housing (Homeless Persons) Act 'to cover all who are homeless' and to offer the homeless 'a choice of accommodation.' It urges, finally – and most ambitiously! – 'a major examination of the whole system of housing finance, including mortgage tax relief,' the object being to 'provide most help to those most in need.'[40]

Briefings prepared by BSR staff personnel for bishops who address housing issues in debates in the House of Lords contain a number of specific proposals. One commentary on the Housing and Building Control Bill which was delivered at its second reading in April 1983 pointed out that the proposed sale of housing units to existing occupants would 'profit individual tenants at the expense of future generations.' Another suggested that such a policy would violate the understanding about the financial need of renters which had informed the thinking of many church groups and individual benefactors and had, in fact, motivated them to donate funds to benevolent housing associations. The further claims were advanced that such sales would involve 'the attaching of conditions retrospectively to the acceptance of Government grants,' and that 'the provisions of the Bill breach charity law' by allowing property to be sold to current tenants at a fifty per cent discount. It was even argued that the Bill 'will make it difficult for some housing associations to continue.'[41]

In 1984, the Church called for the reintroduction of a Private Member's Bill on Houses in Multiple Occupation which 'would have required local authorities to enforce certain minimum standards in such properties.' In April, 1985 Baroness Fisher of Rednall spoke from a BSR brief 'to call attention to the case for investment in public housing and the severe difficulties facing the homeless and badly housed,' and in 1986 Lord Banks drew on a similar BSR document in protesting the inadequacy of existing policy regarding bed and breakfast accommodation for the homeless. The Lord Bishop of Southwark summarized a significant element of the social philosophy of the Church of England on these matters when he declared that although housing associations 'can play – and already play – a vital part in providing new accommodation for the single and homeless,' and that voluntary giving can accomplish some good in this area, 'clearly only local and central government can provide the quite substantial help which is now needed to get some more schemes off the drawing boards and into operation to meet the growing need, [particularly the] wide range of support services and special care required.'[42]

The National Health Service

In 1989, the Social Policy Committee of the BSR produced a position paper which raised a number of fundamental questions about the government's plans to revamp the National Health Service, as these plans had been revealed in a White Paper[43] entitled *Working With Patients*. This thirty-page BSR document, printed without a cover as GS 887, is called 'Working for Patients,' and was distributed to all members of the General Synod as an item for discussion at its meeting in July 1989. The first half is devoted to an introduction which places its appearance in the context of the welfare state principles articulated in *Not Just for the Poor*, a review of the history of the NHS and a summary of the government's proposals for altering its structure and operating processes. The evaluative comments which comprise the second half of the paper are organized under four main headings: (1) questions about specific features of the proposed changes, (2) an assessment of what has been proposed in terms of their own stated aims, (3) a listing of significant omissions and, finally, (4) a reiteration of two fundamental concerns which are especially important in the light of Anglican ethical thought.

The BSR's 'Working for Patients' echoes the complaints and qualms of many medical professionals in pointing out that 'the very tight time schedules [envisaged] will leave little time for consultation.' It points out that although 'implementation of the proposals will mean large increases in the bureaucracy of the NHS, no indication of the associated costs or the sources of additional funding is given.' It also warns that 'there may be difficulties in recruiting and training staff,' and that the proposals are marred by 'a lack of detail which often obscures the intentions' underlying them.[44] Further commentary on this point reveals a pervasive anxiety about 'a "hidden agenda" aimed at financial savings by imposing financial stringency and transferring responsibility to local management.'[45] This fear about governmental intent is augmented by the White Paper's proposal for the establishment of NHS Hospital Trusts which can be run on a for-profit basis: this measure would create a two-tier system in which NHS units under the old dispensation will have to bear a disproportionate responsibility for indigent care, it would exaggerate the dubious effects of the already existing two-tier payment policy for professional and non-professional employees: 'To balance the budget, the wages of unskilled workers may have to be kept as low as possible. These effects are likely to be most severely felt in the self-governing hospitals where competition will be keen because of the emphasis on the profit motive.'[46] An additional fear is that the care of patients in general practice will be undermined by budgetary pressures: 'Cash limits, downward pressure on expenditure on drugs and effects of contractual arrangements with hospitals are potentially harmful to the doctor-patient relationship.'[47]

Other provisions of the White Paper regarding the structural and budgetary dimensions of the NHS seem to undercut its own stated purposes. After noting that 'the intention to improve the hospital service by reducing waiting lists, introducing a better appointments system, and by giving more rapid notification of the results of tests . . . is to be welcomed,' the BSR critique contends that patient access and choice may be eroded instead of enhanced. It points out that 'the offering of services in other Districts [i.e., a District in which a patient is a not a resident] depends on a degree of mobility not available to many people,' and it expresses concern about the probability that 'people with "expensive" conditions may have difficulty in registering with different doctors because of their unlikely demands on budgets.' It voices similar concerns about the prospect that people will have to go without treatment when their general practitioner's budget is overspent, and about the probable curtailment of expensive diagnostic tests based on a hard-pressed doctor's hunch that the test for a given patient will prove negative. It also acknowledges the persistence of social-class factors which virtually ensure that the historical differential in usage of the NHS will continue because of the fact that 'more articulate, more affluent people [are] able more readily to command treatment.'[48] It asks, in short, 'What will happen to the trust between a doctor and a patient if the decision to treat is inextricably bound up with the decision to spend?'[49] Another complaint is that the proposed delegation of responsibility to the local level is more than cancelled out by the centralization of power and authority in the Secretary of State and the Regional Health Authorities. 'What will be lost,' one fears, 'is any vestige of democratically accountable decision making within the management structure,' because

If the NHS is to be increasingly subject to the discipline of the market at the same time as the service becomes less democratically accountable then it will be important for 'consumers' to be provided with the information and access to decision makers they will need to defend their interests.[50]

Several omissions are troubling: an adequate appreciation of something which is emphasized in *Not Just for the Poor*, namely, the state's crucial role as the setter and supervisor of adequate health care standards; adequate provision for (and stress on) preventive health care; several proposals for improving the quality of primary health care advanced in a 1987 government White Paper called *Promoting Better Health* (proposals which were, lamentably, ignored in *Working With Patients*); and some policy suggestions put forth in another government-commissioned report on *Community Care: An Agenda for Action*, published in 1988 but thereafter ignored by the government.[51]

The BSR's 'Working for Patients' closes by reiterating the traditional ethical distinction between active euthanasia (which it condemns) and the affirmation that one is not required to take heroic measures simply to maintain biological existence in dying patients. This statement of an important element in Christian social witness is made in connection with a brief discussion of the allocation of scarce medical resources and a rejection of the bias towards glamorous 'high technology medicine which is seen to be exciting and satisfying in a way that the routine alleviation of minor illnesses or the care of elderly or mentally handicapped people is not.'[52]

In July 1989, the General Synod devoted itself to a discussion of *Working With Patients* and to a consideration of the BSR's response. It voiced its participation in 'the considerable history of Christian concern for an involvement in the provision of medical services' by going on record with a statement to the effect that the General Synod

(a) urges the Secretary of State to ensure that health and not cost is the prime objective and the requirements for economy in the use of time and money as set out in *Working With Patients* do not undermine the provision of effective treatment;

(b) believes that the changes proposed are likely to affect adversely the access of vulnerable people to adequate health care;

(c) calls on the Secretary of State to extend the consultation period and only to introduce the changes if their feasibility has been established through trial projects.[53]

* * *

As we noted at the beginning of Chapter 1, the Church of England has been attacked for refusing to acknowledge the futility of the welfare state. But in calling for a continuation (or even an expansion) of the crucial services of the welfare state, the leadership of the Church is in tune with the British public, which remains convinced of the value of the programmes and does not want to see them discontinued or crippled. Moreover, in opposing proposed cutbacks and changes in the National Health Service, the Church is also in tune with most of the doctors and public health authorities in Britain, who have protested what they consider to be the counter-productiveness of the changes favoured by Mrs Thatcher. So when it comes to the central concerns of the welfare state, the social witness of the Church echoes expert opinion as well as the public pulse.[54]

The Stance on Specific Issues

Work

Since 1975 the BSR has issued several position papers which deal to a significant degree with the topic of *work*.[55] The policy recommendations set forth in these publications include support for *full employment* as a crucial social policy goal, an affirmation of *technological innovation*, a suggestion that the traditional work ethic needs to be supplemented by a *life ethic* which affirms that one may achieve dignity and worth without holding a conventional job, and a tentative endorsement of *work-sharing* (conditional upon maintenance of existing rates of pay and no loss of wage income). In addition, two publications have explored questions pertaining to union-management relationships. One sets forth in a surprisingly tentative and almost apologetic way the case for the legitimacy of the closed shop; the other tries to explain why strikes are sometimes inevitable and are frequently a legitimate expression of grievances or demands which cannot and should not be suppressed. In *Winters of Discontent*, the BSR takes a position on three significant issues: (1) it says that the government's ban on secondary picketing puts labour at an unfair disadvantage, since employers are free to seek secondary suppliers, workers, etc.; (2) it declares that no strike ought to be called unless it is genuinely the will of the union members (therefore, it calls for a secret ballot vote before any strike action is taken); and (3) it argues that supplementary benefits (under the welfare system) ought not to be taken away from strikers' families, for doing so would put them in a lower status than prisoners, whose families are not similarly deprived.

In addition, *Winters of Discontent* offers a theory of 'the just strike' which uses the notion of proportionality to interpret what happened in the 'dirty jobs' strike in 1979. It shows commendable insight into the rage that relatively weak persons and their organizations often feel when arrayed against institutions of vastly superior power. The main point is that the general public ought not to be so censorious against workers who sometimes exhibit rage.

A special problem was addressed in a 1986 booklet called *And All That is Unseen*, which dealt with some of the issues concerning work which are of particular concern to women. Although it was subtitled 'A New Look at Women and Work,' it said almost nothing about comparative worth, flexitime, day care or pregnancy leave. Its summary of the facts of the matter stresses that women have been one-third of the labour force for over a century, and have been over 40% in the 1980s. Trends (as of 1984) indicate that an ever greater number of women will spend their adult years in the labour market in the future, much of this time being spent in part-time jobs.[56] Since 1975, the pay scale for women is only slightly more than 70% of that for men; however, that percentage seems to be very stable; it has not risen lately (and, in fact, has gone down just a little).[57]

Its discussion of underlying attitudes suggests that women's work is still considered to be of secondary significance, for females receive lower pay and have lower status. Furthermore, women are still 'two-shift workers': they are expected to do the housework when they come home. This goes with prevailing stereotypes about women as belonging to the private sphere, and finding their true fulfilment there. It should be noted, incidentally, that the booklet calls housework 'unpaid.' It also points out that house/homework includes caring for the sick or old, children of relatives, etc.: this labour is dubbed 'quiet, unseen caring,' a choice of words which helps to explain the title of the booklet. It proceeds to observe that the burden of house/homework makes it difficult for women to participate in union endeavours and similar activities, and it disguises the extent of their unemployment: if their work does not matter very much, and/or is part-time, their not being at work (even though they might want a steady job) is relatively unnoticed.

The theological assumptions of the study are revealed in its statement to the effect that theology must take experience as seriously as traditional or 'revealed truth,' and this means, among other things, that the world is not really the way men have usually portrayed it: it looks very different from the standpoint of women. Values such as stewardship and servanthood are endorsed – with the proviso that these are just service (i.e., service aimed at promoting justice), not subservience. 'The latter,' it contends, 'is not a Christian virtue.'

Environmental Concerns

For moralists whose primary concern is economic justice, ecology tends to be a secondary interest. If feeding the hungry and housing the homeless is your top priority, then wealth creation is good, and so is the technology required to produce the goods and services human beings require. It is not surprising, then, that until recently Christian social ethics has said a great deal about promoting growth and distributing its dividends fairly, but relatively little about the limits to industrial growth.

The social witness of the Church of England fits this pattern. Even if we expand the temporal scope of our study and go back as far as 1970, we find only two BSR publications which deal with ecological issues. The first is *Man in his Living Environment*, which was issued by a working party of the BSR as a contribution to European Conservation Year 1970. It declares:

> We are seeking nothing less than a cultural revolution in which it is affirmed that despoiling the earth is a blasphemy and not just an error of judgment, a mistake; in which proper concern for all living creatures . . . becomes righteousness and not mere sentimental kindness.[58]

It goes on to proclaim that 'Only the perspective of eternity, combined with a heart-felt conviction of man's accountability before God,' will suffice to overcome contemporary man's insatiable demand for 'an even higher material standard of living in the secular city.'[59] The 'perspective of eternity' is then defined as in part a determination 'to enlist our youth and employ our wealth to build the mature, enlightened civilization that now eludes us' by exemplifying the 'kind of faith that says to the mountain "Be thou moved" and then moves it a spadeful at a time.'[60]

Following this statement of lofty aspirations, the booklet concentrates on investigating specific dimensions of the limits-to-growth problem – population, food, pollution, resource depletion and appropriate technology for sustainable economic growth – and the formulation of policy recommendations designed to implement necessary reforms. As the authors wisely observe, the desired cultural revolution necessitates 'a conversion which subordinates immediate gains to future good . . . [and] challenges the cult, though not the fact, of social and industrial efficiency.'[61] It warns that although 'people and governments might be stirred to action by disasters, . . . a series of disconnected alarmist moves is not good policy,' and it asserts that

> provisions for vigilance and for achieving dynamic conservation of the world's resources should, and must, be built into the established ordering of our society and become a regular and recognised part of management [which] involves

specific programmes concerning water, soil, air, populations, animals and the rest.[62]

The theological rationale for this stance is worked out in impressive detail. After making the familiar point that the biblical view of humankind's relationship to nature is that of stewardship, not domination, it postulates 'throughout mankind biological and emotional needs that require, not the conquest of nature, but rather harmonious collaboration with its forces.'[63] It proceeds to contrast the 'good, rational, desirable change' that results from 'natural birth, growing old and dying' with the sort of 'death and decay brought about through the practice of the deadly sins of avarice, greed and pride [which] destroy the earth.' Insights drawn both from the humanism of Julian Huxley and the process philosophy of Alister Hardy are invoked to reinforce an organic view of the wholeness of all life forms, and an ethic of animal rights is articulated along with that of environmental protection.

Our Responsibility for the Living Environment appeared sixteen years later. Its review of the biblical record includes a direct challenge to the hyperbolic charges levelled by writers such as Ian McHarg (who calls Gen. 1.26-8 a 'declaration of war on nature') and Lynn White, Jr., who inveighs against 'the Judaeo-Christian belief that . . . humans can treat the natural environment as they like, . . . [since] it is God's will that man exploit nature for his proper ends.' It demonstrates a commendable recognition that both poverty and wealth lead to environmental damage, and that the very desire for technological and economic development which is so essential to global economic justice is in itself a danger to ecological health against which safeguards must be instituted. It also shows a prudent awareness of the complexity of what it terms 'the dilemmas of environmental decision making' which contains a very illuminating discussion of animal rights (in food production, in medical experimentation and in wildlife conservation areas).[64] It ends with a summary of the general conclusions of a 1983 British publication entitled *The Conservation and Development Programme for the United Kingdom*, which set forth no fewer than 169 specific policy recommendations for a World Conservation Strategy.

International Dimensions of Economic Justice

A striking diversity is apparent in recent Church of England publications in this area of concern. This is no doubt a reflection of the fact that the Industrial and Economic Affairs Committee and the International Affairs Committee (IEAC) of the BSR rely on rather different sets of experts. In the latter, the strongest single influence is probably that of Charles Elliott, the sole author of *Comfortable Compassion*, the principal author of *Let Justice Flow*, and the writer of the final chapter in *Reflections on Brandt*. In contrast, the IEAC's booklet on *Transnational Corporations* contains essays by seven different authors who express widely varying points of view.

Transnational Corporations (TNCs)

In 1982, the IEAC put together a working party which produced a booklet called *Transnational Corporations: Confronting the Issues*. After an opening chapter which explains the publication as a manifestation of the widespread ecumenical interest in the topic which had led to a five-year study of TNCs by the World Council of Churches, and to parallel studies by other church and academic groups in various parts of the world, the booklet offers a balanced commentary on TNCs and their impact on Third World countries. Two chapters describe the performance of TNCs in a very

optimistic and benevolent light; two are quite critical; and two are filled with suggestions about what British Christians can do to improve performance.

In the serene conviction that 'investment funds now flow to where they can earn
the highest return, *that is, create the greatest wealth* [italics added]' and that 'only
by operating in this way are TNCs efficient,' a former TNC executive argues that
TNCs elevate the standard of living by following the imperatives of economic
rationality. Thus he sees no reason why they should not retain full power to make all
decisions affecting prices, purchases and employment; indeed, he is convinced that
'the best help to be given to the poorest nations must include assisting them to provide the preconditions for attracting TNCs.'[65] A former World Bank functionary
allows that 'there have undoubtedly been instances when TNCs have been insuffi-
ciently sensitive to the needs and aspirations of the third world, . . . for few things
are wholly evil or wholly good,' but he contends that 'the impact of TNCs in Africa
and Asia is overwhelmingly positive,' and he concludes that 'they have made an
indispensable contribution to raising world living standards and need to be encouraged rather than denigrated.'[66]

A different perspective is expressed by Tina Wallace, whose experience as a student of agriculture and land ownership in Nigeria underlies her article on 'The
Damaging Impact of TNCs on the Third World.' She challenges six claims often
advanced in connection with the notion that TNCs contribute to optimum economic
development throughout the world:

1. New local capital is *not* always generated, especially in situations where (to
quote an advertisement for investment) tax concessions and 'guaranteed repatria-
tion of profits' provide 'a proven and budding economic climate.'[67]

2. Inappropriate technology is often installed in defiance of local needs.

3. A net gain in employment opportunities does not always result from the
advent of a TNC, for some existing job-holders are usually displaced and 'TNCs
everywhere very often create fewer jobs for the capital invested than would be
created with equivalent investment in local production.'[68] Moreover, working
conditions and pay in relation to profits are often deplorable, for they are a part
of the economic incentive for establishing a plant in a Third World country.

4. 'While the new industries may produce "quality" products for export and
earn foreign exchange, . . . they frequently undermine alternative producers and
methods of production' and retard healthy diversification.[69]

5. New products (Coca-Cola!) are not always beneficial.

6. The 'stability' which TNCs are said to provide may actually bolster a
government which does not function in the best interest of the majority of
citizens.

In sum, says the author, two key questions must be answered: 'How much can
we expect TNCs to bring to areas of the world where *poverty* is the rule?' and 'How
far does their presence in a country inhibit alternative models of development?'[70]

After a chapter on TNCs and labour unions, which points out that labour organizations often make workers in different parts of the world aware of the advantages
enjoyed by others and therefore serve to promote better working conditions and pay
on a worldwide basis, the booklet closes with a pair of essays on what local churches
ought to do in regard to the issues raised by a study of TNCs, and on how these
issues ought to be understood from the standpoint of Christian ethics. Mike West
urges his readers to concentrate their attention on the food and beverage sector of the
economy, in which 'the contrast between the unmet needs of millions and the

resources devoted to the complex business of processing, packaging and advertising . . . raises many questions.'[71] He urges that more energy be put into lobbying the corporate headquarters of large TNCs, that consumer pressure be exerted both locally and nationally, and that investment policies be used as one of the tactics in this struggle to promote corporate social responsibility.[72] Above all, say the editors of the volume, it is necessary for Christian people 'to do everything possible to press upon governments and private companies their public accountability within the framework of law and good professional practice,' and 'to learn ways of participating intelligently, effectively and faithfully in a vital debate' on these matters.[73] They quote with approval an interim report from the WCC which declares:

> The Churches want to point insistently to the fact that a growing number of people are living outside of any 'market,' and will not be satisfied with abstract development indicators such as acceleration of economic growth, rising prosperity and wealth, etc. Human development only takes place if the following questions find positive answers: Has poverty decreased? Has unemployment decreased? Has the income distribution gap decreased? Are more people getting a better education? Are their cultural traditions being respected? Do they have legal security, human rights, and the possibility of participating in the decision-making process? . . . From a global point of view, the present path of economic development must be challenged, because it tends to leave a growing number of people in poverty.[74]

Global Economic Development

It is not surprising that one of the six principal publications on the international dimension of economic justice during the period under review is entitled *Reflections on Brandt*, for the kind of thinking found in the two highly publicized books put out by the heralded Brandt Commission is highly congenial to that of the social action leadership of the Church of England. The Brandt Commission itself was an exercise in European corporatism, for its list of participants included the cream of social democratic establishmentarianism in Western Europe, and its optimistic idealism struck just the right note with many highly educated mainstream Christians who wanted very much to believe that a more equitable sharing of the world's economic resources was in fact a matter of enlightened self-interest on the part of the have-a-lot nations, and could be sold to their ruling elites on that basis. It follows, then, that BSR publications on these issues voice genuine alarm about the 'common crisis' in which both North and South (the two hemispheres) are mutually involved. It also follows that they call for prompt reforms of policies governing trade, loans and aid, and for individual life-style adjustments in the patterns of consumption and resource utilization characteristic of those who live in the North.

The 1983 BSR pamphlet on *The Common Agricultural Policy and World Hunger* is typical of this Brandt-like approach in its condemnation of the European Community's import restrictions and unused surpluses, and is very much in harmony with a basic contention concerning current international trade practices which is found in both *Reflections on Brandt* and *Let Justice Flow*. In a situation described by a former president of the World Bank as an 'absolute poverty . . . so limited by malnutrition, illiteracy, disease, high infant mortality and low life expectancy as to be beneath any rational definition of human decency,'[75] the need for increased aid and for some escape from the debt trap which presently imprisons many Third World countries is desperate. But the need for change in international trade practices is even more fundamental, for

> Two features [of international trade] call for attention. First is the contrast between prices developing countries receive for their raw materials and particularly their agricultural commodities on the one hand and the prices they pay for manufactured imports and oil on the other. . . . The purchasing power of their exports to the developing world has been eroded at approximately 2 per cent a year since 1950.
>
> . . . No more powerful mechanism, except perhaps for slavery, for transferring wealth from the poor to the rich has ever been invented in the history of the planet.[76]

The 'orthodox' solution to the plight of developing countries is for such countries 'to process their raw materials and export manufactured goods.' But this solution often fails because of protectionism. Despite the Generalised Scheme of Preferences (which is supposed to mitigate this tendency), the ability of First World blocs such as the EEC to declare certain products 'sensitive' makes it possible for them to exclude manufactured goods from Third World countries whenever they choose to do so.[77] This

> causes great resentment in many developing countries, who point out the hypocrisy of the rich countries campaigning for free trade in those areas where it suits them and then imposing extremely restrictive regimes in areas in which the developing countries can actually compete effectively.[78]

As a matter of fact, of course, Brandt offers no panacea. As a conference discussion of a paper on 'Food, Survival and the Balance of Payments' reveals, 'the needs of the poorest nations . . . could not be met entirely by mutual self-interest,' and there remains 'an urgent need for official government aid, not geared to political and commercial interests. . . .'[79] The Brandt Report made an overly sanguine assumption about the ability of international consultations, or even bilateral negotiations, to produce adequate solutions, for 'the basic logic of the negotiating procedure after Brandt is that of a horse fair,' in which 'if you take nothing to it, you bring nothing away from it': thus 'those with least to offer will actually get squeezed out of the negotiating process.'[80] A tremendous load is put on Brandt's appeal to enlightened self-interest, for implementation of its trade reforms really 'depends crucially upon the rich countries ceasing to manufacture those goods that the poor countries can manufacture more cheaply.' Thus the New International Economic Order which Brandt joins Third World spokespersons in asking for cannot come into being without domestic innovations which are necessary to support what is done on the international scene:

> If we – middle class Christians to a man, I guess – if we are really saying . . . that *you* lose *your* jobs in order to help developing countries, we have to go one stage further and say we are only prepared to push that, to lobby for it, if at the same time we lobby for a vastly better deal for those whose jobs are going to be destroyed. . . . Let us go much further and much faster to protect the poor, the weak and the vulnerable in our own society who are the people who will get most hurt in our enthusiasm for helping those overseas.[81]

By far the most significant single volume on global economic justice to be published in Anglican circles during the past fifteen years is Charles Elliott's

Comfortable Compassion.[82] This admirable book makes the point that aid is far less significant in affecting the fate of a developing country than trade, military policy, diplomacy and the management of debt, and it urges Christians to use their ingenuity and energy to change the standard operating procedures now prevailing in business, government, tourism, etc. Its critique of typical church policies regarding education, aid and technical or economic assistance in Third World countries is particularly acute.

Miscellaneous Policy Matters

The foregoing commentary is selective, not exhaustive. It does not include, for example, any coverage of the considerable body of literature that was produced in an intriguing campaign (in the mid-1980s) to 'Keep Sunday Special' by resisting *some* of the attempts being made to change or eliminate traditional British laws restricting economic activity on the Sabbath. Nor does it include a number of publications whose significance is difficult to assess, namely: three publications of the Industrial and Economic Affairs Committee of the BSR which deal with Industrial Mission and related concerns, and a pair of booklets on 'upcoming events' which require some interpretation.

The 'Keep Sunday Special' campaign (KSS hereafter) is more significant than a typical 'sophisticated' Christian might assume at first glance. It raises absolutely fundamental questions about the extent to which human nature can be summed up in the concept of *homo economicus*, and about the extent to which society shall be allowed to 'degenerate from commerce into commercialism which distorts the quality of relationships between people and, even more seriously, their relationship with God.' Freedom is an extremely important human value, of course, but 'The emphasis on the freedom of the individual to consume, trade or work has nevertheless to be measured against other freedoms, . . . [and] the laws which govern society must somehow reflect the concerns of individuals in their totality not in their partiality.'[83] Even humankind's relationship with nature is brought into the picture as a vital consideration, for 'the future of creation, as a project of hope, requires us to learn the art of "desisting."' And

> Sabbath acts in this sense as a 'counter-balance' to men and women's infinite capacity to turn genuine creativity into those selfish acts of sterile manipulation or lustful rapacity which increasingly endanger our planet earth. . . . It is about keeping faith with future generations, . . . [and thus] Sabbath is . . . a matter of covenantly living, of profoundly respecting what is to come as well as what is already at hand.[84]

The KSS campaign avoided both extreme Sabbatarianism and unqualified deregulation. On the one hand, Sunday observance is seen as merely one part of an overall way of life in which all time is hallowed by remembrance of the presence of God. Sunday should be 'a sabbath of delight, not a burden to be endured.' On the other hand, however, it would be a tragic error to 'open up the high street and change, in a significant way, the public face of Sunday.'[85] To do so would 'seriously accelerate the shift from full-time to part-time working, especially amongst women' – and this might prove dangerous if it led low-income families to 'rely on Sunday trading to supplement their income,' or if it encouraged the state to 'look towards part-time working on Sunday as a means of easing the level of social security entitlements.'[86] Moreover, restricting economic activity on Sunday helps to promote a certain quality of life which is rightly considered precious: it provides an occasion for visiting one's extended family, for visiting the sick and elderly and for simply relaxing after an exhausting week of work. Small wonder that public opinion polls show that as many as 62% of the respondents oppose total deregulation.

The review of Industrial Mission commissioned by the IEAC in the mid-1980s began with a very substantial document of 138 pages named *Industrial Mission – An Appraisal*. It was continued in a collection of responses to that publication called *Dear Mr Green*, and it was brought to a conclusion in a pair of pamphlets entitled *Church and Economy* and *Ministry and Mission Examined*. The former offered models for 'the management and structure of IM and for the employment, deployment and training of IM personnel.' It dealt with strategy and organization at both the local and national levels, and it concluded with a set of recommendations regarding diocesan support for IM, optimally effective organizational structures and staff development. The latter articulated a rationale for IM as a specialized mission activity and a description of noteworthy new directions in IM (based on an account of distinctive emphases elaborated by particular IMs in the UK).[87]

Another group of (usually very brief) BSR publications deal with important events 'on the horizon' concerning which it is felt that some comment from the Church is appropriate. The logic of these offerings seems to be, 'Let's be sure we keep abreast of what's happening so that we can alert the Church constituency to upcoming challenges, problems and opportunities.' A pamphlet on the Eurotunnel says, for example, that this construction will provide 'substantial overall benefits to the UK economy, especially to areas which are at present most afflicted by unemployment.' It adds: 'The Church should not merely seek out compromises, but should ensure that changes which communities are compelled to make are seen as opportunities for mature growth.'[88]

Another document on the Single European Market raises questions such as: the relationships between economics and politics; the willingness of rich member nations to share resources and opportunities with other member nations which are poor; environmental protection; and the complications resulting from cultural diversity. On the first point, it observes that existing documents are silent on the need to regulate the operations of TNCs (and on the possibilities of dangers from concentration of economic power in general). On the second, it points out that the existing European Community never did a good job of helping the poorer members with problems of poverty, and asks if there are any assurances that the social policies of the Single European Market will be more enlightened. On a related point, it asks, 'Should there not be a major revision of the European Community's total North-South policy, focussing on such unsolved problems as Third World debt, hunger and militarisation?'[89]

A Concluding Observation

Various persons of good will, including Christian people who differ in their understanding of the faith, will disagree with some of the particulars contained in the Church of England's pronouncements on economic justice during the Thatcher era. But no one can rightly accuse the social action leadership of abdicating its responsibility to take the initiative in articulating a prophetic witness on the vital issues at stake. And no fair-minded critic can maintain that the Church has not made a serious and sustained effort to ensure that this witness is based on careful study involving systematic consultation with competent scholars and thinkers, and with men and women who have had extensive experience in business and government.

The next chapter presents some analytical insights which serve to explain the content of the pronouncements summarized in this chapter. It addresses the intriguing question of 'Why the Church Took this Stance' regarding Christian responsibility in economic life.

4

Why the Church Took this Stance

Having given a rather exhaustive account of what the Church of England had to say on economic justice issues in the Thatcher era, we now face the task of analysing and interpreting this stance in terms of the context in which its pronouncements are generated. After a few remarks on some of the specific policy matters addressed in the documents that have been examined, the analytical focus will shift to three major aspects of these pronouncements, viz.: (1) their curious lack of commentary on the qualitative aspects of wealth creation, (2) certain organizational variables and pervasive characteristics of the ecclesiastical institution and (3) the ethos of 'cautious moderation' which is often regarded as typical of British national character. The chapter concludes with a related discussion of the social action leadership's thinking on the subject of 'putting down markers.'

Specific Areas of Economic Policy

The merits of the publications speak for themselves, and the positive contribution they have to make is usually self-evident. The documents we have summarized represent a conscientious attempt on the part of the BSR to fulfil its mandate – because in taking a stance on these matters, church agencies have 'put down markers' for Anglicans to use in orientating their thinking and their behaviour in regard to the matters under discussion. The Church can no longer be accused, as it was in Denys Munby's day, of ignoring its obligations to provide leadership of this kind, or of showing egregious stupidity in what it has to say on economic affairs.

Even so, certain questions must be raised. The questions are of two kinds, i.e., those having to do with the particulars of church pronouncements on work, Sunday trading and miscellaneous topics such as the Eurotunnel and the European Community, and those having to do with fundamental concepts such as the social market economy and the welfare state.

Work

If remuneration and the opportunity to earn it through employment in a market job are the two salient factors to be considered in articulating an ethical assessment of work, the BSR has done a commendable job during the past fifteen years in its social witness on this vital aspect of life. But one cannot help being struck by the lack of attention given to two issues that receive a lot of attention from secular analysts: the humanization and the democratization of work. One senses that those who guided the BSR deliberations on the subject of work have a tendency to accept the traditional biblical view that work is both a punishment and remedy for sin. Because it is a punishment, one should not expect it to be terribly pleasant, let alone fulfilling –

so one does not grumble very much about alienation, so long as the pay and the benefits are good. (The Marxist assumption that work is inherently alienated because it involves the sale of one's labour, and in that sense one's *self*, is conspicuous by its absence in the BSR publications.) And a job is evidently much more than just a remedy for the sins which idleness might induce if it provides opportunities for one to be reasonably secure in his or her ability to put bread on the table, and if it provides a *place* in society through the companionship of mates who are reasonably congenial. This is in contrast to the many examples of the literature on work which shriek with indignation over dangers to health and safety and over the dehumanization wrought by jobs which are boring, nerve-wracking or insulting in their failure to facilitate the worker's development of her highest capacities as a thinking, aspiring being created in the image of God. It is also in contrast to writings on work which call for the kind of 'participative management' or 'industrial democracy' which allow workers to have a great deal of say in determining how work processes will be organized, how prices will be set, how profits will be distributed and, in general, how the institution which employs them will be run.

The 'Keep Sunday Special' Campaign

A description of the KSS campaign raises questions that force us to acknowledge two broadly political facts of life which the social action leadership must take into account. In the first place, as noted in Chapter 1, the Church of England is not a monolithic organization, and the mainstream leadership of Church House and Lambeth Palace does not control everything that is done in the way of social witness by Anglicans. So if a certain faction within the Church gets aroused on an issue which is regarded as peripheral by the liberal ascendancy, this group is perfectly free to mobilize rank-and-file parishioners to do something on the issue. That, it appears, is exactly what happened in the KSS movement. Second – as we observed when commenting on the ambiguous character of Industry Year 1986 – giving support to a movement which is dear to the hearts of a numerous faction within the Church may be a relatively cheap and innocuous way for the leadership to gain a bit of credibility (even popularity!) in the eyes of this non-mainstream group, which may tend to be unenthusiastic about its ruling elite or downright suspicious of it. Lending a measure of support to the KSS campaign may have been doubly expedient for several Church House staff persons because (as the KSS literature shows) it can be related to environmental concerns, and to the 'voluntary simplicity' movement.[1] Thus enlisting in the campaign to resist wholesale change in the laws concerning commercial activity on the Sabbath could be seen as eminently worthwhile by reformers who want to give top priority to 'ecojustice' (meaning both ecological sanity and distributive justice).

Miscellaneous Publications

The last two documents mentioned in Chapter 3 deal with forthcoming events of enormous importance, the Eurotunnel and the Single European Market. The fact that the BSR takes the trouble to study and report on them is a good sign in the eyes of all who believe that a church's social witness must of course go beyond those social problems and policy debates which pertain to 'moral issues' in a narrow sense, or to the institutional self-interest of the ecclesiastical entity. *Not* to call attention to the momentous upcoming developments might be construed as a failure to live up to the BSR mandate 'to collect information and think through problems and formulate the results so as to provide background material for the General Synod's debates, the decisions and statements that Church leaders have to make, and the guidance of both the Christian public and wider public opinion.'[2] On the other hand, however, an extremely brief and insubstantial commentary on a momentous topic can hardly be seen as a solid fulfilment of this charge – and one cannot help but wonder about the usefulness of such *minimal* statements on complex issues.

The Social Market Economy and the Welfare State

Ecumenical Protestant thought since the third decade of the twentieth century has tried to avoid both of the totalitarian extremes represented by communism and Nazism, and it has also tried to steer a middle course between pure *laissez-faire* and a collectivized economy. It is not surprising, then, that recent Anglican pronouncements assume the validity of a mixed economy in which the strengths of free enterprise are appreciated and reaffirmed. Nor is it surprising to find continuing support for the welfare state.[3]

Qualitative Aspects of Wealth Creation

Recent BSR publications on the topic of wealth creation are rather astonishing in their failure to provide a more rigorous examination of the *qualitative* aspects of wealth creation. One must certainly recognize the validity of their attempt to affirm the importance of productive economic activity, and one should not fail to notice their stress on the need for moral restraints on acquisitiveness, on the importance of some kind and degree of moral assessment of the goods and services produced, and on the Christian imperative requiring just distribution of the fruits of economic endeavour. But the strongest statement along these lines was in the very brief reply to Mrs Thatcher's Sermon on the Mound, not in one of the BSR documents intended to make a positive declaration of the Church's position. In most of the documents we have reviewed, one senses an overly sanguine attitude towards the presumed benefits of wealth creation, and extraordinarily optimistic hopes for the exercise of 'corporate social responsibility.'

I find it alarming that so little was said about the absolutely crucial importance of evaluating the utility of (presumed) 'goods' and 'services' in meeting *real human needs* (as opposed to spurious wants created by insidious advertising). For example: how could the BSR endorse a statement as patently misleading as the one which was quoted in Chapter 3 regarding the presumed *identity* of profits and wealth creation? How could the BSR go on record with a misleading half-truth to the effect that 'investment funds now flow to where they can earn the highest return, *that is, create the greatest wealth* [italics added]'? How could they endorse the notion that 'only by operating in this way are TNCs efficient'?[4] And how could they seem to endorse so uncritically the plans for a Single European Market without *insisting* on what they mention only tentatively when they ask (so feebly) if it might conceivably be appropriate to inquire into the desirability of 'a major revision of the European Community's total North-South policy, focussing on such unsolved problems as Third World debt, hunger and militarisation'?[5]

When rhetoric of this kind is joined with simplistic remarks which suggest that promise-keeping and honesty in carrying out contracts constitute 'going most of the way' in business ethics, a very dangerous *counter-suggestion cue* has been given. A counter-suggestion cue is a manner of speaking or acting which seems to belie one's allegiance to officially proclaimed ethical ideals and guidelines – and that is exactly what happens if 'the weightier matters of the law' are ignored or trivialized. It is a counter-suggestion cue to imply, for example, that mere truthfulness and observance of accepted rules *in a deeply flawed system of economic activities and interactions* exhausts the demands of ethical responsibility or fulfils the spirit of Christian teachings about the mutual obligations of the covenant relationship uniting all human beings.

But a critique of the inadequacies of the Church's social witness on the subject of wealth creation must go further and deeper than a catalogue of problematic statements in BSR documents. These are only the 'sins of *commission*' in dealing with the topic – and they are far less serious than the 'sins of *omission*' which are evident. What I have in mind here concerns the fundamental fallacy of equating a rise in the GNP as genuine (or optimal) *wealth* creation. The fact that corporation ledger sheets show a handsome profit, or that the dividends of stockholders increase, begs most of the most important questions about the ethics of resource allocation. Apart from the fact that there is *sometimes* (not always!) a net increase in jobs when new business enterprises are started, people who are interested in the rational development of economic resources and their just distribution in a humane society have little to rejoice about in the spectacle of a supercharged high-consumption society where a great deal of what is produced and sold is either superfluous or damaging to consumers, to the poor and to the natural environment on which the very survival of the species depends.

– Is it a fitting act of stewardship to increase the GNP by marketing commodities which are harmful to those who can be persuaded to purchase them, and all kinds of experiences which are degrading to those who partake?

– Is wealth creation morally justifiable when access to whatever is produced is disproportionately unequal, so that the presumed 'consumer heaven' of two-thirds of the population is based on the exclusion, deprivation, stigmatization and exploitation of those who are least advantaged?

– Is is right, or even sane, to boost the GNP by engaging in reckless pollution and depletion of non-renewable resources?

– Does it make sense to count the balance-sheet consequences of leveraged buy-outs and other kinds of mergers and acquisitions as 'wealth creation,' when the only purpose of such manipulations is to increase the speculative value of certain financial instruments (and to reward the guile exhibited by a handful of successful manipulators with enormous windfall profits)? Such machinations are the antithesis of genuine wealth creation.[6]

I am also fearful about the presence of counter-suggestion cues in some of the decisions which have prompted the BSR to expend its energy in easily misunderstood efforts to ratify capitalist ideology and certain ambiguous undertakings justified on its terms. It strikes me as unnecessary – or unwise – to spend a great deal of time or energy in the glorification of 'Industry Year 1986,' and the same may be said of the investment of church resources in the Docklands enterprise. I presume, of course – as a comment from a highly placed adviser to the princes of the Church suggests – that the participation of the churches in Industry Year 1986 was approved as a symbolic gesture of fundamental good will towards the powers that be which could be justified on pragmatic grounds: we can, with very little effort, scratch their backs on a matter of great concern to them, in the hope of receiving a reciprocal scratch at a time and place which is decisive for us. But the pernicious effects of counter-suggestion cues must be taken seriously – and the cost, in terms of time, money and symbolic alignment, must be carefully calculated.

I also find it puzzling that the documents on wealth creation seem to be written as if the limits-to-growth problem (particularly what some would call the ecological *crisis*) did not exist. The two publications on environmental protection are good – but their insights seem to have been arrived at in isolation from the work on economic issues done by other BSR study groups. Surely it is a serious mistake thus to compartmentalize these two topics of concern, for this, too, is a deplorable counter-suggestion cue. On this particular point, the BSR output suffers by comparison with a recent Methodist pronouncement on 'The Ethics of Wealth Creation,' which not only develops a more profound critique of the ethos of acquisitive individualism but also does justice to the environmental damage created by unregulated market operations.[7]

Structural Problems

Since organizational analysts are constantly assuring us that the institutional structures and processes adopted by any sociological unit are of decisive importance in determining their output, we must now turn our attention to this aspect of the social witness of the Church of England. We may be able to glean some valuable insights by analysing the composition of the General Synod, the status and role of the bishops, and certain pervasive limitations on the ability of top-line leadership to define Christian discipleship and persuade rank-and-file parishioners to live in accordance with this definition.

The General Synod

Pundits seem to agree that the compartmentalization of the work of different boards and agencies sometimes results in the rule of 'technological bureaucratic imperatives' instead of dedication to the ultimate goals of the organization. But bureaucracy may not always be the decisive culprit, for sometimes organizational structure is the key factor. As Moyser has wryly pointed out, 'the Board(s) may propose, but it is the Synod which disposes.'

When Moyser examined the 1975 General Synod elections, he found that those elected were overwhelmingly middle-class, middle-aged males. The social-class composition of the *parishes* from which members were elected was pretty evenly balanced, with about as many working-class parishes as middle-class. However, if one examines *congregations* rather than *neighbourhoods*, a different picture emerges: 46% came from 'mainly middle class congregations,' whereas only 14% came from mainly working-class congregations. Moyser concluded by saying that 'the centre of gravity of the General Synod's parochial base is not so much the urban parishes of England as the middle class urban parishes. This means, more than likely, that these ties are to suburbia rather than to the shires or the city centres.'[8]

When Moyser studied the 1980 election, he found a similar picture, which he summarized by quoting the 'blunt words of a recent report of the Partners in Mission Consultation chaired by the Archbishop of York':

It seems to us that the Synod represents the Church of England as it is – middle-class and middle aged/old and male dominated. If the Church of England seriously wishes to move away from this sort of Church, it will have to change . . . . Its Synod . . . must move away from meeting during the week so that its meetings are open to the working class. . . . It should also build in a young and female element if it wants to be sensitive to the needs of these people.[9]

Bishops

The Church of England has always expected some of its bishops to speak out on social issues, and certain sees are regarded as having a special responsibility in this regard. But 'the interventions of most spiritual peers are spasmodic,' both in the House of Lords and in other forums.[10] This is due in considerable measure to the fact that the episcopate has undergone a 'conversion into a specialized ecclesiastical elite, more concerned with "domestic" pastoral matters than serving within one relatively coherent governing class' – and this tendency has grown more pronounced as a result of the rapid increase in the administrative burdens of ecclesiastical housework during the present century.[11] Bishops are discouraged from playing a consistently prominent role in the House of Lords because of the fact that 'contributors to debate are expected to await official replies,' and this may mean 'neglecting important diocesan business for up to two days.' Moreover, 'for ecclesiastical leaders with full engagement diaries, dropping commitments [in order to participate in parliamentary affairs] can be administratively burdensome and pastorally damaging.'[12]

A low level of involvement is also reinforced by the custom which decrees that bishops in the House of Lords may speak *but not vote* on issues perceived to be partisan. This is part and parcel of the aforementioned assumption that church leaders should 'stick to pastoral concerns and not meddle in politics' and the parallel distinction between 'issues of principle' and 'technical issues.' As a result,

> Specific issues come onto the agenda of the Synod, the Board and other Church agencies because people decide to put them on. . . . Debate initiated by the Board represents in many cases a late stage in a process which may have been initiated several years earlier. . . . The decision represents an implicit assessment of the intrinsic importance of the issue, its 'political' significance within the Church, and the resources available to the Board.[13]

Pervasive Characteristics of the Life of the Church

Difficulties attributable to the General Synod are compounded by a number of general features of the Church of England, some of which are so obvious that we might overlook their significance. When we examine its laity, for example, we must not fail to notice several noteworthy facts.

For one thing, the official active membership of the Church is really very small, comprising less than 2% of the country's population – and according to R. H. Preston, the drop in membership is matched by a decline in the importance of secular Anglicanism.[†]

Second, as a Church House veteran contends, the laity's low level of sophistication is a significant obstacle. Effective communication is a constant problem, and necessitates the watering down of reports published by the BSR.

[†]'Secular Anglicanism' is a term used by sociologists to refer to the fact that many British people who never attend services in the Church of England nevertheless have considerable respect for the institution and what its leaders say on social and cultural matters. (A fuller explanation is given on pp. 98–9.)

This consideration was forcibly brought to my attention in an interview in which the discussion came to focus on a BSR publication called *Perspectives on Economics*. I had been inclined to see this booklet as the very epitome of triviality, because it seemed to do nothing more than to summarize a bit of elementary information and a variety of competing views that cancelled each other out. Yet my interviewee saw *Perspectives* as a very helpful document. 'Unfortunately,' he said, 'the average parishioner is so ignorant about economics that a booklet of this type serves a very important educational function – far more important than a thoroughly knowledgeable person would realize at first glance.'

Third, Preston cites the *parochialism* of the Church as a drawback: the fact that each local unit often feels detached from and uninterested in what the apparatus of the national denomination is doing. The Church is seen as the *parish*, and local concerns define the Church's agenda, not some larger national or ecumenical vision.[14] This is yet another reason why the Church of England can hardly develop a single, unified voice in which key spokespersons speak for the institution as a whole. Moyser and Medhurst cite three other variables which make it unlikely that the Church will find success in its quest for a 'new, clearly expressed and agreed upon ecclesiastical identity':[15]

1. An Established Church is always going to have certain 'pastoral' duties to perform for the state, and this will always inhibit the prophetic thrust.

2. The variety of opinions within the leadership of the Church of England (and its people) is very real, and it would be hard to cover this over or ignore it in order to arrive at some one unified (progressive) identity. It is unrealistic 'to expect the Church to speak with a single voice about major issues on its agenda.'

3. There is a significant gap between leadership and constituency. 'Usually, it represents class-based loyalties on the part of those rural or suburban middle- and upper-class groups who have been the chief source of local Church members.'

Moreover, since the top leadership of the Church must avoid any hint of excessive clerical interference, it must frequently resort to 'indirection.' Many an Archbishop of Canterbury has upon occasion made an exceedingly bland or irenic statement on a controversial issue, while at the same time signalling behind the scenes that he would not object to a stronger statement by some other bishop. On the subject of unemployment 'the Archbishop may encourage bishops from industrial areas to protest whilst keeping his powder dry.' This is a way of making known 'the pastoral concern of Church leaders for the unemployed . . . without drawing the institution's chief leader into open conflict with the incumbent government.'[16] And since church leaders must take pains to avoid identification with the secular left, they must be careful about entering into 'embarrassing alliances' – that is, they must try not to bestow an aura of 'ecclesiastical goodwill [that is] used to legitimize the objectives of groups whose ultimate goals may be different from those of their Church-based allies.'[17]

It should be noted, incidentally, that *Faith in the City* is an exception to the pattern just described, for it is a manifestation of the Church's 'taking on more of an independent role and of articulating its own position more fully and clearly.'[18]

It could partly be construed as a redefinition by churchmen of their own Christian insights in the light of changing circumstances. It could also, at least for a while, have been construed as a matter of the Church's leaders being constrained to accept the role of a surrogate political opposition.

[Yet] subsequently, efforts were made, from both sides, to mend the partially broken fences. A well-publicized meeting between the Archbishop and the Secretary of State for the Environment worked to this end.[19]

Cautious Moderation and Balance

Social scientists are often accused of belabouring the obvious. But what we frequently refer to as 'the obvious' (or 'common sense') is seldom as 'inevitable' as we are tempted to suppose, and it is always more nuanced than a superficial reading reveals. Moreover, the further question must always be asked, 'How *significant* are the "obvious" connections between social class and values or habits we discern . . . and how *unalterable* are they?' We hope to find some of the answers we seek in an admittedly speculative description of the ethos of 'cautious moderation' underlying the perceptions, interpretations and actions of Church of England leaders, and in a 'Portrait of a Church House Bureaucrat' which attempts to trace the consequences of this ethos in the attitudes and the behaviour of a member of the BSR staff.[20]

Cautious Moderation

If there is such a thing as an ethos of 'Anglican establishmentarianism,' surely one of its major elements is a concept of *reasonableness* which translates into an image of the well-bred, good-mannered fellow whose quiet cheerfulness is an outward expression of an inner conviction that orderly observance of good form and patient willingness to hear all (important) points of view will lead to a wholesome outcome. This very image is often alluded to by those who admire (or dislike!) it as the 'reasonable chaps' approach to social witness.

Now, this notion of reasonableness, and the image of the fair-minded, well-behaved person which goes along with it, is something of a cliché in drawing-room conversations about the national character of the English people, and it has been satirized unmercifully by foreigners and Britons alike. It is certainly easy to use this aspect of English culture as grounds for dismissing the English as a race which is altogether too content to 'muddle through' (or perhaps incapable of doing anything else).

But it is also possible to see reasonableness and cautious moderation as a legal, moral and philosophical heritage of which the British people can be justly proud. The conservatism of Edmund Burke is usually regarded as the supreme articulation of a kind of British folk-wisdom which stands in favourable contrast to excessive faith in abstract reason or utopian ideals. According to Burke, the heirs of the Anglo-Saxon political tradition ought to be grateful for their historical experience; indeed, they should have a respect that borders on reverence (but not idolatry) for the accumulated body of law and custom which guides the nation. By contrast, they should be properly sceptical of pretentious visions of a Perfect World that call for sweeping changes in the way things are done: the dreams of abstract Reason advanced by the French *philosophes* might look wonderful on paper, but the enthusiasm generated by them was excessive and misdirected, and the French Revolution was far less beneficial to the cause of human progress than faithful adherence to the Anglo-Saxon heritage.

To rehearse these familiar givens of Burke's political philosophy is to call attention to the fact that the traits of reasonableness, patience, calm optimism and cautious moderation we associate with British national character have solid historical and cultural roots which serve to enhance its credibility in the minds of many twentieth-century Britons. If British people 'hold these truths to be self-evident,'[21] it is not merely psychological or cultural inertia which prompt them to do so: they are inclined in this direction because of a collective history which leads them to believe that such traits have certified their value in promoting the common good on the whole and in the long run. As Giles Ecclestone has written, the pronouncements and the actions of the Church of England seem to

> reflect a belief in the possibility of bringing about political and social change by rational argument (though not by that alone), and in the worthwhileness of incremental, piecemeal improvement. In this respect the Church is not fundamentally at odds with the dominant values of British society . . . [and] . . . our national ideology. The Church does not envisage any significant transfers of power and responsibility away from its present holders to new groups. . . .[22]

So far, we have spoken of national *character*, and we have asserted that the moral *substance* of these traits is of great significance. But the implications for 'personality' or 'style' are of almost equal importance. A proper Briton is polite because politeness expresses the citizen's duty to treat her fellow human beings with respect and consideration – so being good-natured while maintaining an orderly queue is a way of showing that one is a *civilized* person. One prefers understatement to exuberance because – well, experience shows that it usually works out better this way (perhaps because far too many individuals are creatures of impulse who would benefit from having or taking a little more time to think things through, and because they are easily seduced into intemperate outbursts or injudicious actions on the basis of first impressions which have not been duly considered).

The optimism alluded to above may have its roots in the Enlightenment notion of 'moral sentiment' which was so eloquently articulated by British philosophers such as Francis Hutcheson and Adam Smith. If one believes that every human being has an innate capacity for admiring the good and being repelled by evil, it is possible to believe that time is on one's side in the struggle for a just and humane society: one can trust in the likelihood that good results will ensue if only each party to a conflict has a little more time for reflection, a little more patience in negotiation, and a resolute refusal to denounce one's adversaries in language that will leave a lasting wound or – God forbid – to consign their spirits to hell. Smith's famous doctrine of the Invisible Hand is now seen to be hopelessly naive, but its wishful thinking made at least *some* sense in the context of Smith's faith in human decency, as recorded in his earlier book on *A Theory of Moral Sentiments*.

I would argue that the entire process of study-group deliberation to be described in the next chapter is an interesting manifestation of this concept of appropriate behaviour. Thus one should not be surprised that many of the documents which emerge from such processes are characterized by a 'both/and balance' of conflicting data and interpretation which encourages readers to perceive them as food for (further) thought rather than a call to action. That is why *Perspectives on Economics* simply pulls together essays offering opposite interpretations of economic reality without attempting to explain or account for their disagreement, and that is one reason why the publication on transnational corporations begs many of the most important questions by doing exactly the same thing.

Changing Britain

But the most noteworthy single illustration of calm reasonableness in a typical BSR publication is *Changing Britain*. This 1987 book was not analysed in Chapter 3 because of the fact that it is not devoted primarily to a treatment of economic issues. Instead, it is an appeal for civility, toleration and resolute co-operation in the face of trends and temptations to polarization and strife; moreover, it presents this appeal as a reaffirmation of some of the most important values of British civilization and of its dominant religious tradition. It argues that the findings of a European Value Systems Study Group which *might* be interpreted as 'suggest[ing] that British society is living on a deposit of religious values which are slowly but surely being exhausted' might equally be regarded as

> evidence of a level of *human* morality – a morality widely accepted across groups with divergent religious beliefs or with none – which has been articulated for centuries, for which various philosophical explanations have been provided, and below which most people most of the time would not be disposed to sink, and which is regarded as more or less self-evident.[23]

Changing Britain proceeds to deplore the 'narrowness of vision, vested interests, confrontational styles, unreflective polarisation and the distorting effects of the mass media' which tend to 'make disputes, both genuine and artificial, seem irreconcilable, and diminish the chance of mutual enrichment through the recognition of differences.' Warning that mere *tolerance* is not enough to avoid counter-productive confrontation, it points out that civilization requires a *moral basis* in which values such as 'respect for persons and personal life, the enhancement of individual freedom, responsibility and equality' can only be attained in a society which aspires to genuine *koinonia* (community) and has mechanisms for developing and extending it.[24] It ends by maintaining that the Church of England has a particularly vital role to play in promoting these values and the community without which they cannot flourish:

> Any Christian church, and especially a national one, courts particular dangers, but it ought to have special gifts, qualities and insights to bring to the issues this study has considered: breadth of vision, the ability to handle complexity and to live with polarities, moral concern rooted in basic principles rather than detailed prescriptions, wide pastoral contacts and commitments, a recognised place both in the voluntary sector and as an integral part of national life, a sense of responsibility for the whole nation constantly tempered by broader international and religious perspectives, a realistic appraisal of our human capacity to deceive ourselves and serve our own interests, a message of hope in the face of failure, cynicism and despair – all these and more.[25]

It should be noted that the cautious moderation and reasonableness of *Changing Britain* did not meet with universal approval when it was discussed by the General Synod. Gareth Bennett denounced it for assuming that 'the end of man is in physical and mental wellbeing' (which might be 'sufficient for a political programme but . . . is not the essence of Christian faith'); furthermore, he bridled at the fact that 'in this report Christian doctrine is continually treated as a kind of illustration of human activity.'[26] Various critics found the document 'jolly weak' on a variety of counts: it ignores conflict, especially that arising from sexism and racism (in regard to which its patronizing tone is especially offensive); 'there is no discussion of power, very little discussion of communities, only very simplistic treatment of the family, or the State, of unionism, of the relationship between institutions'; it is filled with useless platitudes; and it breathes the malodorous spirit of a moribund functionalism. (This last indictment is particularly damning, for it amounts to the accusation that *Changing Britain* is obsessed with social unity, and wants the Church to concentrate on 'cementing society, providing the moral basis, the moral unity, . . . stopping society from disintegrating.')[27]

Putting Down Markers

The mandate of the Board for Social Responsibility is, as we have noted, to ensure that Anglicans are aware of the vital issues of the day and have some guidance from the Church in discerning the moral dimensions at stake in these issues, and in deciding on a faithful Christian response. Now, how is this mandate translated into the job description of a BSR staff person, and how does he or she incorporate it into the daily tasks one is called upon to perform and the organizational roles one is called upon to play?

One thought-provoking answer to this question is to be found in a phrase used by several prominent BSR staff persons in describing the purpose of publications they had been instrumental in producing – i.e., 'putting down markers.' The phrase was usually spoken with assurance and satisfaction; it referred to one aspect of their work, and one clearly identifiable feature of each staff member's job description, which they felt good about, because they were sure (amidst the complexities and uncertainties of their vocation) that it was *right*: doing this was one thing they knew they were supposed to be doing – putting down markers.

This means, I believe, that a BSR staffer is constantly on the lookout for significant social issues which seem to pose a special challenge to Christian people, or which can be illuminated in a particularly helpful way by the wisdom of the faith. Thus BSR staffers devote a good deal of energy to identifying crucial issues and arranging for a study group to analyse it and come up with a report that will touch the minds of ethically sensitive readers (especially church people, of course), and stir their consciences towards appropriate action.

This way of conceptualizing one's own role-responsibilities can be seen, I believe, not only in the documents we have examined but also in the description of social witness activities that is presented in the following chapter. The concern for balance which we found in publications such as *Perspectives on Economics* or *Changing Britain* is also exhibited in the attempt of BSR staff persons to 'cover all the bases' which fall under their jurisdiction; i.e., not to fail to do what the staff person can to persuade the committee he works with of the importance of a given issue, and not to fail to see to it that something is done to put down a marker delineating the Church's stance on that issue.

A noteworthy illustration of the consequences of this imperative is found in the publication of slender booklets on topics such as the Eurotunnel or the Single European Market, for if one complains that these enlarged pamphlets do not really say anything terribly useful, the BSR can reply, 'Well, yes, you are right – but at least we have reminded the Church that a marker *needs* to be put down on this topic!' Another illustration of the force of the pressure to cover everything is found in the account of Chris Beales' attempt to arrange for effective lobbying on the government's plan to institute a poll tax (see Chapter 5). The overall dynamics of such a dilemma may be analysed in the following effort to imagine what goes on in the mind of a BSR professional as he or she tries to decide what the job demands from day to day. It represents an attempt to lay out a few plausible correlations between the typical mind-set or personality type of the Church House employee and the pattern of behaviour which usually ensues.

To be a BSR staff person with major responsibility for a certain area of social concern is to work in a system where one is supposed to *prepare certain documents for denominational approval*. To bring before the Synod materials which that body would perceive as outrageous (or simply unreasonable) would be to violate the tacit contract entered into at the time of employment. The staff operative, being somewhat more progressive theologically and politically than the typical Church of England parishioner (or the typical member of Synod), is apt to chafe a bit under the necessity to tone down what is said in a given report, or to clothe it in palatable rhetoric – but he is also apt to think in terms that are not drastically different from those of his employers because of his education and class position (which incline him to be more or less in agreement with established – and Establishment! – notions of reasonableness, both as to goals and 'politically realistic' strategy).

If we should try to make the same point in a somewhat more down-to-earth way, and especially if we should attempt to 'get inside the head' of a well-meaning Church House employee confronted with this responsibility, what might we find?

Well, of course (like everyone else) he is a person with many different psychological (and pecuniary) needs, and many different goals. One of his most important needs is to be able to feel that he is a good person, a faithful servant of God whose work is a vocation, not just a job, and this means his goal in whatever he does is to do God's will by serving and advancing those purposes believed to be in accordance with the will of God.

But the plausibility structures of his job and his life will encourage him to believe that all kinds of actions which appear to be dubious when viewed in the uncompromising light of the Christian vision of the good life and the good society are nonetheless *regarded and treated* as necessary, legitimate and (therefore) at least instrumentally good. Thus many programmatic goals of the Church – or of the Anglican Church, or of that particular agency of the Church of England for which he labours – come to be regarded as in line with the ultimate ends of Christian endeavour. In any case, it is these programmatic ends which he is expected to help actualize, and it is by his success in doing so that he will be judged and rewarded. For example:

– Even though he realizes that co-operation with high-ranking members of commerce, industry and government has its hazards, the long-standing tradition of corporatism (personified, over time, in men and women whom he regards as role-models of the very best sort) persuades him that it is a part of his job to 'lunch with power.'[28] In view of the fact that heady gratifications are involved, one is inclined to try this approach again and again: it is exciting, and if you *win*, the gains may be quite substantial.

– He realizes that Establishment-funded research often has crippling strings attached, but the hazards may dim by comparison with the ready availability of money, the prestige associated with adding to the fund of (scientific!) knowledge and the programmatic goal-attainment represented in successful fund-raising and publication.

– He realizes the difficulties created by the need for balance in the setting up of a study-group process, but since this is the only fair and reasonable way to proceed, he follows this administratively mandatory path and hopes that managerial finesse will enable him to produce a report with *some* degree of bite and punch to it.

Even if he is not aflame with career ambition, he will certainly value the good opinion of his colleagues and respond to their cues by attempting to deliver the verbal and behavioural responses which he knows they will see as appropriate. In short, he very much wants, and needs, credibility in the eyes of his co-workers, and if he desires to stay and advance in the sort of career track upon which he has embarked, he will pay special attention to what his superiors say and do and expect of him.

There is nothing intrinsically insidious in this, and unless the disciplines of psychology and sociology are completely erroneous in their perception of the laws of human thought and action which they purport to codify, it is true of every person in every social system. But it is highly significant for analytical purposes to acknowledge that sincere would-be servants of God exercising their vocations in an ecclesiastical bureaucracy are not above these laws, and that their effectiveness in attaining the worthy goals they aspire to – and their very definition of these goals – will be greatly affected by the psycho-cultural variables which they are committed to perceiving, evaluating and, where advisable, transcending. The question is, how well can they sort out the imperatives of Christ from those of culture – and how often will they be misled by rationalizations which somehow manage to equate the two, or at least bring the former into acceptable alignment with the latter?

Even more basic, perhaps, is the lack of power which comes from being a part of the bureaucratic scramble for scarce funds, and for the scarce attention of the powerful ecclesiastical (and secular) leaders who can make or break what the staff generate by 'putting it on the agenda' or not. Moreover, as Hoare notes, the lack of funds is aggravated by a lack of management skills (as revealed, for example, in the BSR's apparent inability to make their publications sufficiently attractive to readers in the Anglican Church or in the British public at large). These lacks are related, perhaps, to the lack of clout within the power structure of the Church of England: the counterpart board in the Methodist Church has a lot more power (e.g., it can speak in the name of the denomination on social issues). In addition, limitations of budget and clout also manifest themselves at the diocesan level. Social Responsibility Officers in the dioceses have difficulty in (1) getting a spot on the agenda and (2) getting any funds to pay for the purchase and distribution of BSR publications (let alone money for follow-up study programmes on the issues covered in these publications).

What that means, practically, is that every Church House staff person is bound to feel that his or her adequacy as an employee is to some extent a function of the ability to achieve acceptable programmatic goals with the resources at his command – or (even worse? or even better!) that the possibilities must be expanded by spending a certain amount of time in fund-raising.

Even theology is affected, of course, by this psycho-cultural dynamic. But commentary on this point will have to be postponed to Chapter 7.

5

What Church Agencies Did

When parishioners volunteer to participate in the social witness activities organized by Church agency staff personnel, these are some of the things they are actually involved in doing:

– A working party or a special study commission meets regularly over a period of several months to gather information about an important societal problem, and to formulate policy recommendations for dealing with it. The appointment of such groups is no simple matter, for 'it takes experts to pick experts' – and both the composition and the deliberations of such groups must be perceived as fair (i.e., relatively unbiased and representative) by all of the major 'parties' in the Church. After consideration in the next meeting of the General Synod, the finished report (if approved) is disseminated throughout the ecclesiastical institution's Social Responsibility Officers network, and it is also sent to appropriate policy-makers and opinion leaders outside the Church.

– A press conference is held and, over a period of time ranging from months to (in the case of *Faith in the City*) years, follow-up conferences and meetings are held to publicize the findings of the study group. In addition to loyal church members of various sorts and classes, the audiences for these events are likely to include influential government officials, business persons, labour leaders and professionals of many kinds.

– BSR staff persons and key members of BSR committees engage in conversations with government officials or community leaders about policy matters within the sphere of authority of the person concerned. There is a two-way exchange of information, of course – but there is also an explicit *lobbying* agenda which the church spokespersons are trying to communicate.

– Staff members conduct research and prepare a position paper intended to help a bishop who is speaking on a particular piece of proposed legislation in the House of Lords the following week.

– Men or women recruited by staff (ranging in rank and public visibility from bishops to civil servants to academics or little-known church functionaries) volunteer their services in attempts to mediate a labour–management dispute which threatens to lead to a disruptive strike and subsequent resentments in the affected groups and the populace at large.

– An *ad hoc* study group meets to consider a White Paper on legislation being proposed by the government. The outcome of their endeavours is a statement concerning the social action leadership's point of view on the provisions of the forthcoming bill, with recommendations for changes and a justification of why they need to be made.

– A Church House official (e.g., the General Secretary of the BSR) joins with the bishop who is in charge of overseeing the relevant agency in making a public response to a newsworthy statement or action by a prominent government or business leader (e.g., Mrs Thatcher's 'Sermon on the Mound').

Activities of this kind are not included in the traditional definition of 'works of mercy' undertaken by churches; indeed – as pointed out above – they are an occasion for offence in the minds of conservative churchpeople who deplore ecclesiastical involvement in 'politics.' As a very indignant critic of the Church's recent social witness put it in an interview, 'Imagine the good that could be done if only that army of church bureaucrats would stop meddling in political affairs and spend the same amount of time and energy ministering directly to the needy!'[1] To understand the logic of this remark (and the emotional intensity with which it was spoken!) is to appreciate the importance of a characteristic of this study which was stipulated in Chapter 1: it is a study which concentrates on prophetic social witness aimed at analysing and influencing policy on economic issues at the national level, and it devotes particular attention to the ordinary (regularized, routinized) activities of the BSR, the extraordinary initiatives of the bishops and the special work of Industrial Mission. Furthermore, it focuses on *incremental reform activities of a prophetic nature in the economic arena*. In doing so, it must perforce say very little about those many worthy efforts made by dedicated churchpeople to provide pastoral relief to the poor and other victims of the ups and downs of the market, and even less about the efforts of revolutionaries to reshape the structures and processes of society in radical ways. This is a study of attempts to *reform* social policy, not of *relief* or *revolution* – but reform sometimes manifests itself indirectly as church *renewal* or *rehabilitation* (e.g., training the suddenly unemployed in new job skills), so activities of this kind are also taken into account.[2]

The Board for Social Responsibility

As noted in the previous chapter, the Board for Social Responsibility has a mandate to collect information, think through social problems and report findings in such a way as to stimulate reflection and furnish guidance 'of both the Christian public and wider public opinion.'[3] The BSR offices in the corridors of Church House (the headquarters of the Church of England, located right beside Westminster Abbey, in the shadow of the Houses of Parliament) provide a workspace for staff representing several major committees charged with responsibility for covering the following areas of concern: industrial and economic affairs, social welfare, the criminal justice system, housing, international relations and racial justice. Each of these committees acts in co-operation with staff to carry out the BSR mandate by producing a steady stream of reports, pamphlets and books which offer thought-provoking commentaries on particular social problems. In addition, each office maintains contact with various leaders in church and society who are involved in setting and implementing policy in the relevant sphere of societal affairs, and staff and committee members (including bishops and other church officials as well as lay authorities) are constantly engaged in both long-term and short-term, *ad hoc* lobbying on specific legislative proposals, administrative procedures, funding decisions and the like. There is, moreover, a national network of Social Responsibility Officers (SROs) who are employed at the diocesan level for the express purpose of making sure that the agenda developed by the BSR is transmitted to clergy and parishioners throughout the land.

The output and activities of the BSR represent the Church of England's effort to *institutionalize* a regular, consistent, systematic analysis of ethical issues arising in the life of the nation and appropriate actions designed to shape the thinking and guide the behaviour of secular policy-makers. Most of its operations can be classified, in fact, under two headings which are of the very highest significance for this entire study of the work of the social action leadership of the Church of England: *issue analysis* and *lobbying*. The latter topic is so important that it deserves special treatment at the end of this chapter – so the discussion of the BSR which follows will concentrate on three aspects of its work: (1) the process of generating and disseminating a study document, and (2) the activities of the BSR committee which is of the greatest interest to this study, namely, the Industrial and Economic Affairs Committee and (3) the programmes carried out by diocesan SROs.

Producing a Publication

Most public pronouncements of the BSR are contained in publications which are produced by a well-established process that originates with the appointment of a study group (or a task force) and ends with the dissemination of a report which has been approved and recommended for study by the General Synod.

The current practice is to appoint a working group composed of clergy, representative lay persons and technical experts to study a social problem and formulate a statement regarding the Church's responsibility in regard to it. The inclusion of professionals who are fully informed about the technical, political and economic aspects of the problem under discussion is a logical corollary of *intelligent* social concern which aspires to contribute to a *relevant* social witness which secular decision-makers will listen to with respectful attention; indeed, it is an example of that same realization of the importance of technical wisdom which helped to bring about social Christianity and which led many would-be clergymen (and sons of ministers) to go into sociology and other social science fields in the nineteenth century.[4] As noted in Chapter 2, the Church of England owes a great deal to the administrative ability of William Temple in its current emphasis on technical expertise as a *sine qua non* of valid studies of social problems.[5] Given Temple's belief in the efficacy of corporatism, his influence may also be seen in the fact that BSR study groups usually reflect a considerable diversity of viewpoints.

Working groups almost always follow a well-established pattern of study and discussion. After a period of general discussion which is carried out 'in a rather undisciplined and wide-ranging way,' the moderator guides the group in devising an agenda, appointing a chairperson and 'arrang[ing] to hear expert evidence.' A participant in the study group which produced *Peacemaking in a Nuclear Age* described the ongoing deliberations in the following way:

> We approached our task open-endedly, and I believe all of us changed our minds in some respects during the exercise. After the third meeting, I noted privately that two of the seven participants were pacifists, two seemed to accept the conventional case for a nuclear element in deterrence, and three were difficult to pin down.[6]

Customarily, the next step is for each person to prepare a first draft of some section(s) of the projected report. When a composite first draft of the entire report has been examined by the entire working party, revisions are made and, following procedures similar to those followed on the first round of actual writing, a second draft emerges. The winnowing proceeds until a penultimate draft is agreed upon, whereupon it is printed and distributed to all members of the group for a final critical reading and 'last chance' suggestions for a minor alteration here or there (with the tacit understanding that at this point it is not quite cricket to ask for anything more than a slight alteration of style or tone). When a final polishing of the report has been completed, the report receives official approval by the working group and is ready to be published.

Needless to say, a document intended for review and approval by a body such as the General Synod undergoes a good deal of anticipatory censoring before it is approved by the working group. The result is likely to be within the boundaries envisaged by the person(s) who appointed the task force: it will almost certainly be a balanced report, one whose wording is couched in terms of cautious moderation and balance. To be sure, advocates of a minority opinion have a certain kind of veto on the inclusion of findings and recommendations which are *drastically* different from what their conscience or their technical expertise will allow them to endorse. But this veto power is rarely exercised – and such action usually raises eyebrows. For example, a well-known journalist who served on the working party for *Changing Britain* declined to approve the final version. She was criticized for this on the grounds that (1) one should be able to see fairly early in the game that a report is not going in a direction one can endorse, and should resign from the group before the work of hammering out compromises has gone very far, *or* that (2) if one attends all or most of the meetings and has a fair chance to voice one's opinions all along, one ought to have the grace to accept whatever compromises are arrived at and be willing to ratify a report that does, after all, include consideration of the facts and arguments one has brought to the table.

The final version of the report is distributed to members of the General Synod and is debated at one of its sessions; if approved, it is 'commended to the members of the Church of England for discussion, reflection and appropriate action.' The report is then disseminated to an appropriate distribution list of religious and secular leaders and is made available to the general public through parishes and bookstores.

Reliable information on the actual dissemination of BSR materials is hard to come by. My examination of sales records during the three-year period from 1986 through 1988 indicates that only a few of the publications available during these years sold more than a hundred copies. The exceptions were *Not Just for the Poor* (1621 copies in 1986, 748 in 1987 and 160 in 1988); *Let Justice Flow* (1855 copies in 1986 and 278 in 1987); *And All That is Unseen* (900 copies in 1986 and 975 in 1987); *Growth, Justice and Work* (172 in 1986); *Changing Britain* (895 copies in 1987, 146 in 1988) and *Peacemaking in a Nuclear Age* (710 copies in 1988). These figures do not include copies given free distribution to readers considered to be especially important or especially interested in a given topic, but the number distributed for these reasons would not have exceeded 500 copies for any of the publications named (and probably would have been closer to 200 in most cases). In any case, it is apparent that even the best of the BSR's output receives a very limited circulation, and that little money is budgeted for systematic dissemination and use. The meagreness of this phase of the BSR's role in social witness can be judged by comparing the figures just summarized with the figures for *Faith in the City*: when a major study was undertaken under the auspices of the bishops, with the full authority of the Archbishop of Canterbury behind it, close to 50,000 copies were sold – and the follow-up volume (*Living Faith in the City*) sold more than five thousand copies.[7]

Two Illustrations of the Operations of the BSR

In order to breathe some life into the rather abstract account of the work of the BSR just given, it may be helpful to provide an example or two. First comes a description of exactly what was done in issuing *Not Just for the Poor*, one of the most ambitious publications put out by the Church of England during the 1980s. This is followed by a summary of the highlights of a report from the Industrial and Economic Affairs Committee on its activities and its output during the four-year period between 1985 and 1989.

The Creation of *Not Just for the Poor*

The process which ultimately led to the publication of *Not Just for the Poor* began with a consultative phase that was much more elaborate than usual. The first step was taken in the autumn of 1984 when a twenty-page collection of questions and theses for debate called 'The Future of the Welfare State' was sent out to several hundred church leaders and secular opinion-makers. More than a hundred letters of response were received, and the concerns voiced in these letters then became grist for the mills of the working party which investigated the issues from late 1984 until early 1986. Various members of the working party produced position papers on particular topics which were debated, refined and ultimately used in the drafting of the final version of the report. The sales figures compiled in the publications division at Church House indicate that more than 2500 copies of the book were purchased and dozens of additional copies were distributed *gratis* to influential individuals or agencies.

The General Synod's deliberations on *Not Just for the Poor* were conducted on 25 February 1987; they take up almost forty pages in the published account of the proceedings at this meeting of the Synod. In order to allow for as much discussion as possible, speakers wishing to address the report were allowed only ten minutes, and a wide range of well articulated and occasionally passionate opinion on the merits of the book was expressed. Its theology was applauded by some and challenged by others; it recommendations were welcomed by some and deplored by others – but in any case it was evident that the publication was taken very seriously by those who took the trouble to prepare these brief but tightly packed commentaries.

The Industrial and Economic Affairs Committee (IEAC)

In 1989, the IEAC circulated a report on its activities during the past four years. This document provides a useful glimpse into the 'normal' operations of the single most important organizational branch of the BSR for an understanding of the Church of England's ordinary (routinized) attempts to create a social witness on economic issues.

Heading the list of its activities is a paragraph describing its fulfilment of its obligation to relate to and support IM in Britain.[8] The most important of the endeavours discussed in this connection was an inquiry into 'the current state of IM' which was implemented by a working party that produced six study documents between its establishment in 1985 and the publication of its final report in 1988. This report, a 138-page booklet entitled *Industrial Mission – An Appraisal*, was produced in conjunction with the Church Consortium on Industrial Mission, and was distributed to everyone in the IM movement in Britain and to a large audience of ecclesiastical leaders. The report was sent out with a cover letter which invited a critical response from all recipients, and the highlights of the thirty-odd letters which it elicited were compiled in a publication called *Dear Mr Green*. 'Meanwhile, a small group had been set up by the Committee to take further the wishes of the Board and the Committee for specific recommendations about the future of the

Church's work of ministry and mission in the field of economic affairs' – and this group produced *Church and Economy: Effective Industrial Mission for the 1990s* and a companion volume named *Ministry and Mission Examined: Stories and Reflections on Industrial Mission Today*. These documents were received by and discussed in subsequent meetings of the General Synod, and the IEAC committed itself to 'work out a strategy for implementing the recommendations [of *Church and Economy*]' (including an amendment calling for 'work in relation to the City of London and financial institutions').[9]

A response to the amendment noted above was already in the works, for in 1987 the Committee had commissioned a consultation on mergers and acquisitions, the report of which was published as *The Ethics of Acquisition* in 1990. The usual working party/publication sequence was also followed in a 1984 investigation of 'Women and Employment' which resulted in the publication (in 1986) of *And All That is Unseen*.

Some of the Committee's work had to do with lobbying. It made a formal response to the government's proposals in 1985 and 1989 'to reform or abolish Wages Councils,' and it 'contributed to responses to proposals from the Labour Party and Low Pay Forum on these matters also.'[10] It was represented in meetings of the Department of Trade and Industry's Industry-Education Committee, and '[worked] for two years on developing the churches' participation in industry-education links.' It was instrumental in organizing a one-day conference in November 1988 on this topic, and has been following through on plans to implement some of the recommendations coming from this conference. In addition, 'several meetings have taken place with Lord Young while he was secretary of State for Employment, and then Trade and Industry.' Subjects discussed 'have included employment and unemployment, youth and adult training, enterprise, inner cities, industry and education, mergers and takeovers, and 1992.' As the section of the report headed 'Meetings with Government Ministers' declares, 'Meetings have also taken place with Norman Fowler (at the Department of Employment) and officials in the DE, DTI, Cabinet Office and DoE.'[11]

Especially important are the activities undertaken as a means of supporting and implementing the recommendations of *Faith in the City*. Included here are sponsorship of entrepreneurial endeavours undertaken in co-operation with the Community Roots Trust, an examination of Urban Development Corporations and the mounting of a very ambitious area development programme called Linking Up, which involved the use of government, industry and church funding in hiring five full-time staff who have worked for three years on a variety of entrepreneurial and job-training projects. On the intellectual side, there was a consultation on the question 'Can a Christian Support a Social Market Economy?'[12]

Also included in this four-year report of committee activities are accounts of attendance at meetings with ecumenical groups and with 'ginger groups' such as Church Action with the Unemployed (CAWTU).[†] In the 'Miscellaneous' category are conversations with the Industrial Christian Fellowship, an important IM agency which has always maintained a close relationship with the IEAC, contact with UNIAPAC, a Brussels-based Christian organization which holds a symposium for European Church and Transnational [Corporation] leaders every two years, and

---

[†]A ginger group is an organization which devotes itself to research and lobbying on one main issue, thus creating 'heat' on more broadly-based organizations which (in the opinion of ginger-group members) might otherwise neglect this key issue.

reports on developments leading towards the Eurotunnel and the Single European Market.[13]

This report is notable for several reasons. The variety of interests and activities recorded is a reliable indicator of the BSR's ambitious attempt to keep abreast of an impressive number of developments affecting economic life, and to maintain contact with a variety of organizations in all major sectors of British society which are responsible for devising, implementing or criticizing economic policy. It shows the BSR is doing what it can to engage in fundamental theological reflection on the issues concerned, while at the same time it is also attempting to understand, criticize and influence social policy on these issues. The report contains a reference to most of the significant kinds of activities and topics which are examined in more detail throughout this study.

Mobilizing the Troops: Diocesan Social Responsibility Officers

Implementation of the BSR agenda for the Church is carried out to a considerable extent by diocesan Social Responsibility Officers (SROs) throughout the country. The importance attributed to the work done by diocesan SROs is revealed in an important symbolic way by the fact that the newly appointed General Secretary of the Board for Social Responsibility, David Skidmore, comes to his new post from several years' experience as SRO for the St Albans diocese.

Anglican social workers in Britain have for many years been organized into a national network which has enabled them to keep in touch with each other and with what is being thought and done by colleagues of various ages, with different backgrounds in education and experience, throughout the country. But it was not until 1986 that diocesan SROs formed the Anglican Association for Social Responsibility to guarantee that the work of the BSR is effectively translated into education and mobilization activities in parishes throughout the country.

The fledgling organization seems to be off to a good start. When its first convocation was held, in 1986, all but six of the dioceses in Britain had an SRO, and (as its first Annual Report announces) attendance at meetings of its newly formed steering committee was virtually 100%. A 1988 report highlights three indices of the organization's growth and development since its inception: the expansion from one-day meetings to two- or three-day residential meetings; the forging of strong ecumenical ties; and the transition 'from speaking for the Church to Partnership with the Church.' This third accomplishment is particularly important, because it represents an extension of a trend in 'thinking about the nature of social responsibility work and who should be doing it' already noted above:

> When Edwin Barker was secretary of the BSR (until 1974) it was assumed that the Board spoke for the Church to Government and Whitehall. In Giles Ecclestone's time, it tried increasingly to help the General Synod speak both for the Church and to the Church, and began to establish Social Responsibility in the widest sense as a mainstream part of the Church's normal agenda.
>
> Since 1982, while John Gladwin has been Secretary of the Board, there has been increasing awareness that Social Responsibility 'done' at national level needs to be closely in touch with similar work now being done locally in most of the dioceses. There has been, for example, consultation with local Churches [sic] before Board reports have been written and published [as in the case of Not Just for the Poor]. A representative of the Social Responsibility network sits in at

Board meetings as an observer, [and] resolutions passed by the General Synod increasingly urge further study and action in dioceses, deaneries and parishes.[14]

The Chelmsford Council for Social Responsibility

The potential significance of this trend, and of the work of diocesan SROs, can be illustrated by outlining the activities sponsored and engaged in by a single diocesan Social Responsibility office.[15] Its programme strikes a wholesome balance between the pastoral and the prophetic, and the 1987 Annual Report speaks with pride of the fact that increasingly its service to the parishes is matched by an ability to speak with 'a corporate diocesan voice on issues of concern.' Its pastoral work is carried out on a very impressive scale, for it employs five area social workers in five locales away from diocesan headquarters, and it has five additional centres where residential, nursery and other community services are offered.[16] In addition, there is a full complement of services under the rubric of Counselling and Community Social Work (such as care for pregnant teenagers, care of the elderly and day care for small children). A programme on Christian Renewal for Education and Social Tasks, which has been in operation since 1971, has just received a boost in resources, for it is a good example of the kind of pastoral outreach effort to Urban Priority Areas called for in *Faith in the City*.

On the prophetic side, the Council sponsors six issue groups, each of which engages in sustained study and periodic action (and calls to action) on a particular social problem (such as, to use the titles in effect up to 1989, Unemployment, Family Life, Poverty, Countryside and Rural Issues, Race and Community Relations and International Affairs).[17] These groups contribute to the rather amazing array of council publications on a lengthy list of important topics. Sometimes it is only a four-page summary of an important BSR book (e.g., *Not Just for the Poor*, which served as the basis for many a parish study group); sometimes it is a major report (such as the one on 'Church and Society in Essex and East London' which was prepared to brief the bishops attending the 1988 Lambeth Conference as well as for use in the parishes); sometimes it is a bulky study packet (such as that for a five-session study group on 'Christians, Poverty and Wealth'); and sometimes a survey (such as the one on 'Responses to Unemployment' in the nineteen municipal areas around Chelmsford). More often it is a flyer designed to make people aware of some community service offered by the Church, or a relatively small pamphlet filled with essential facts about a significant moral issue. All in all, one has the impression that if churchgoers in this diocese are not exceptionally well informed about social problems, and given innumerable opportunities to render service in regard to them, it is certainly not the fault of the Chelmsford Council for Social Responsibility.

The Bishops

Any bishop of the Church of England can count on receiving press coverage of almost any public statement he makes on a public issue. 'Whatever the bishops say is news' – and if the substance of their remarks is presented at an announced press conference, or even available to the press after a sermon on some newsworthy issue, notice will be taken. Where serious efforts are made to give wide distribution to such statements, it is a virtual certainty that they will be brought to the attention of those who make policy in the area under discussion; indeed, it is equally certain that the press will attempt to elicit a *reply* from policy-makers upon whose toes a bishop may have trod.

It follows that during the fifteen-year period under examination the bishops of the Church of England have made a substantial number of newsworthy comments on economic issues. This is true in part because the media *always* tend to deal in personalities, and 'this extends to bishops even in an age that is widely termed secular in its approach and outlook.' As Peregrine Worsthorne, former editor of the *Sunday Telegraph*, has written, 'Bishops are public figures and legislators in the House of Lords. They are grist to the mill of journalism and are no different in that respect to any other group [of public figures].'[18]

It also follows that the *most* newsworthy of these pronouncements are the ones in which the leadership of the established Church appears to challenge the thinking of well-known elected officials or the policies of powerful political and economic institutions. This has of course led to an atmosphere of confrontation between church and state. It is, on the whole, true that 'David Jenkins has gone further than most of his fellow clerics,' to the point of labelling Mrs Thatcher's legislative initiatives 'wicked,'[19] but as the highly regarded journalist (and Thatcher-watcher) Peter Jenkins has observed,

> The Thatcherite modification, whereby consensus has been thrown out and conviction is the thing, has in many ways carried all before it. This thrusts the church, especially the established church, though with others assisting, into the centre, not of straightforward political opposition, but of speaking up for the issues that are being ignored, overridden, or for the moment settled in a way that up to now would not have been thought of as the right way.[20]

As the authors of *Believing Bishops* declare, 'It is not simply that the bishops have entered the political debate in the Thatcher years that has angered Ministers and prompted widespread media attention.' Beyond that it is 'the comprehensive and detailed nature of the bishops' rejection both of the substance of government policy and the philosophy that underpins it.'[21]

So a meticulous listing of episcopal pronouncements on economic issues during the period from 1975 through 1990 would include criticisms of the government's housing policy by the Bishop of Bradford in 1988, an attack on the probable effects of the poll tax by Bishop Stanley Booth-Clibborn of Manchester in 1989, Bishop Jenkins' comment (at an Industrial Society Conference in 1987) to the effect that 'industry and community in this country cannot long survive with viability and future potential under the current market myth' and a considerable number of similar criticisms.

These *ad hoc* indictments of particular government policies, and of the moral worldview on which they are based, are of great significance for anyone who would presume to chronicle the social witness of the Church of England during the Thatcher years. They comprise a major ingredient in the prophetic protest which the Church has voiced since 1975. The lobbying done by bishops may be equally significant; it is summarized in the last part of this chapter. But by far the most important action taken by Church of England bishops during the past two decades (perhaps the past *five* decades!) is the *Faith in the City* enterprise, which began with the appointment of a special Archbishop of Canterbury's Commission on Urban Priority Areas (ACUPA) in 1982. The deliberations of the Commission were only the beginning, for the ACUPA follow-up process is one of the most elaborately organized and substantially funded undertakings of the Church of England during the twentieth century, and its work is supposed to continue for a period of no less than twenty-five years. Hundreds of speeches have been made, dozens of conferences have been held, and numerous publications have been issued since the 1985 publication of *Faith in the City* in an effort to identify exactly what church people in particular localities need to understand and do to address the ills and right the wrongs of the urban poor. It is significant, incidentally, that these efforts are conceived of and initiated with an eye to co-operation with other religious bodies and also with appropriate secular agencies. Thus several of the local conferences designed to mobilize resources for action in a given locality have had not only the participation of local government officials, business leaders, academics and other human-service professionals, but the partial *sponsorship* (read financial support) of these non-church entities as well.

Faith in the City

The moral ferment which finally produced *Faith in the City* began as early as 1981. Canon Eric James, whose work as Executive Director of a ginger group named Christian Action had made him all too familiar with the dire distress of the UPAs, wrote a letter to the Archbishop of Canterbury urging him to take dramatic action on the matter. The appeal to the Archbishop came shortly after a letter to the editor of *The Times*, in which James had expressed amazement at an article by its religious affairs correspondent Clifford Longley – written just after the Brixton Riots of 1981 – which declared that 'all manner of things are well' in the Church of England. James pointed with alarm to the fact that inner-city parishes were being rapidly deserted by Anglican parishioners and clergymen. He wrote:

> I should myself like to see the immediate appointment of an Archbishop's Commission – to report within a year – called the 'Staying There' Commission. . . . It would report on the Church's strategy for the inner-city, and would need of course to consider the theology and spirituality of the church in the inner-city, not just finance and manpower.[22]

Later that year (1981) the summer issue of *Christian Action Journal* reprinted the letter to *The Times* and added the proviso that 'for the church to stay in places like Brixton means sustaining varieties of ministry there,' by which the author meant not only full-time priests and '"priest-workmen" of all sorts,' but also 'Christian laymen and women who will identify with the joys and pains of the inner-city.'

A few months thereafter (April 1982), the Bishop of Stepney invited James to address this topic at a meeting of the urban bishops of the Church of England, to whom the Archbishop of Canterbury had referred the matter. As the Bishop of Stepney noted in his letter of invitation, 'a preliminary sounding suggests that quite a few of us [bishops] do not think a Commission is the way forward'; nevertheless, he thought James would be just the right person to lead the bishops into a discussion of the problem, and he felt obligated to see to it that the session would 'come up with some positive proposals to put to the Archbishop.'[23] James addressed the urban bishops for two hours, broadening the focus to include a consideration of all kinds of political and economic actualities such as widespread unemployment, racial tension, conflict with the police, cuts in social services (especially the Health Service), the decline of public education, etc. As a result, proposals concerning an inner-city Commission were drafted and presented to the Archbishop of Canterbury, who officially set the process in motion.

One of the key leaders in carrying out the study which led to the publication of *Faith in the City* was Richard O'Brien, a staunch Anglican with extensive experience at the highest levels of government, including a stint as head of the Manpower Services Commission. O'Brien cites the following features of ACUPA as crucial to its dramatic success:

1. It was patterned after Royal Commissions, which have an honourable history and constitute a respect-demanding precedent in the mind of the public even today. It was a blue-ribbon panel, with adequate representation from some of the most important questioners of mainstream Anglican liberalism and high-level expertise in all requisite areas.

2. It used government statistics, so that no one could accuse the Commission of stacking the factual and statistical cards against official perceptions of reality.

3. Getting John Pearson to be the executive leader of the Commission was extremely important. This highly regarded civil servant was possessed of great administrative finesse, invaluable contacts, and all of the seasoned abilities needed to run the entire operation. Pearson's work was decisively important in three specific ways: his experience in politics enabled him to interpret 'the mind of a government official' to the clerics and academics who made up such a large percentage of the members of the Commission; his position in the Department of the Environment, from which he was seconded, enabled him to speak with special knowledge and authority on matters pertaining to Urban Priority Areas; and his contacts in the Thatcher administration made him aware of 'inside information' concerning the intentions, strengths and liabilities of ruling elements in the party in power.

4. A remarkable panoply of intellectual and political ability was assembled, not only in the membership of ACUPA, but in the research personnel called upon to prepare position papers on particular topics of concern to the Commission. One must always be wary of the myth-making instinct which comes into play whenever one assesses the strengths of an 'all-star' team of any kind (i.e., the tendency to proclaim *this* year's goalie as the *greatest* goalie of all time!), but it is tempting to describe the individuals who represented relevant institutions such as The William Temple Foundation (John Atherton), Christian Action (Eric James), the Evangelical Committee on Urban Mission (Michael Eastman), Lambeth Palace (Graham Howes) and the BSR (John Gladwin) as the very cream of Protestant social action personnel in Britain – and similar claims might be made concerning the members of the Commission drawn from British academic circles. In addition, the other two civil servants seconded for the task were men of exceptional insight and ability.[24]

5. The credibility of the report was strengthened by the well-publicized visits of commission members to inner-city areas. The advance publicity created curiosity about the report and guaranteed an attentive audience in press and public. In addition, the visits actually changed the thinking and the emotional intensity of many commission members: they looked and listened without pontificating to the poor, and they were often shocked by what they saw. As a result, they developed a robust determination to produce a report and a process which would change things.

The Follow-Up Process

An elaborate follow-up process (already envisaged and planned at the time of the Commission's appointment) began immediately after the publication of *Faith in the City*. This work was guided by a full-time staff of two persons, two honorary part-time workers of great experience and ability who were in a position to donate many hours of labour to the Church, and by an Archbishop's Advisory Group consisting of about twenty-five representatives of various churches, professions and interest groups whose co-operation was essential to the success of the venture. The Advisory

Group met five times a year, but its members were in contact with one another, planning and carrying out specific projects, much more frequently than that.

The follow-up network featured a *Faith in the City* 'link officer' in every diocese of the Church of England. Some link officers were especially appointed for the post; others assumed the responsibility as a part of their duties as an officer or adviser for the BSR. It also included a representative from each of the central boards of the Church and a number of academics, civil servants, political officials and community leaders from urban areas. Financial support for follow-up activities was assured by the setting up of a Church Urban Fund intended for church renewal and community service activities *other than maintenance of existing facilities* (a stipulation made necessary by the fact that there are so many old buildings for which the Anglican Church is responsible that local parish leaders are always looking for money which can be used for up-keep). Administrative attention was provided by directing all parishes to conduct a 'Parish Audit' designed to help 'churches generally (not just in the UPA's) . . . become more "local," more outward-looking and more participative.'[25]

In addition to these inwardly directed activities, the follow-up also involved systematic efforts to influence public opinion and social policy in secular institutions. The BSR, for example, made a special effort to respond to *Faith in the City* by using its already established contacts with leaders of government and industry to lobby for some of the specific policy recommendations set forth in the report, and by adjusting its own research agenda to include themes highlighted in the report. A follow-up conference on 'The Challenge to the Nation' was held in May 1987, and representatives from government agencies, corporations and other community institutions were able to share experiences and ideas concerning what had already been accomplished and what might be accomplished in the future to implement the imperatives of *Faith in the City*. One of the workshops at this conference led to the publication of a remarkably detailed paper on 'Faith in the City and Local Politics' by a social scientist named Richard Farnell,[26] who found that a follow-up conference on *Faith in the City* had been held in no fewer than thirteen cities in the first eighteen months since the publication of the report. These gatherings often enjoyed the official support of local government and industry, and they usually elicited the participation of local universities.

Industrial Mission Activities

The special work of Industrial Mission is an aspect of church social witness which is far less clearly defined than the operations of the two centres of initiative we have just examined. In order to appreciate the distinctive contribution of IM, one must appreciate the importance of *rehabilitation* as a type of *indirect reform* which has a special place on the 'relief/reform/revolution' continuum (which is explained at the beginning of this chapter and in note 2).

The significance of this typology was forcibly brought to my attention during an especially fascinating conversation with several Social Responsibility Officers and Industrial Mission personnel in the Manchester diocese who obviously felt that what they were doing went significantly beyond 'relief.' They prided themselves on doing something *concrete* which would be of immediate assistance to the unemployed in their area, and for them there was a decisive difference between their area development activities and what is usually meant by 'pastoral' activities (e.g., visitation of the sick and the elderly, soup kitchens, providing shelter for the homeless, etc.). They saw what they were engaged in as 'rehabilitation,' and in explaining the difference between activities of this kind and mere 'relief,' one member of the group made reference to the familiar distinction between 'giving people some fish to eat' and 'teaching them how to fish.'

On the other hand, however, it is clear that there *is* an important difference between a voluntary association's undertaking to mount special programmes to help the unemployed and that same voluntary association's attempts to get public- or private-sector institutions to take it upon *themselves* to remedy the problems of those whose lives have been dislocated by the operations of the market (and by the failure of the society as a whole, acting through the state, to regulate the market in such a way as to prevent, minimize or remedy the effects of such dislocations). It is activities of this kind – calling the megastructures of the economy and the polity to fulfil their vocations more effectively – which I consider especially worthy of being called prophetic, and it is prophetic activities that we are *most* concerned with in this study. Even so, it makes sense to recognize that rehabilitation effects reform indirectly; indeed, rehabilitation activities are a form of 'lobbying by *demonstration.*' For surely programmes which are designed primarily to give direct aid to victims by equipping the unemployed for new jobs or enabling a small business to get started have a sort of multiplier effect of their own: they not only benefit neighbourhoods (and, cumulatively, whole geographical areas) as well as the individuals and families most directly affected; they also tend to have an indirect effect upon subsequent policies. Experimental projects which are successful open up new avenues for later policy to pursue, and those who devise especially successful *means* for carrying out current policy (e.g., employment training) create models of action to be followed by public- and private-sector agencies which are occupied with similar tasks.

Thus it ought to be acknowledged that *indirect* reform may be just as 'prophetic' as *direct* reform, for lobbying and rehabilitation should be seen as two different tactics employed on different fronts for different objectives: lobbying directly attacks the inadequacies of structures and policies by showing how government and industry can (and ought to) operate more humanely; area development programmes affect structures and policies indirectly by demonstrating the effectiveness of new approaches and by showing the capabilities of new sponsoring coalitions. It might even be argued that the kinds of frontline work 'in the trenches' of the war against need and deprivation in Urban Priority Areas is a particularly important way of recognizing the indispensability of wealth creation, and that as such it is an absolutely essential complement to the emphasis on just distribution of economic resources reflected in the pronouncements and the lobbying of the BSR and the bishops.

Now, to say all this is to say something important about the reasons why Industrial Mission is far too important to the concerns of this study to be ignored or set aside as peripheral. It may be true, as a generalization, that most of the practitioners of Industrial Mission like to pour their energies into 'remedial' work at the local level – but it is also true that some of the best theological and political/economic theorizing in the Church of England arises from IM circles. The movement has always seen itself as an exercise in 'action/*reflection*,' and it has always promoted the kind of systematic theological dialogue which receives an appreciative hearing in the academy and in the highest circles of ecclesiastical leadership.[27] It is hardly surprising, then, that the last two secretaries of the Industrial and Economic Affairs Committee of the BSR have come from Industrial Mission (Paul Brett and Chris Beales), and that a glance at the agenda undertaken by the IEAC and the publications it has produced in the Beales years (1983–91) shows a heavy investment in IM concerns and in the future of the IM movement. There is, in fact, a great deal of over-lapping in the work of the theoretically separate and distinct branches of the Church of England whose activities are analysed in this book. Area development programmes which are discussed under the rubric of Industrial Mission because they represent a special concern of the IM movement and because they are staffed primarily by IM-trained personnel may actually be under the remit of the IEAC Committee of the BSR – and they may be described in the latter's annual report as an activity which was undertaken in response to the priorities and the agenda announced in *Faith in the City*. Another indication of the closely intertwined rela-tionship between the 'routine' work of the BSR and the specialized work of Indus-trial Mission may be found in the fact that so much of the activity of the BSR's Industrial and Economic Affairs Committee in recent years, and so many of its pub-lications, have centred on IM.[28]

In sum: Industrial Mission is a movement which addresses both the needs and opportunities of those in power (who formulate policy in corporations, government agencies and labour organizations) and of those who are relatively powerless (ordinary workers as well as the poor, the unemployed and the homeless). It is a crucial element in the overall social witness of the Church of England. As the fol-lowing description of the evolution of IM in Britain will reveal, the emergence of the concept of a Local Economy Based Industrial Mission as IM's 'Fourth Gener-ation' may be of great significance, for it is linked with an attempt to formulate a set of priorities and an efficient division of labour in the Church's social witness. And if IM does in fact evolve into the fourth stage envisaged by one of its leading theoreticians, it may be more important than ever in the future.

The Evolution of Industrial Mission

Even though Phase 1 of the IM movement included recognition of the need to influence the 'principalities and powers' which govern the world of industry at all levels of national life, it was essentially evangelical and pastoral, because it was orientated towards enabling and enhancing existing structures and patterns of indus-trial life. Phase 2 featured greater emphasis on influencing the policies instituted by those principalities and powers,[29] whereas Phase 3 was a reaction to the new eco-nomic, political and cultural situation caused by deindustrialization, high inflation and unemployment. It involved a strategic retreat in which a good deal of IM energy had to be invested in 'picking up the pieces' of the wreckage caused by the decline of the old basic industries. One of the key ingredients in this phase is the eagerness of the Manpower Services Commission to contract with voluntary agencies at the local level to do some of the job training it promoted.[30]

According to Mostyn Davies, Phase 4 will see the rise of 'local economy based Industrial Mission.' It is differentiated from Phase 2 by virtue of the fact that 'the central determining realities' of life have changed (i.e., from prosperity to reindustrialization along new lines), and differentiated from Phase 3 because the focus is broader than repair work: local economy based IM seeks to be both pastoral and prophetic in a relentlessly practical and altogether manageable sense. In Davies' words:

> Fourth generation IM is trying to clarify what has been learned to date and take a broader, more experienced, view of how the whole local economy is creating the central determining reality conditioning people's lives and values. . . .
> Nowadays, the local economy is much more plural, its commercial structure

looks very different and the workplace is no longer martialled into massive armies of industrial workers. Where yesterday the central determining realities created a collectivised working class culture and trade-union solidarity, now they create a new world of offices, shops and warehouses, an aspiring middle-class culture and a spirit of property-owning individualism . . . at least for the 'haves.' The 'have-nots' form a twenty per cent underclass of dependent, pressurised people for whom the central determining realities are the DHSS rules, Family Credit, Income Support, Restart Interviews, housing problems, debt and low-paid work.[31]

The vanguard of the movement now appears to see its top priority as that of initiating projects which are both rehabilitative and political: they are ambitious local coalitions which seek to promote a new configuration of public-, private- and voluntary-sector resources in *area development programmes*, an approach which has been very much emphasized by the IEAC of the BSR in recent years.[32]

Area Development Programmes

The two most prominent area development efforts made by church agents during recent years are probably those undertaken in the London Docklands and in a new programme called 'Linking Up.' The former involved church participation in (or cooperation with) one of the most highly publicized urban renewal projects ever undertaken in Britain. The project's public relations spokespersons see it as the creation of London's 'Wall Street on the Water' and (once the Channel Tunnel is finished) of 'Britain's diving board into the Common Market.' But most of the 15,000 new housing units being constructed are too expensive for long-time residents, who are simply pushed out by gentrification, and the as yet very small number of jobs being created are mainly transfers from the City into the Docklands, for there is 'a mismatch between the types of new jobs and the skill structure of the local people.' The Newham Docklands Churches Group which was supposedly formed to provide a Christian voice in the development of the area finds itself doing little more than 'linking the old community with the newcomers.' A study of the churches' involvement in the Docklands project concludes that 'the work is similar to the Red Cross, which has to take care of the victims on both sides of the gap. That means: traditional parish work, which does not address the power structures.'[33]

'Linking Up' is an ambitious programme undertaken by the BSR in response to *Faith in the City*. Funded by privately raised money, under the joint sponsorship of CAWTU, it is aimed at improving the situation of inner-city folk both directly and indirectly (i.e., in mobilizing Christian people to improve the conditions of life in UPAs). It seeks to create jobs (by stimulating small-business development),[34] help the unemployed cope on the benefit system, find new ways to enlist 'local authority, private and voluntary support for the unemployed,' improve national policy (by reporting what works and what does not), and to do something similar at the local level by establishing close communication with local government and business leaders, and get the educational system to do a better job of 'contributing to local economic regeneration and promoting an "enterprise culture" which relates to community needs and is compatible with them.' Linking Up works closely with CAWTU, Evangelical Enterprise and the Church Urban Fund (CUF), helping the CUF 'in identifying the best projects to support.' Among the specific objectives pursued by Linking Up are these: establishing 'community enterprises, small businesses and cooperatives, . . . encouraging the formation of credit unions,[35]

[and] helping church sponsors in the adult employment field to adapt from Community Programme to Employment Training.'[36]

Other IM Activities

The shift within the IM movement away from earlier emphases towards area development coalitions is the most dramatic recent development in the evolution of that exceedingly significant specialized ministry, and it is certainly accurate to highlight its significance. On the other hand, of course, it would be a mistake to overlook the fact that earlier emphases have by no means been utterly abandoned. Thus industrial chaplains still help to mount rather more conventional job-training programmes under the auspices of the Manpower Services Commission, and they still take a lead in familiar repair programmes such as neighbourhood improvement. They still carry out adult education programmes within the churches whose intent is (at least in part) to help Christian people see their daily work as a form of Christian vocation or mission. And they still do important work in the area of labour–management relations.

In regard to the labour–management front, the historic posture of church representatives begins (in the twentieth century) with idealistic appeals for co-operation, coupled with protection of the right to strike. The corporatist assumptions implied here carry through right to the present in the pastoral laments regarding the Winter of Discontent and the delicately worded acceptance of the closed shop contained in the BSR document on that subject.[37]

Lobbying

Lobbying may be defined as an attempt to persuade some policy-maker (someone who creates legislation, or administers an institution or a programme, or designs and executes organizational processes) to see or do things connected with his or her job responsibilities in a somewhat different manner. Of course, this definition is so broad that it raises the opposite question, 'What can *not* be construed as lobbying?' Whenever one publishes a study, that may be seen as 'long-term lobbying,' for one hopes that its readers will be influenced and thus will be stimulated to move in a new direction, sooner or later. When the BSR, for example, puts out a minimally informative and altogether bland pamphlet on the Eurotunnel or the Single European Market, is it merely *reminding* its constituency of developing events which are already familiar to all who are in contact with the media – or is it encouraging them to *take a certain point of view* about these developments? (If it fails to do the latter, a critic might complain that it is falling short of its mandate.) Or when church officials attempt to drum up support for some worthy cause by soliciting contributions from churchgoers, as they did in their '1% Drive' on behalf of international charities, their official designation of 'One World Week' and their campaign to establish the post of Diocesan Development Officer, is this an activity which fits the description of 'lobbying'?

Consider the activities of bishops. They are probably engaged in lobbying for something with someone in most of the conversations they have with representatives of the press or of the government. *Believing Bishops* analyses the influence of the bishops in terms of their appeal to the mass media and to politicians. They get the attention of the media because 'Bishops personify something more than the cut and thrust of the world of politics; they are thought to be above personal interest, and they carry that weight with them in public interventions.'[38] Moreover, it is interesting to note that 'church leaders who do not hold the title of bishop' are often ignored (or cropped out of a photo) unless the bishops make sure that the lesser church leader is photographed in the middle, between the two bishops!'[39] Politicians pay attention, too – partly because of the 'size of the flock that they lead.' 'Individual bishops holding forth in the cathedrals still have the attention of a crowd that any Minister would be proud to gather at a political meeting. Religion retains the power of numbers, if a diminished one.'[40] Bishop Jenkins may pooh-pooh this as 'regressive nostalgia,' but Gummer calls it 'a great desire for moral values.'

There has certainly been a good deal of effective lobbying behind the scenes. *Believing Bishops* lists four kinds of activity as especially noteworthy means of lobbying by bishops: informal, behind-the-scenes conversations (as in lunches, shared rides in a taxi, etc.); visits to a government official (e.g., the Home Secretary) to ask for something specific (e.g., a request that new evidence be considered in a case such as the Guildford pub bombings); and 'drawing parameters for action in the moral sphere.' For example: 'Graham Leonard has used his inbuilt and obvious conservatism and hence acceptability to the government benches to persuade them to modify some of their legislative schemes – most notably in the field of education.'[41] In general, though, 'interventions by bishops tend to be more wide-ranging: delineating legitimate areas of government activity, for example, rather than getting down to the nitty-gritty of clauses in legislation.'[42]

The quest for a perfect definition of lobbying is futile, and the multiplication of examples would be intriguing but not very edifying.[43] I have elected to seek a rough clarity without comprehensiveness by focusing the analysis of lobbying on two sets of data. The first is an overview provided by one of the BSR's most experienced and astute participant-observers; the second is an examination of proactive and reactive aspects of six different kinds of lobbying for some type of economic justice.

Ecclestone's Map

In 1980, the BSR commissioned its General Secretary, Giles Ecclestone, to write 'a document which would introduce new members [of the General Synod elected that year] to the matters and presuppositions with which the Board works,' one that would be 'a reflective survey on the Church of England's involvements in social and political affairs.'[44] After this report was 'duly produced and debated in the Synod,' it was published (in 1981) under the title *The Church of England and Politics*. It is only fifty-eight pages in length, but it remains one of the most informative and helpful sources ever written on this theme, and its account of the Church's lobbying activities may well serve as our point of departure in discussing this aspect of its social witness.

Ecclestone's analysis covers four main types of lobbying, i.e., attempts to influence what is done in Parliament, in executive branch agencies, in the mass media and at the local level. The two most important activities aimed at parliamentary outcomes are BSR responses to the 'White Papers'/ 'Green Papers,' and the BSR input into debates in the House of Lords (e.g., the briefing of bishops who hold a seat in the House of Lords and are willing to put on record the view of the BSR on some vital topic currently under consideration). In discussing interaction with executive agencies, Ecclestone highlights conversations with a Home Office official regarding proposed legislation on immigration (which was actually a follow-up to the BSR's formal response to the Labour government's Green Paper on Nationality Law Revision) and conversations regarding policy on Rhodesia (in which the BSR's International Relations staff person played an extremely important role as a communications broker and mediator between British and African policy-makers). In speaking of media relations, Ecclestone alludes to the importance of press coverage of General Synod debates (where valuable publicity is sometimes given to BSR publications being debated in Synod) and of press conferences in which the Church of England's view on a specific issue is aired. He also mentions political activity at the local level (using a church-sponsored campaign entitled 'Unity Against Racialism' in Leicester as his key illustration) – but he ventures the opinion that 'in regard to the Church's engagement with the political life of the nation and the world the parish hardly figures.'[45] This pessimism about lack of effectiveness at the local level leads, in the concluding part of the book, to a recommendation that more attention be given to 'community politics,' which will 'give to deprived communities a sense of their own resources and capacity to shape the conditions of their lives.'[46]

Ecclestone's analysis still exudes the comfortable aroma of the days when the first General Secretary could pick up the phone and call a government minister and tell him where the Church of England stood on a matter then being decided. But it also shows the shift to a more participative and less corporatist pattern which started in Ecclestone's incumbency as General Secretary and continued throughout the 1980s.

The definition of lobbying adopted here means that matters pertaining to use of the media and other activities intended primarily to shape public opinion are discussed elsewhere, and the focus on national policy means that activity at the local level is dealt with only sketchily. But the analysis which follows is certainly true to the spirit of Giles Ecclestone's understanding of the Church's role, and owes a great deal to his thinking on all these topics.

Lobbying in the 1980s

The individuals who actually manage the operations of the BSR – its staff and the key members of the committees with which they work, and on whom they rely for statements and action on particular areas of concern – must endeavour to be *au courant* on a bewildering diversity of issues and they must be ready to swing into action in response to an infinite number of specific eventualities. They are expected to make sure that vital moral concerns which are often neglected (or mishandled) by the powers that be are somehow brought to the attention of their religious constituency and of the general public, not to mention the relevant policy-makers – so a portion of their energy has to be spent in doing research and reflection on a number of 'deeper issues' on which the Church has a special responsibility to bear witness. On the other hand, they have to be ready to undertake up-to-date study of issues and policy recommendations put forth in White/Green Papers, and they have to be able to make *ad hoc* responses to events *and pseudo-events* (i.e., speeches or press releases or ceremonial occasions which media publicity make into an issue which must be confronted or a challenge which must be answered).

I have chosen to highlight the most salient considerations pertaining to this topic by describing six activities which illustrate the main kinds of lobbying undertaken by the Church of England. The campaign to influence social security reform involves the preparation of a substantial position paper on a theme which the Church had already been studying and is constantly in a position to comment on. Protest against curtailment of certain NHS policies which are vital to effective preventive medicine is a specific manifestation of a larger social witness regarding a government White Paper which was covered in the preceding chapter. The attempt to mobilize opinion on the proposed poll tax is a good example of the sort of 'reactive' lobbying which deals with problems or issues that arise rather suddenly and call for a quick *ad hoc* action of some kind, and the same may be said of the protest against Unilever's decision to close a large plant in Northern England. The efforts to influence the outcome of the ambulance workers' strike through mediation is a form of conflict resolution which requires a special approach to lobbying. And church support for Industry Year 1986, although it lies on the extreme border of our definition of 'lobbying,' is too interesting and important not to be included.

Social Security Reform

As the following chapter will reveal, the BSR has made a very serious effort to register the Church of England's best thinking on a number of policy questions under deliberation in Parliament or within the civil service bureaucracy of an important ministry. It would be impossible for us to give a detailed account of each of these campaigns, and to do that is hardly necessary, so long as the reader gets some idea of the pattern of activity which is typically carried out in similar situations by church agencies. I have chosen to make the point by discussing the BSR's campaign to influence the outcome of deliberations concerning a proposed change in the laws governing social security in the mid-1980s.

When it became clear, in 1984, that the government was going to propose legislation entailing significant changes in the country's social security system, the Social Policy Committee of the BSR offered testimony to the Department of Health and Social Security. In early 1985, after the appearance of the government's Green Paper describing its plans, the same committee responded by submitting a commentary which was also used to generate a discussion of the issues at stake in the General Synod meeting of August, 1985. In keeping with established precedents, this response did not attempt a detailed critique of the recommendations, but endeavoured instead (see Chapter 3) to 'reflect on the underlying principles.'[47]

In addition, the Social Policy Committee of the BSR also issued a briefing paper on The Social Fund set up by the proposed social security reforms, pointing out that a number of absolutely fundamental questions were raised by this highly problematic innovation. It attacked certain features of the new plan, in particular its redefinition of the concept of need and its practical requirement that 'the basic needs of more people will be met in future from charitable funds.' Likening this feature to the infamous Poor Law of bygone days, the briefing paper declared that 'Even if they wanted to comply, it is difficult to see how agencies could make the financial commitment necessary to meet the likely level of need.'[48]

Protest Against Curtailment of Preventive Health Care

In 1988, the government announced its intentions to carry out a fairly extensive reform of the National Health System. One of the first moves in this direction was to start charging a fee for eye and dental examinations, which had previously been free. Some of the voices raised against this change in policy were those of Anglican leaders, who joined a host of protesters in denouncing this step as a frightfully ill-considered attack on preventive medicine which would, in the long run, have serious counter-productive consequences. Not only would people be discouraged from keeping a close check on the condition of their eyesight and their teeth, but lessened use of the NHS's 'early warning system' would ultimately mean greater expenditures: instead of correcting problems early at minimal cost, more expensive treatment would be required further down the road for defects which had been allowed to develop into serious problems.

John Gladwin's description of efforts to line up speakers in the House of Lords in opposition to proposed charges for eyesight and dental examinations provides a fascinating insight into the delicacy of some lobbying efforts. It was essential, said Gladwin, to get *just the right number* of bishops to speak:

> We wanted enough to make a significant statement on the drawbacks of the proposals, and on the Church's theological and moral reasons for speaking out – but we did not want *so many* bishops speaking that the Government could have created a boomerang effect by claiming that it was just one more attempt on the part of the liberal Church leadership to sabotage whatever the Tories try to do![49]

The Poll Tax

As anyone who follows media accounts of life in Britain knows, there was probably nothing initiated by the Thatcher government that caused a greater furore in the populace than the poll-tax legislation of the late 1980s. (The poll tax was so unpopular, in fact, that John Major, Mrs Thatcher's successor as prime minister, deemed it expedient to *abolish* the levy, and to lop more than £200 off every voter's tax bill for 1990!) In essence, the poll tax replaced existing patterns of raising revenues for municipal administration with a new system of taxation based on the obligation of each person to pay, not (as before) on property ownership and wealth. It was roundly criticized from the beginning by a great variety of critics as being capricious and demonstrably unfair to many readily identifiable segments of the population, and the BSR devoted a considerable amount of time and effort to the task of documenting the grounds for dissatisfaction and rallying the opposition. There were two principal outcomes: the first was the publication of a very modest position paper (printed in the cost-cutting format of BSR Annual Reports) which raised a number of issues in a decidedly non-partisan manner; the second was an attempt to contact local activists around the country to see what sort of national campaign against the poll tax could be devised.

Chris Beales, the BSR staff man who works with and for the Industrial and Economic Affairs Committee, was in charge of both of these activities. He realized rather quickly that the attempt to mobilize a national campaign could easily consume virtually all of his time, so he felt both relieved and hopeful when he found a dedicated colleague who declared his willingness to take that responsibility upon his own shoulders. That left Beales free to concentrate on the preparation of the position paper to be used in guiding the General Synod's discussion of the issues concerned.

The Ambulance Drivers' Strike

In the autumn of 1989, the ambulance drivers employed by the National Health Service went on strike over wage negotiations. A broadly based coalition of religious groups, which included the Roman Catholic Church as well as all of the Protestant churches affiliated with the British Council of Churches, rather quickly got involved in the dispute by offering their services as mediators. On 9 November, Chris Beales wrote to the General Secretary of the union to express his desire to help (knowing that a similar letter was being written by his Catholic counterpart to another union leader). A 4 December meeting with union representatives led to pursuit of informal contact with the Department of Health. On 6 December, the

Bishop of Manchester delivered an address to the House of Lords in which he urged the government to settle the dispute speedily. Efforts to get an appointment with a key NHS executive proved to be somewhat frustrating, but on 12 December Beales was able to talk with this executive's private secretary; however, any hopes for a smooth compromise were dashed by word from the minister in charge to the effect that the government would not budge from the position it had taken earlier. On 19 December, the Church of England issued a public statement asking for a prompt resolution of the dispute – and, when it was not forthcoming, many church leaders participated in a well-attended public rally in Trafalgar Square on 13 January 1990. When the stalemate continued, the churches issued another statement calling for an independent inquiry into the matter, noting that the strike is, 'daily increasing the risk to the health and welfare of thousands of men, women and children.'[50]

When the strike was finally settled on 22 February both sides claimed victory. Comments on this outcome, and on the significance of the churches' mediation efforts, will be given in the following chapter.

The Unilever Dispute

In March 1989, Unilever announced its plans to close its Bird's Eye factory in Kirkby, England (near Liverpool), and at the end of September this action was implemented. When the Liverpool Anglican Diocesan Synod held a meeting on 7 October, the following resolution was put forward for consideration: 'The Liverpool Diocesan Synod recommends that the Church Commissioners withdraw their 21 million pound investment from Birds Eye's parent company, Unilever, in the light of Bird's Eye's decision to close its factory in Kirkby.'[51] Papers by spokespersons for the company and the union, as well as by a representative of the Kirkby team ministry and the Senior Industrial Missioner in that locale had been distributed in advance, and a lively debate ensued. As a result, an amended resolution was passed with no negative votes, calling for the Church Commissioners to review their Unilever investment in the light of the plant closure, and to 'consider how as shareholders in major companies they may best promote sustained investment in areas of high unemployment.'[52]

The vote on the diocesan resolution was the penultimate link in a chain of activities going back to 10 March, the date of the announcement concerning impending closure. When the local Anglican clergy met a few days later, they 'felt a clear duty to respond,' and decided to 'try to form a joint ecumenical response with our Roman Catholic and Methodist colleagues.' They quickly discovered that 'our local links to industry, our ecumenical colleagues and industrial chaplaincy were largely informal – not unusual for parochial clergy – and were not geared for such a delicate undertaking'; nonetheless, they decided to push ahead.[53]

Their first response was a five-hour silent vigil held during Holy Week outside the factory gates; it was intended as 'an act of witness, not of blame.' The vigil was followed by meetings with management and with unions, and the ecumenical group issued a joint statement on the situation which received extensive press coverage. The statement concluded:

This decision [to close the factory] has been based on a system of values which idolise market forces and profit margins, ignoring the local community from which the labour force is drawn. We believe that the values of justice, of community and of human dignity are of paramount importance. . . . It is time that this community is given a fair share of the nation's prosperity, rather than the

cosmetic measures it receives – such as 'training for jobs' that do not exist
here. . . .

In the light of this, we ask the management of Unilever and Birds Eye to
reconsider their decision to close the factory.[54]

The decision to alter the wording of the resolution submitted to the Church Commissioners may have been in good measure the result of a nicely argued paper by
Robert Dew, the Senior Industrial Missioner. Acknowledging the unavoidable significance of productivity, and measures designed to increase productivity, as well as
the probable futility of disinvestment, Dew urged his readers to challenge the
Church Commissioners to exercise their moral imagination in using shareholder
power positively, e.g., 'to seek to get and monitor a positive Unilever policy of
commitment to disadvantaged areas.' He urged the Commissioners to demonstrate
the validity of their own avowed commitment to 'ethical investment' by developing
(and acting on) 'a much wider understanding of that phrase which encompasses commitment to communities.'[55]

The resolution was conveyed to the First Church Estates Commissioner, Sir
Douglas Lovelock, who 'raised the matter with the Chairman of Unilever.' The
Chairman reiterated the company's reasons for its decision, expressed regret and
concern about the dislocations which had been caused, and 'said that no categorical
assurances could be given about future developments because [we] operate in such a
highly competitive market.' He also voiced his confident opinion that 'Unilever had
a record of social responsibility and future changes would be handled with that fully
and properly in mind.' The Commissioners then decided against disinvestment in
this particular case (noting that such a step had upon occasion been taken in the
past), and reiterated their commitment to the primary aim of the Commissioners'
investments, i.e. 'to support the parochial ministry.'[56]

Industry Year 1986

While the Archbishop of Canterbury's Commission on Urban Priority Areas was
preparing the report which was ultimately released under the title of *Faith in the
City*, The Royal Society for the Encouragement of Arts, Manufactures and Commerce was making plans for a fairly ambitious exercise in cultural consciousness-
raising of its own. The Royal Society's programme was called 'Industry Year 1986,'
and its prime objective (as explained in Chapter 3) was 'to increase public awareness
of the role of industry and its service to the community.' It was to be 'part of a continuing programme to encourage a better understanding of industry [and to encour-
age] industry to project itself more effectively.' Its slogan was 'Thanks to Industry,'
a phrase which reveals quite candidly its 'challenge to a society which is insuffi-
ciently aware that almost everything we do depends on industrial activity and which
shows little appreciation of such activity.' The project enjoyed the support of
'Government, CBI, TUC and other major industrial organisations and the professional and educational institutions'; indeed, it was hailed by HRH The Duke of
Edinburgh as an undertaking which 'can only be to the benefit of all the people of
Britain' because of its nature as a timely reminder that 'Industry is by far the most
important activity in our national life, . . . and it can do no good at all to give it a
bad reputation or to call it a "rat race."'[57]

Churches were brought into the planning process very early in the game. In
September 1984, more than fifty ecclesiastical leaders gathered at St George's
House, Windsor, for a conference whose stated aim was 'to stimulate thought and

prayer about what the response of the Churches should be to Industry Year 1986.' Participants insisted that 'the Year has to be seen as something which will change industry as well as our view of industry and thus in no way be simply a static promotional exercise'; however, given that caveat, they suggested a variety of ways in which the churches could co-operate: devising liturgical innovations which would 'affirm God's interest in industry and link liturgy with real life as people experience it today,' putting together 'a package of material for discussion which parishes could take – probably suggesting a five-week discussion programme,' and forming an ecumenical Church Group for Industry Year 1986 that would include representatives of the Industrial Mission Association, the Industrial Christian Fellowship, and others.[58]

In early February, 1986, a service of thanksgiving and intercession for industry and commerce – a service at St Paul's Cathedral featuring a sermon by the Archbishop of Canterbury – inaugurated the programme. A sample sermon for the guidance of those who might want to plan similar services throughout the country was prepared and given wide distribution. Flyers designed to stimulate awareness of the Church's support of Industry Year 1986 were circulated in many dioceses (notably that of the Greater Manchester Churches). The sample sermon and the flyers were part of an extensive follow-up programme called 'Industry Matters' which was launched in 1987, its ultimate aim being 'to lay the foundations for a more prosperous economy' by changing attitudes in such a way as to overcome the incongruity of the world's only 'industrial country with an anti-industrial culture.'[59] It sought to utilize and expand the network of 300 working groups throughout the country established by Industry Year 1986, and to reap the fruits of a tripling of the links between secondary school and industry ('from a level of 25% to over 75% by the end of the Year').[60]

A Wise Investment of Church Resources?

An impartial observer can hardly fail to be impressed by the range of activities carried out by a wide range of people at all levels of membership in the Church of England. But crucial questions remain: To what end? What is the point of all this running hither and yon to proclaim this or that as a guide to thought and a call to action by Christians and by socially concerned citizens? What good, finally, has been accomplished?

It is questions of this kind which are answered in the following chapter. It attempts to assess the *impact* of what the Church of England said and did on matters pertaining to economic justice during the Thatcher years.

6

Impact Assessment

A useful analysis of a church social witness must attempt to assess its societal impact. It is interesting, of course – and of great theological importance – to evaluate the stance and activities of a Christian body in terms of their faithfulness to the best resources of the tradition. But *ethical* analysis requires a judgment about *effectiveness* – for if the moral positions advanced, and the policy options advocated, have no impact on what happens in the world, what good are they?

Unfortunately, it is extremely difficult to measure the effectiveness of social witness, for organizations are notoriously inattentive to impact questions, and to the need to carry out research on questions of this kind. This may be particularly true of social reform agencies, because they are not always enthusiastic about having their own operations subjected to systematic evaluation, and they understandably prefer to invest their limited resources in action, not programme reviews. In any case, my experience in ecclesiastical and academic life suggests that it is seldom possible to establish a cause-and-effect relationship between Christian social witness or the teaching of values in programmes of applied ethics and the hoped-for adoption of more enlightened and ethically responsible policies on the part of corporations, government and professional groups.[1]

The present study is no exception to that rule. In interviewing the leadership of the BSR, I quickly discovered that some of the questions I was asking were questions they had not spent a great deal of time in addressing, and to which they had no answers that went beyond educated guesses. When I asked, for example, about the number of copies of a given booklet which had been published, its distribution and the programme of constituency education undertaken to publicize its findings and recommendations, there was no authoritative reply which could be advanced. I was given an impressionistic account of a sermon here and a speech or a conference there, and I was told to consult with such-and-such a diocesan social responsibility officer (who was known to have taken the booklet seriously and made some effort to disseminate its findings in his jurisdictional sphere), but very little *hard evidence* concerning the pay-off of such activities was already assembled and available for examination. I must therefore introduce this section of the study with a caveat: do not expect scientific accuracy or comprehensive coverage of the relevant data. All I can do is to advance some reasonable judgments and suggestions, and pose certain questions and hypotheses for further study.

Anecdotal Criticisms and an Analytical Reply

The place to begin, I believe, is with some arresting comments which were made by friendly critics of the social action leadership of the Church of England. All of these interviewees must be classified as colleagues who are themselves involved in and committed to church social witness and the goals towards which it is presumably directed, but who have serious misgivings about what is actually being done. Their impressionistic observations will raise troubling questions which cannot fairly be addressed without a reconsideration of our expectations regarding what can realistically be attempted or hoped for.

Impressionistic Observations

Item: The speaker is an Anglican who feels tremendous moral passion about what he sees as the Church of England's clear duty to adopt a more prophetic stance, and to fight to change those forces in contemporary British society which perpetuate scandalous economic injustice. He complains that the average member of his Church's social action leadership seems to be a person with distressingly little *vision*, the kind of person who tends to get preoccupied with programmatic goals which may be (somewhat) important for the short-term instrumental goals of institutional maintenance, but which are relatively trivial, perhaps counter-productive, in comparison with the ultimate consummatory goals of a Christian church. He deplores their lack of theological *profundity* and their lack of clarity about what is *really* important in a Good Society, and what sweeping changes would need to be made in Our Ordinary Way of Doing Things if such a society were to be established on a global basis.

Item: Another devout Anglo-Catholic decries what he terms the 'civil servant' mentality of Church House employees. What he means by this, first and foremost, is acceptance of the notion that a BSR staff person has very little right to inject his or her own interests or preferences (or convictions) into the deliberations of whatever organizational entities the staff person works with or for. Just as faithful civil servants merely carry out the directives of the elected or appointed officials whom they have been hired to serve, so the Church House bureaucrat seems to think one ought to confine him/herself to the role of an *enabler* who implements whatever is ordered by the committee or agency for whom one furnishes staff support.

Item: A prominent ecumenical executive is writing to a friend of his who works for one of the nonconformist churches of Britain. He speaks admiringly of a manifesto on economic injustice which has just been issued by his friend's denomination – and he declares, with particular admiration, that he knows one can count on the wholehearted commitment of the denomination's social responsibility staff to the goals outlined in the manifesto. 'I know,' he says, 'that all those who work for your church will devote themselves energetically to implementing what the manifesto calls for' – and then he goes on to observe, somewhat ruefully, and more in sorrow than in condemnation, that the same cannot be said of all denominations, including his own (Anglican) church. 'We frequently say all kinds of good things,' he writes, 'but one often has to acknowledge, if he's honest, that we have no serious intention of actually attempting what would have to be done to make these things a reality.'

To enter these comments into the record is seemingly to suggest that Church House functionaries are at best dull plodders who have neither the creativity nor the energy to imagine or accomplish what *really* needs to be accomplished to make the world just and humane, and/or that, at worst, they are disingenuous careerists whose heart is not in their ostensible vocations. There may be an element of truth in such charges; indeed, there are very few persons who understand themselves as Christians who would claim that they are not sometimes guilty of bad faith as well as culpable dullness of mind, spirit and imagination.

But there are simpler explanations which are both more charitable and more plausible. In the first place, the bureaucrat, who has probably been exposed to the benefits of higher education (and has undergone the socialization process involved in finishing secondary school and college, perhaps even graduate or professional school) is likely to believe that Establishment ways of doing things are really the *best* way of doing things, most of the time. He may be deeply convinced that the so-called middle-class virtues – such as punctuality, reliability, honesty, conscientiousness, etc. – really *are* virtues, and that anyone who does not possess such traits is to some extent defective (although not necessarily unworthy, let alone contemptible). Moreover, it is possible to believe quite sincerely (and tenably) in at least two models of church social witness which fit very nicely with the empirical realities we have discerned. If one is dissatisfied with the 'predictability' (i.e., the lack of vision or imaginative flair) of Church of England statements, one is likely to view its pronouncements as a sort of 'for-the-record tokenism' which is not actually expected to have much immediate influence, certainly not on the policies adopted in secular institutions. On the other hand, one might explain this same characteristic of church pronouncements as an attempt to help bring about 'realistic incremental reforms' which at least have a chance of being enacted fairly soon by the powers that be in government, culture or some particular social institution. Each of these fundamental postures can be justified by certain descriptive and normative presuppositions, and each can be a part of a scenario which sooner or later leads to significant societal improvement.

What a morally indignant critic calls 'lack of vision' may be perceived (from the inside) as conformity to the 'rational actor' paradigm of organizational decision-making.[2] The widespread acceptance of this paradigm might itself be seen as an altogether plausible (almost *inevitable*) incorporation of the scientific-technological worldview, with its doctrine of 'the one best way' of analysing, comprehending and taking action in regard to almost every contingency in life.[3] To be sure, one might judge this pattern of thinking and acting to be seriously flawed, and one might want to protest against it and propose more fruitful presuppositions and action paradigms in its stead. But it might be extremely helpful (as, among other things, a safeguard against misplaced disdain and overweening self-righteousness) to cultivate an awareness of the pervasiveness and the power of the dominant cultural assumptions which seem to spawn or substantiate tokenism, if that is what it is – or, more charitably, faith in realistic incremental reform. It might serve, also, to accentuate the importance of the sociological perspective which illuminates the nature of the General Synod and defines what is almost certainly going to emerge from an organizational unit composed of its class, age, gender and socio-educational elements. It might serve to remind us, in fact, of the need to be realistic in our expectations.

What Can We Realistically Hope For?

An overly idealistic set of assumptions will lead to an unduly pessimistic assessment of impacts. So before we draw any conclusions about effectiveness we need to attain greater clarity about the context in which judgments of this kind will be made. We can do this by (1) sketching the historical shift from the existence of an 'old boy network' to the situation in which the Church's social witness is just one more example of interest-group politics; (2) reviewing the previous record of the Church of England's social witness, with particular reference to some encouraging 'success

stories' – i.e., some of its most noteworthy accomplishments; and (3) by summarizing 'expert opinion' on future prospects for successful church social witness.

From the 'Old Boy Network' to Interest Group Politics

The Church of England used to be fairly aggressive in its attempts to influence
government. This was true in part because of corporatism, for in a relatively small
country, where the ruling elites in business, government and key areas of culture
(especially higher education and religion) are composed of men who have attended
the same schools and universities, belong to the same clubs and see or hear of each
others' doings in a variety of public or quasi-public activities, it seems natural for
leaders in one area of collective life to 'check with' leaders in other areas before
making far-reaching policy decisions. If they typically 'move in the same circles'
and are acquainted with one another, by name if not by friendship or associational
interaction, they may come to see it as 'good form' to consult with one another
regularly. Thus

> Even after the social basis of the Anglican Church's public influence had been
> substantially eroded, a prelate like Randall Davidson [Archbishop of Canterbury
> in the 1920s] was able to discuss informally ecclesiastical and State business with
> the most senior members of the national political elite. Indeed, Davidson's
> opinion was quite frequently sought by political leaders, and not least in times of
> political crisis.[4]

When William Temple was Archbishop of Canterbury, he was often consulted by
government ministers or captains of industry about matters concerning which they
had reason to believe that Temple had strong convictions and might want to voice an
opinion before significant policy decisions were made. In the 1960s, as noted above,
it was not at all outlandish for the first General Secretary of the BSR to execute the
social witness of the Church by means of strategic telephone calls.[5]

Since these days, however, a number of changes have transpired, the most important of which is the decline of corporatism and, therefore, decreased contact with
and influence on policy-makers. The princes of the Church no longer have the sort
of automatic access to the secular decision-makers which the top leaders of the
ecclesiastical elite used to have, because the country is no longer run to the extent
that it used to be by an old boy network. In Parliament, for example, there is a new
wariness about 'church interference.' In matters concerning the Established Church
over which Parliament has some power, there is an Ecclesiastical Committee in
Parliament which deals with the Legislative Committee of the General Synod, and
things usually go pretty smoothly here, except that in the last few years the Tories
have retaliated against what they perceive as the Church's opposition by subjecting
church matters to exceptional scrutiny and delay. And in matters concerning society
where the Church is critical of government (e.g., *Faith in the City*), the party in
power has often reacted strongly against what it sees as 'a more generally disturbing
tendency on the part of Church leaders to call into question the institution's traditional political alliances and to adopt more pronounced, socially critical positions.'[6]

There is also an analogous decline of receptivity on the part of policy-makers in
the civil service and in the world of business. Roger Clarke of the William Temple
Foundation documents this point in commenting on the changed relationship between
church representatives and the executive agency of the government which deals with
employment and employment training. The Church of England had some luck in

lobbying the Manpower Services Commission when Richard O'Brien was its chairman, and church spokespersons can still 'discuss options' when conferring with government officials – but they cannot very often contribute to the formulation of policy (or influence legislative proposals). This was particularly true in the Thatcher era, because Mrs Thatcher ruled with an iron hand and decided everything herself in consultation with a very small, tight little circle of trusted lieutenants.[7]

This means, among other things, that whatever influence the Church is able to exert is likely to be in connection with 'opinion formation,' not with direct or immediate changes in behaviour or policy:

> In the absence of widespread public support, or of specific institutional inter-
> ests that the state recognizes as legitimate, immediate Church contributions to
> official policy-making have [in recent years] been, at best, very modest. This per-
> haps indicates that the institution's major contribution may be of a much more
> long-term character and could involve joining with others to shift basic attitudes,
> to modify underlying values and, ultimately, to shape the general climate of
> opinion to which policy-makers are constrained to respond. Public utterances
> made in response to immediate short-term problems may contribute to this end.
> But the church's role seems likely, on balance, to be of the long-term strategic
> kind.[8]

This is even true of the BSR. Its aspirations are lofty, and Synod debates inspired by its publications are intended not only to educate the constituency of the ecclesiastical institution, but 'are also ultimately intended to affect public and hence governmental attitudes.' Furthermore, 'its lobbying of officials and politicians, up to prime minis-terial level, is part of a process of sustaining, on the Church's behalf, a running commentary on public affairs . . . [which is] intended to have practical con-sequences.' Thus, although the BSR 'is, arguably, the most politicized of the Church's specialized Boards,' its main function is still that of 'a "promotional" group concerned to advance particular causes.'[9]

So the practical consequences which the BSR tries to bring about 'follow (if at all) because of the Board's impact on ecclesiastical and extra-ecclesiastical opinion rather than as the direct result of Church-sponsored programmes of social action.'[10] Even pronouncements on South Africa have not produced immediate results in government policy shifts, and it may be asserted that the lack of impact on this issue highlights the strict medium-term limits of ecclesiastical influence within the public domain:

> The Church needs to wait for the emergence of a more propitious political
> climate [while continuing] to modify local Church and public opinion. Mean-
> while, the Synod, and especially the BSR's International Affairs committee, has
> helped to keep the issue on the Church's agenda and has kept open policy options
> which may be pressed more effectively on some future government.[11]

On the other hand, however, the potential influence of the Church is still assured by 'secular Anglicanism,' the meaning of which may be summed up as follows:

> The real weight of the Church's presence is not to be found in Lambeth Palace
> . . . but in the 'grass-roots' up and down the length and breadth of England. This
> 'army' of over 10,000 clergymen, and around two million active lay members in
> literally every parish in the Kingdom are arguably far more decisive [than the
> official leaders of the Church of England] so far as the Church's contribution to

English society and politics is concerned. On top of that, however, there is another still larger but more diffuse and tenuously linked diaspora, constituting perhaps a third to a half of all the adults in England, who claim at least a minimal sense of Anglican identity.[12]

Many Englishmen and women still think of England as a Christian country and of themselves as Christian, albeit in a possibly very diffuse sense. It follows, then, that this general cultural vitality of religion has, in turn, some modest political significance – for politicians, both national and local, are likely to share in, and be influenced by, the unspoken assumptions that sustain this prominence. These assumptions, in other words, are indicative of a reservoir of goodwill among such secular leaders towards religious institutions, and instil among them a greater readiness to listen to, and possibly to be moved by, religious arguments. In short, there is an expectation on their part that religion has an important part to play in English public life.[13]

Thus the Church of England can still aspire to be the conscience of the nation – but only in the sense that it is a very special kind of interest group which must seek public support for moral or Christian values by arguing the merits of the case. As Giles Ecclestone has observed:

> In [various kinds of lobbying] approaches the Church of England is engaging in a pattern of activity common to the other British Churches and the British Council of Churches, and indeed to a wide range of community organizations and pressure groups. The combination of public and private approaches, use of the press, collaboration with other interested bodies and communication with one's constituency, is a methodology familiar to lobbies in most free societies. The Church has in addition a privileged place in the political process by virtue of the 26 seats occupied in the House of Lords by the Archbishops and bishops senior by appointment.[14]

Moreover, says Paul Brett, each BSR publication usually appeals to the policy-making elites as well as to its own constituency, for each position paper issued under its auspices usually has three clauses: it renders a judgment about some social problem, it calls upon the government to address this problem, and it urges Anglicans to ponder the report and act upon it. The implication, as we have noted above, is clear: the leadership of the Church of England operates on the assumption that it is entitled (indeed , expected) to make its voice heard on social issues – and that it will be respectfully heard and sometimes heeded by policy-makers, churchpeople and citizens alike.

Success Stories

Despite the difficulties alluded to above, the Church of England has had some success in shaping public opinion and influencing public policy on a number of significant issues.

The Church's study document on divorce law reform provided a blueprint for legislation passed in the late 1960s. A highly controversial report on *The Church and the Bomb* 'drew attention to the weight still sometimes attached to Church opinion in areas of particularly sensitive political or moral concern.'[15] And lobbying by a consortium of religious groups on the Immigration and Nationality Bill of the early 1980s succeeded in obtaining many concessions to the moral point of view expressed by a determined cadre of energetic church social change agents.

Divorce Law Reform

One of the most successful ventures into the public policy arena ever made by the Church of England was its leadership role in reforming British legal statutes governing divorce in the 1960s. It had become abundantly clear, by that decade, that no Christian church could possibly succeed in enforcing its traditional view of the permanence of marriage in a modern pluralistic society. The Archbishop of Canterbury, Michael Ramsey, had the wisdom to see that the Church of England, without abandoning its position that from a religious and moral point of view marriage is indissoluble, could none the less exercise a constructive role in indicating the lines along which reform of the existing law should take place. This led to a rejection of the law's former emphasis upon 'matrimonial offence,' which was a legalistic approach no longer respected in Protestant ethical theory anyhow, in favour of the concept of 'irretrievable breakdown.' A grateful Parliament endorsed this new understanding of the rationale for divorce as a way of allowing hopelessly incompatible persons to gain their freedom while at the same time reaffirming the widespread public sentiment (rooted in centuries of Christian culture) that even though divorce ought not to be entered into lightly, a marriage which no longer possessed the closeness which ought to unite a couple in love and joy was a pointless mockery of what it was intended to be.[16]

The Church and the Bomb

Moyser and Medhurst are convinced that *The Church and the Bomb* had a marked impact on the thinking of high-level policy-makers:

> Recent developments suggest that calculated expressions of Synodical opinion are taken seriously by opinion leaders and even by governments (e.g., the 1983 General Synod debate on *The Church and the Bomb*, which called for 'a carefully staged policy of unilateral British nuclear disarmament'). It was tacitly assumed that an expression of unilateral opinion from the Synod would make it considerably more difficult for defenders of the status quo to dismiss alternative approaches.[17]

The adoption of such a stance shows that E. R. Norman is incorrect in asserting that the recent social witness of the Church of England can be dismissed as nothing more than the treasonous sell-out of a secularized group of intellectuals whose opinions come from the world, not from the formation given to them by the historic teachings of the Church. When church leaders advocate policies which have certain things in common with those of the Labour Party, and when they seem to be drawing on ideas that are frequently considered 'Marxist,' they are not pandering to secular vogues in any simple sense, and allegations of this kind 'overlook the extent to which the views under attack are the product of an ecumenical or even Anglican elite consensus' which has developed from 'reassessed Scriptural understandings.'[18] Furthermore, it is absurd to 'discount theological factors in [explaining] the gap separating ecclesiastical leaders from local adherents' by contrasting 'the latter's common sense with the former's uncritical acceptance of the conventional wisdom of the liberal-minded secular intelligentsia.'[19] There is, in fact, a 'two-way traffic between given theological traditions and given components of the secular culture':

> The results may be attitudes which sometimes owe more than is commonly appreciated to contingent sociological factors but which, particularly at the elite level, also owe more to theologically inspired values than is always allowed. . . . Not least, it seems possible that affinities between particular doctrinal and ideological viewpoints sometimes result from churchmen embracing values of secular provenance that initially became part of surrounding culture as a consequence of Christian influences.[20]

Action Group on Immigration and Nationality (AGIN)

A third noteworthy lobbying effort was carried out by an ecumenical group called AGIN, which was a loose federation of separate organizations, including the British Council of Churches Community and Race Relations Unit, the Catholic Commission for Racial Justice, the Quaker Community Relations Council, and a number of non-ecclesiastical voluntary associations.[21]

AGIN's attempt to eliminate some of the harsh provisions of a government Bill on Immigration and Nationality resulted in only a qualified victory – but this was enough to demonstrate the potential impact of a determined cadre of energetic religious social change agents. It did not succeed in defeating the 1981 British Nationality Bill; however, it did succeed in obtaining many minor concessions and a few important changes.[22] It secured the right of registration instead of naturalization at discretion for certain immigrants; it extended the transitional periods in which wives and Commonwealth citizens can register; it obtained the right of appeal 'to a court for those refused any registration that is an entitlement'; and it achieved important modifications in descent provisions. 'Under pressure from the churches in particular, the Government introduced a "non-discrimination clause,". . . [which] represents a statement of principle.' In short, they demonstrated the overall value of such groups: 'They do not often score great practical successes; they do succeed in getting innumerable small changes made that benefit individuals, and in keeping issues alive in the public mind.'[23]

Expert Opinion

But even in the area of shaping opinion, the Church may be too bureaucratic to promote profundity;[24] indeed, its participation in ongoing debates about social philosophy is both less intense and less appreciated than one might expect, *particularly in regard to economic affairs*. 'Given the centrality of macro-economic debates in contemporary public life, it might be assumed that the Industrial and Economic Affairs Committee is of special importance' – but the situation deplored by Munby in the 1950s and 1960s has not changed completely, because 'the Church in general, and the BSR within it, have tended to eschew involvement in such debates.'[25] And this, say Moyser and Medhurst, fits in with their findings on Synodical opinion: they discerned a 'fairly general acceptance of established economic arrangements,' with 'serious questioning of such arrangements . . . particularly concentrated amongst urban-based and, above all, younger clergy.'[26]

There are three principal reasons for this lack of involvement in macro-economic debate. 'First, the Church may lack the necessary full-time technical experts.' Second, the 'traditionally reformist or even pragmatic Anglican approach . . . has declined to offer alternative models of the good society,' preferring, instead, to urge 'piecemeal change within established frameworks.'

Third, 'the Board, though not itself staffed by advocates of an individualistic Christian ethic, . . . has to operate within an ecclesiastical environment permeated by such assumptions.'[27]

Despite these caveats, however, Moyser and Medhurst remain fairly sanguine about the traditional reinforcing function of religion and its perennial function as a gadfly:

> On the one hand, the Church, through civic rituals, symbolically testifies to a continuing concern for existing social frameworks. On the other hand, the institution's increased autonomy, modified theological understandings, and a sense of responsibility for the powerless impels it to advocate change.[28]

> [This] is complicated by the need to operate at different levels and on different time-scales. Interventions may have such different objectives as the influencing of specific political decisions; the sustaining of dialogue with particular sets of policy-makers; the changing of public attitudes toward specific issues; the modification of current prevailing climates of opinion; and, at the deepest level, the nurturing or challenging of underlying cultural norms.

> In practice, these are not mutually exclusive objectives. Nevertheless, important questions arise concerning priorities. First, there is the matter of which audience the Church, at given moments, should address. In particular, there is the question of whether to give priority to addressing Church members or to commanding wider audiences. Secondly, there is the question of the priority to be accorded respectively to lobbying power-holders and to mobilizing public opinion. Thirdly, there is the matter of deciding for whom Church leaders can presume to speak. Finally, there is the question of the extent to which the institution should 'go it alone' or should coalesce with others sharing similar goals.[29]

Although Moyser and Medhurst are emphatic in declaring that the Church of England needs 'a clearly articulated view of the place of politics within the Church's overall purposes' instead of its present pragmatic adhocracy of approach, and in their conviction that ecumenical dialogue and co-operation are crucial if the impact on society is to be substantial, they applaud the fact that Christian leaders will continue 'to regard contributions to [political] debate as appropriate acts of service to the wider community.'[30] This service may be rendered in the following ways: by 'preserving or replenishing society's reserves of moral wisdom and so, at least indirectly, affecting the temper and terms of public debate'; by furthering the 'quest for a refashioned moral consensus'; by accepting a modest role 'in writing the nation's political agenda' (which means, in part, 'discern[ing] the underlying import of existing trends, [thus putting] on the agenda issues of long-term significance that hard-pressed politicians may overlook'); by helping to resolve particular policy questions; and by occasionally promoting specific causes.

> In this area, there is the danger of platitudinous moralizing or of technically ill-formed judgments. But this has to be set against the danger of too readily abdicating responsibility in favour of narrowly based technical specialists. . . . A merely negative denunciatory role will not, in the long run, enable the Church to be heard in the public arena.[31]

Moyser and Medhurst agree with Ecclestone in saying that the Church of England should be viewed as

> a pressure group alongside other pressure groups – albeit a group which, over a relatively wide range of issues, can count on more than the usual attention. Episcopal and particularly archepiscopal interventions of a personal kind are still possible, and . . . access can be gained to the highest levels of government. But such opportunities are now relatively limited; hence, in using them, churchmen feel constrained to be selective. A recognition that the Church's traditional social base has been much reduced puts some onus on ecclesiastical leaders to conserve those funds of goodwill upon which assurance of an official hearing depends. Indiscriminate or poorly informed interventions can bring the Church into disrepute at the hands of critics anxious to challenge the legitimacy or credibility of its pronouncements.[32]

Michael Fogarty is somewhat less optimistic, but he does assert that 'The public policy role of the churches has moved from the margin of political concern towards centre stage [since the 1960s].' With 131 national boards or offices, research centres and action agencies concerned in one way or another with church and society, the churches are making more public statements on social policy than ever before. Their audiences (secular leaders and the press) are nowadays much more likely than they might have been earlier to react with a public response. Moreover, many social analysts are beguiled by 'the discovery in sometimes unexpected places that values and the way they are translated into action matter a great deal for practical affairs.' His view is that churches may legitimately see themselves as providers of policy guidelines, and that they may be involved in action 'of a non-political sort' – but he asks, 'Where political and economic affairs are concerned, what do churches and their members (for no church is monolithic) think they are about? What business are they in?'[33]

The Impact of Recent Efforts to Shape Economic Policy

So the historical record and expert opinion are in agreement: it is *not* totally unrealistic to hope for effectiveness in church social witness. The time has come, now, for an assessment of the impact of the specific pronouncements and the specific activities which have been described in Chapters 3 and 5. The discussion which follows is organized under two headings, i.e., according to *target audience* and according to *type of activity*.[34] In stressing the significance of target audiences, we focus on three particulars:

1. What impact have the publications and activities under review had upon what is probably, after all, their principal target audience, i.e., the constituency of the membership of the Church of England? This question will be answered by taking a closer look at the endeavours of the BSR network, the efforts generated by the ACUPA enterprise (including the Church Urban Fund), and the programmes undertaken by agents of Industrial Mission.[35]

2. What impact upon 'the world' or 'the nation' can be discerned? Assuming – as one surely must – that the steady stream of BSR publications, and the publicity or follow-up programmes associated with them, are intended to be noticed and pondered by the citizenry of the commonwealth as well as the church constituency, what can be said about the numbers of people reached and the ways in which their thinking and behaving may have been influenced?

3. What, finally, can be said about the effect of the lobbying activities of various agents in the Church of England? What we are interested in here, of course, is the specific and very precisely targeted actions of bishops, clergy, prominent lay persons and BSR or IM practitioners and staff designed to influence particular policy deliberations; actions intended, that is, to affect a certain vote in a legislative assembly, or to modify administrative policy in a government bureau, a corporation or a labour union, or to engage in conflict resolution.

Impact on the Constituency of the Church

As the description of the entire *Faith in the City* follow-up process shows, the activities carried out after publication of the study constitute a remarkable allocation of ecclesiastical energy. The sheer focus of attention upon the report and subsequent events is remarkable. Everybody in the Church of England (and secular Anglicans as well) have been urged to stop for a minute to pay attention to the study, to discuss what the implications may be, to attend follow-up gatherings and peruse derivative publications, to do parish audits, to think of how to tap into the Church Urban Fund, etc. The fact that (as of the summer of 1988) Eric James had spoken about *Faith in the City* more than three hundred times is an indication that somebody has been exceedingly busy setting up meetings which can be addressed by those who can explain the implications of *Faith in the City*.

One of the programmatic suggestions made in *Faith in the City* called for economically self-sufficient parish churches in the suburbs to be 'paired' with less prosperous inner-city parishes. Dozens of pairings were entered into in response to this proposal. Another concerned changes in theological education (for laity as well as clergy), and many innovations of this kind have been undertaken. If we may assume that even a fraction of the agenda items listed in various follow-up conferences and publications are being addressed, thousands of parishioners are being drawn into various kinds of programme activities aimed at achieving the objectives envisaged in *Faith in the City*.

Moreover, existing organizational entities of the denomination are being energized into new initiatives which are related to their sphere of responsibility. Among the numerous BSR activities undertaken in response to *Faith in the City* are these:

1. The Industrial and Economic Affairs Committee's inquiry into the pro's and con's of the social market economy was a direct response to Recommendation 26 of *Faith in the City*.

2. The IEAC's October 1986 conference on 'Regenerating the Local UPA Economy' and the series of meetings with Lord Young of the Department of Employment during 1986 and 1987 were an attempt to deal with the issue of high unemployment in the inner city raised by *Faith in the City*

3. Three other IEAC study processes and subsequent publications are focused on issues of social justice in economic life which are highlighted in *Faith in the City*. They are: the study of women and work summarized in *And All That is Unseen*; the study of the stock market and the world of finance reported in *The Ethics of Acquisition*; and the extensive review of Industrial Mission contained in three recent BSR booklets: *Industrial Mission: An Appraisal*, *Church and Economy* and *Ministry and Mission Examined*.

4. Certain work of the BSR's Social Policy committee is also responsive to *Faith in the City*: the inquiry into 'The Future of the Welfare State' which resulted in the publication of *Not Just for the Poor* deals with recommendations 5, 11, 12, 13 and

14, and with follow-up conversations on these matters with Her Majesty's Government; the July 1986 discussion and action of the General Synod on Child Support is a response to recommendation 12; and recent work on housing is an attempt to implement recommendation 17 of *Faith in the City*.

One final observation is too intriguing to omit – and although it may seem to be somewhat whimsical, I am sure (from the demeanour of the interviewee!) that it was by no means facetious. According to R. H. Preston, one of the signal accomplishments of the BSR in regard to its constituency is this: its studies frequently prevent the bishops of the Church from doing or saying something egregiously stupid![36]

Public Opinion

As reported above, *Faith in the City* was ferociously 'trashed' by certain Tory spokespersons even before its official release – and the attendant publicity ensured that its arrival upon the scene would be noticed by everyone in Britain who reads a newspaper. One theory is that the leak and the attack were, on balance, harmful. It presumably coloured the initial perception of the report, and the first gut reaction to it, on the part of millions of ordinary Britons. Those who hold this view are also likely to believe in the conspiracy theory which sees Rupert Murdoch and other elements of the conservative press as engaged in a deliberate 'disinformation and destabilization' programme through press coverage that is hostile to the Church. Such a theory also fits the picture defined by the government's indignant response to the Falklands Memorial Service. The point is to make the citizenry disinclined to receive sympathetically *anything* uttered by the bishops or the other 'secularized' leaders of Christian churches.[37]

The other school of thought declares that the *intelligent* segment of the public will recognize the absurdity of the red-baiting charges, and that the Thatcherites will simply destroy their own credibility by refusing to recognize Christian concern for justice as something which must remain an operative part of British culture and politics. Whereas the former view worries about having the Church of England marginalized and dismissed as extremist and unBritish, the latter view is that the progressive leadership of the Church will be perceived as 'truly British,' whereas the Thatcherites will be seen as right-wing extremists who are unworthy of handling the reins of government.

What this all adds up to is that *Faith in the City* probably had a double impact upon the public's *general* perception of the Church of England and its leaders. It made some people even more scornful of bishops and preachers, and of the tired old welfare-state measures they endorse – but it made another group more suspicious of the Thatcher government, and more determined than ever not to lose the sense of social solidarity which has historically been articulated and enacted by the Christian patrician wing of the Conservative Party, and by the Labour Party.

It would seem, then, that there are two rather broad (but significant) generalizations which can be advanced with confidence. The first is suggested by Labour MP Stuart Holland, who says that people in his constituency are profoundly grateful for *Faith in the City*, because they feel so defensive and so abandoned by government and by large segments of the populace. They need *somebody* with Establishment credentials to say a good word for the working people and the non-affluent. Their appreciation (and their indignation against Tories, the media and gullible segments of the public) is increased by their perception of the *ironies* and contradictions in Thatcherism: many of the cutbacks in government funding and services hurt small businesses more than anyone else (e.g., less money for housing kills small contractors, and cutbacks in money for transportation and recreation create larger numbers of bored youth who then get into crime and drugs).

A second major impact is implied in the attention given to the report by the many political and professional groups who sponsored and or participated in the array of follow-up conferences referred to in Chapter 3. Richard O'Brien, Chairman of the Archbishop's Commission, is hesitant to claim that there was a direct causal relationship between *Faith in the City* and tangible alterations in government policy. On the other hand, there is a strong plausibility in Paul Brett's contention that debate on *Faith in the City* in the General Synod served to create a new wave of publicity concerning inner-city problems which heightened public awareness of the issues – and local-level conferences involving municipal authorities, professional elites and other civic leaders are a reliable sign that a groundswell of public interest was set in motion. At any rate, as Bishop Thomas Butler observed when speaking at the press conference which launched *Living Faith in the City* in 1990, 'whereas inner-city problems were not on the Government's list of priorities at all five years ago, they are now high on it.'[38] It seems difficult to avoid the conclusion that the Thatcher government's hand was to some extent guided (and forced!) in this particular direction.

Some critics maintain that the report's impact was far from optimal because of the fact that it neglected race-linked issues, and often put forth policy proposals that were boring or stultifying because they seemed to be unimaginative reiterations of familiar demands which had been tried and found wanting. Yet even non-Anglican critics of *Faith in the City* such as Keith Jenkins and John Richardson agree that the report was useful in calling attention to persistent social problems which honest citizens, despite their weary sighs, *must* see the need of addressing.

It is worth noting that many of the items listed under the category of 'Lobbying' in the next section have had a pronounced effect upon public opinion. If lobbying for a policy change is successful, it will always lead to (or involve) certain new explanations to the public by the policy-makers who have been persuaded to undertake changes they have come to see as desirable.

Lobbying

Since *Faith in the City* was an activity launched by the bishops, discussion of the impact of lobbying might conveniently begin with some comments on the effectiveness of the bishops in shaping policy or influencing policy-makers and administrators.

Some would argue, of course, that the impact is usually rather minimal: 'The most often reported interventions by bishops in the political arena have been their criticisms of legislation and their urging that the government alter course. The trophies from these public confrontations are few and far between.'[39] For example: on the one hand, Bishop David Jenkins did not succeed in getting 'a peaceful resolution to the miners' strike, despite his eloquence from the pulpit and his presence on the picket line.' Furthermore, the Roman Catholic Archbishop of Glasgow could not prevent the implementation of the community charge in Scotland, even though he had described it as 'immoral.' On the other hand, however, the Falklands Service was a triumph for the bishops, because 'the Archbishop of Canterbury stood up to Mrs. T. and refused to allow the event to be a celebration of victory and military achievement.'[40] Among the few other victories that might be noted are 'principally those won in the House of Lords': speeches given by bishops prevented the government from abolishing the Inner London Education Authority in 1985 (even though the government won on the same vote in 1988), and there is some evidence that the publications and briefings on housing issues have influenced many votes. (Peter Naish, a housing specialist, asserts that church lobbying on the housing bills of both 1980 and 1987–88 was quite effective.[41])

Especially significant, perhaps, is the informal lobbying which is almost constantly being carried out: there is a great deal of lobbying in 'lunches, dinners, meetings set up with ministers to put a particular case, . . . without the press paying much attention, or with the gathering kept on a strictly private basis.'[42]

If one were to make a list of the concrete policy recommendations set forth in *Faith in the City*, and then ask how many of them were acted on promptly by secular institutions, the analysis might be terribly discouraging. Even when a particular item came up for debate and action shortly after the publishing of the report, its wishes were not heeded – as, for example, in the case of the vote on child-support payments in early 1986. But there have been some significant impacts at the local level, partly because of the *site visits* which were a part of the process used by the Commission in gathering data. ACUPA representatives not only *saw*, but were *seen* by the poor of the inner cities and the public at large, and this in itself had a salutary effect. It is claimed, moreover, that some local government and professional groups have taken *Faith in the City* very seriously, pondered it carefully, and changed certain priorities, goals or *modi operandi* in response to its exhortations.[43] In addition to the activities described in Chapter 5, which were initiated by municipal governments, several universities have had elaborate follow-up meetings on the implications of *Faith in the City* (sometimes being funded in this by local government), and such conferences have often been attended by high-ranking political functionaries and community leaders as well as academics.

An assessment of the impact of the BSR activities highlighted in Chapter 5 must concentrate on the following efforts: social security reform, conflict resolution in the ambulance drivers' strike and in the Rhodesian crisis, the Unilever plant closure, and protest against the poll tax.

Bowpitt credits the campaign on social-security reform with at least three important achievements: it educated churchgoers and promoted informed reflection on the ethical issues at stake; it convinced many secular leaders that the Church has a role to play in formulating policy (and that it is going to exercise its vocation in this regard!); and it '. . . reminded politicians of the need to spell out the moral basis of political judgments hitherto dominated by economic arguments.'[44]

Attempts to mediate the dispute involving ambulance workers were a brave effort to overcome stalemate by persuading the government to give a serious hearing to the claims of the workers. It was not 100% successful, but it had some noteworthy consequences: it showed the Church of England fighting on the side of the workers in a dispute where the bulk of public opinion was on their side, yet doing so in a reasonable way that could not possibly have been described as 'Marxist Thatcher-bashing'; in addition, it put the Church in the role of helping to obviate a strike which was causing considerable hardship, and which might have caused a great deal more had it not been settled speedily.

In the final analysis, it must be admitted that lots of people suffered because of the disruption of services, so the need for an inquiry still exists (to lessen the likelihood of such strikes in the future by giving the workers a fair settlement). But the mediation efforts of the BSR probably shortened the strike and helped to keep public feeling from becoming too intense; furthermore, these efforts constitute an encouraging illustration of ecumenical co-operation, for 'throughout the dispute the churches spoke with one voice and worked closely together.'

An even better example of effective behind-the-scenes mediation was that carried out by church leaders at the time of the crisis in Rhodesia. BSR staff persons were able to secure the participation of a number of trusted intermediaries who played a crucial role in communicating messages from one party to the other which could not have been transmitted through official channels.

As for the Unilever campaign, it showed the Church's concern for a group of employees being severely hurt by management decisions made in the name of economic rationality. Thus it represented a challenge to the idea that 'business is business and a company has to do whatever the market requires' without any consideration of the impact on those who are gravely affected as a result. It must be admitted, however, that the Unilever action turned out to be a rather fruitless protest. Unilever did not change its decision, and the Church Commissioners decided not to disinvest in the company (although they reserved the right to do so at some point in the future, and they pointed out that such disinvestment actions had occurred in the past). The final sentence of the report shows the triumph of 'fiduciary responsibility [to] support the parochial ministry' over tough lobbying in the thinking and actions of the Church Commissioners.[45]

The poll tax protest offers important insights into the practical difficulties of the BSR in allocating scarce resources of staff time. After doing considerable research on the matter, and formulating some solid ideas on how to explain and mount a viable protest, Chris Beales (staff person for the Industrial and Economic Affairs Committee of the BSR) relied on others to provide effective leadership in a continuing campaign on this vital issue. But unfortunately the protest had little impact. This outcome serves to illustrate the dilemma often faced by a BSR staffer: you cannot do everything yourself, so you have to yield the initiative to colleagues on lots of issues (so that you can shift your energies to something else which will not get off the ground unless you give it your personal attention). But when your colleagues fail to deliver, it is too late to redirect your energies to the task you had counted on them to do. Thus the incident reveals some of the difficulties created by lack of resources and personnel in the BSR. It lends support to the notion that the BSR might be wise to concentrate on simply putting down markers, for then at least the record will be clear, and the long-term pattern of the social witness will be something that future analysts *and activists* can sink their teeth into (enabling them to say, for example, that a particular action or lobbying attempt being considered *now* is congruent with a series of statements – markers! – put on the record over a lengthy period of time).

To make the point more concretely, consider the plight of a staff person. On the one hand, the overall mandate of the BSR is inclined to make one feel that the BSR (or the IEAC) ought to say *something* (put down a marker) on virtually *every* issue of any importance that comes along, or even looms on the horizon – e.g., the Eurotunnel or United Europe in 1992, or even Docklands (and other significant Area Development projects). And there will be *someone* who is a significant player in one of the reference groups to whom one feels responsible (and in whose eyes one is going to be judged) who will be *pushing* for a high priority on most of these developments in the world of politics and/or economics. So the pressure to keep jumping from one issue to another is formidable.

The trade-off here is the inability to do a *maximally* effective lobbying job on any particular issue which is at a crucial fork in the road. You are 'damned if you do and damned if you don't': if you insist on preserving 'balance' and 'comprehensiveness' on a range of issues and events, your participation in any given campaign may be limited – but if you decide that a given campaign is decisively important (and that your full effort is critical in effecting the outcome you desire), you will fall behind on comprehensive marker-setting.

The logical strategy of time and resource allocation in this situation is to do exactly what Chris Beales tried to do in regard to the poll tax: you try to find a colleague whom you can trust (whose intensity of commitment, shrewdness in organizing and negotiating, and overall *ability* looks adequate) to carry the ball on a particular campaign. It appears to be a *necessary* strategy, and when it works, everything looks good and you will feel good about the way you have managed your time and allocated your resources. But when it fails – well, you may second-guess yourself and resolve to be more careful next time about your choice of a colleague to take over an especially important project/issue/task.

The Church of England's participation in Industry Year 1986 is a noteworthy example of an investment of staff time which was made as a necessary gesture towards a group of less-than-ideal supporters who might have been alienated by a refusal to join in what they saw as a momentous initiative. And once you have said 'Yes, we'll support it,' you have to show a *respectable* amount of zeal for the project, so you end up spending a certain amount of your time in mouthing a rhetoric which you would really like to qualify drastically, in the interests of a cause about which you have weighty reservations!

One final comment concerns the irony of programmatic success in a vain effort. Charles Elliott reports that the Church's campaign for support of expanded foreign aid in the late 1970s was extremely well organized and spectacularly successful in bringing out large numbers of marchers in demonstrations favouring increased economic assistance to developing countries. Unfortunately, however, these manifestations of public opinion did not actually influence government policy one little bit![46]

7

Evaluation

This book began by asserting that true Christianity in our time must be social Christianity; i.e., that it must exercise an ethic of responsibility which seeks a more just and humane world here and now. It has taken the position, moreover, that the Church's social witness must be prophetic, not merely pastoral: it must endeavour to influence the policies of secular institutions, not just personal morality. In the light of these fundamental convictions, Chapters 3 and 5 summarize the pronouncements and the implementation activities of the Church, and Chapters 4 and 6 present an interpretive analysis of these aspects of its attempts to fulfil its role as 'the conscience of the nation' in regard to economic affairs. This final chapter strives to evaluate the effectiveness of this social witness: How good are the Church's pronouncements (i.e., how faithful to the best resources of Christianity, and how astute in terms of wise policy recommendations and/or cultural commentary)? Which endeavours were on the whole successful, and which were not? What, finally, can be learned from the Church of England's recent experience that will enable Christian people in other denominations and other countries to mount a more valuable social witness of their own in the years ahead? In sum, the book concludes by asking the normative question, 'What *ought* the Church to strive for?' and '*How* can this best be done?'

I propose to address this task in the following way. First, I shall outline the most important elements of the critique of the Church of England's social witness which has been set forth by the religious New Right and by Christian radicals in Britain. This will bring to the fore the most important controversies regarding *major* emphases and issues as formulated 'from the outside' (i.e., by critics who do not share some of the fundamental assumptions of the mainstream leadership of the Anglican Church). Second, I shall raise the most important questions and offer the most important suggestions for constructive change which arise in my own mind. This will bring to the fore a number of the recommendations for 'fine tuning' the Church of England's social witness which can be made from the *inside* (i.e., from the standpoint of an observer who *does* share many of its theological and sociological assumptions).

Criticisms from the Right and the Left

Since many of the principal tenets of the New Right have been summarized in Chapter 2, and since my differences of opinion with this school of thought are apparent throughout, the analysis of its critique which follows will be brief. I want to affirm, however, that I respect the authenticity of the convictions of New Right thinkers; moreover, I must admit that if they are right about both economics and Christianity, Protestant ethicists of my stripe are terribly and disastrously wrong. In addition, as the statement of my own position will reveal, I believe that the Church of England would be wise to accept the validity of certain themes put forward by the New Right, and to address their implications.

My treatment of the Christian Left is also brief, but the reason in this case is that I have incorporated a good deal of its thinking into my own. I share some of its fundamental assumptions and I agree with its constantly reiterated insistence that the Church should be bolder in speaking the truth and more radical in stating social goals. My differences with Christian radicals would parallel Reinhold Niebuhr's differences with exponents of the social gospel whom he regarded as sentimental or utopian – furthermore, like Niebuhr, I recognize the need to be realistic and pragmatic in identifying particular policy options and programmes as worthy of support at particular moments in history, and I see the necessity of bureaucratic organization, power and compromise in moving towards tolerable justice as rapidly and surely as possible.

The New Right's Attack on 'The Kindness that Kills'

The New Right's most fundamental complaint is that the social action leadership of the Church of England are guilty of double offence in being both arrogant and basely motivated. Their arrogance is said to be a function of their ignorance: they do not understand economics, and they do not really understand Christianity either! Their motivation stems from resentment and envy, which they attempt to disguise through the adoption of a posture of moral superiority. They are, in fact, insincere if not downright hypocritical: for if they spent all the time and money they are currently wasting on illegitimate lobbying for *state* intervention into economic affairs on behalf of the poor, they would be able to give and accomplish all that is necessary (and all that is wholesome) through private charity, directly given to the *deserving* poor. 'Remember,' the New Right critics admonish, 'every hour debating is an hour not visiting the sick, the bereaved and the lonely.' It is scandalous, they contend, to 'contemplate the spectacle of a Church so keen to talk about the importance of persuading politicians to solve the needy's problems that it has no time actually to do that itself.' What church people should be doing, of course, is stressing the importance of orthodox belief, faithful observance of traditional sexual morality and the virtues of good character and hard work. When bishops, theologians and BSR personnel do the exact opposite, they reveal themselves to be apostates as well as meddling fools – and they show that they deserve the appellation 'Procrusteans' with which one New Right thinker has saddled them![1]

Thus a second complaint of the religious New Right concerns the trend 'from individual devotion to criticism of social structures.'[2] In sounding this lament, the sociologist David Martin echoes E. R. Norman's charge that the current leadership of the Anglican Church is nothing more than a contemptible group of hangers-on who have committed theological treason for the sake of ingratiating themselves with the secularized sub-culture of left-wing intellectuals. Quoting Charles Sisson with approval, Martin says:

> The emphasis on individual conscience, which was uniquely achieved in Anglo-Saxon cultures, has been subtly revamped as the collection and advancement of *opinions* about what *somebody else* ought to be doing or have done. Guilt no longer inheres in the responsible person, but in blameworthy collectivities.

Christian examination of the self is thus transformed into a giving forth of opinions, vaguely certified as of Christian provenance.[3]

This pseudotransformationist pietism is combined with a truly remarkable other-worldliness in the thought of the New Right philosopher Roger Scruton, who goes even further than E. R. Norman in his notion of the Church as 'a body which legitimates and sacralises the existing order of things, an embellishment of the Establishment.' Scruton sees religion as 'the possession of that belief [in God] which enables men to direct their most profound dissatisfaction away from the ruinous hope of changing things to the peacable hope of one day being redeemed from the need to do so.' For him, 'there is nothing more dangerous to the State than the transfer of frustrated religious feelings to petty secular causes.'[4]

Christian Radicals

Left-wing Christians are frequently so impatient with their more moderate brothers and sisters that they come very close to calling them knaves or fools. In any case, they reproach them for their lack of moral imagination or their *naïveté*.[†] Both types of criticism are evident in the following statement by a highly regarded spokesman of the Christian left who deplores both the culpable disingenuousness and the wishful thinking expressed in *Faith in the City*:

> Why didn't they call a spade a spade? Why didn't they *tell the truth* about the distribution of power in contemporary British society? It is pointless to keep on deploring the same evils without identifying the *causes* of those evils, and the *structures* which perpetuate them – especially, of course, the unequal power of various persons and groups. It is foolish, and self-defeating, to keep on putting out laundry lists of desirable policy options without saying anything pertinent about the obstacles which insure that these options will not be implemented. Moreover, it is fatuous to assume – or to pretend to assume – that we live in a society where the haves and the have-a-lots are benevolently disposed towards the have-nots, and will be only too glad to share resources generously once the areas of need have been named. That simply isn't true: neither the British people nor the membership of the Church of England are full of so much good will and compassionate concern.[5]

The *naïveté* about the presumed benevolence of Britons which is pilloried in the second half of the above statement is echoed in a number of criticisms of *Faith in the City* voiced by several observers representing varied political/theological positions. In Kenneth Leech's *Struggle in Babylon*, for example, the theology of ACUPA is assessed in these terms:

> At the very beginning of the report the authors tell us of the 'basic Christian principles of justice and compassion which we believe we share with the great major-

---

[†]'*Naïveté*' is a word which stands as a surrogate for a whole continuum of possible adjectives ranging from '*naïveté*' to 'false consciousness' to 'disingenuousness' or 'bad faith' to 'dishonesty' or 'hypocrisy.' Since I am opposed to psychological reductionism (see below, note 20), I want to use the least judgmental word I can. But (as the discussion of reductionism shows) I believe it behooves *all* would-be social analysts and social reformers (especially, following Reinhold Niebuhr, Christians!) to search their own souls to discover their own sinfulness and – therefore – the extent to which other, less charitable, nouns might apply!

ity of the People of Britain.' This is a revealing and significant statement, for it excludes from the start the view that Christian principles and values might be in conflict with those of the dominant society. The authors are very committed to the view that the mass of people, if not the government, share certain assumptions, for example that compassion should be a governing feature of our society. . . . [But] it is not self-evident that the values of the gospel *are* common to society as a whole. Indeed the evidence to the contrary is considerable.[6]

This criticism of cultural *naïveté* is already, to be sure, a criticism of political *naïveté*, and it is echoed by John Austin in a commentary on *Faith in the City* which he delivered at a follow-up gathering:

Its basic assumptions were of consensus politics; in other words, the report assumed that churches and the government have the same ultimate aims and objectives – of working for justice and the improved well-being of all the people. This in turn assumed that it was enough for good men and women to describe what was happening to certain sections of the community for policies to change. The report failed completely to perceive that a very different body of people were in the driving seat of government and guided by attitudes and assumptions very different from its own.[7]

In Leech's words: 'There is therefore a fundamental conflict of interests – between the powerful and the powerless, the wealthy and the poor, those who control the means of production and those who produce the wealth.'[8]

Also under attack is the *naïveté* of a psychological self-understanding which is virtually powerless even to *conceive* of the fact that 'good form' may be defined in such a way as to incapacitate well-bred church leaders from seeing evil and being able to speak out against it boldly and efficaciously. A commentary on the 1988 Lambeth Conference of Anglican bishops from all over the world ventured the opinion that the Church of England's 'impotent caution and misplaced decency will do more to endanger it than any external attack.'[9] Perhaps the most laughable (and at the same time the most *appalling*) example of this subtle obstacle to prophetic vigour is portrayed in an incident involving Kenneth Leech several years ago. In a talk-show debate on British television, Leech reacted civilly, but with considerable feeling, to a blatant misrepresentation of his views (actually, a totally inaccurate 'quotation' from something Leech was alleged to have said) by his studio adversary. Leech received an angry telephone call from an Anglican viewer who denounced him for his impoliteness – and when he asked, 'But wasn't it right, and important, for me to set the record straight by making it emphatically clear that I had *not* said what I was accused of having said?' he was told that *nothing* could be more important than observing the conventions of middle-class propriety![10]

The obsession with 'good form' expressed in this not altogether amusing anecdote has affinities with the partiality towards reasonableness analysed in Chapter 4. In so far as there is an ethos of 'cautious moderation' which characterizes Anglican Establishmentarianism, its principal significance is summed up in Charles Elliott's perceptive critique of the American Catholic bishops' pastoral letter on the US economy. Contending that a two-level problem is caused by the fact that 'a lot of America is rich, and even more of America is comfortable,' Elliott writes:

First, there is the pastoral/prophetic problem of persuading the rich and the comfortable that the Gospel demands a radical shift in priorities, resource allocation, legislation, labour law which will hurt them.

Second, and much more profound, the Bishops find themselves in a cleft stick. . . . They are obliged to ask a question that would be almost unutterable in middle class Catholic circles, [namely this:] Even assuming that American anti-trust legislation is tough enough in concept and implementation to preserve genuine competition (and the Pastoral sometimes reads as though it doesn't want to make that assumption, probably rightly), is competitive capitalism *intrinsically capable* of so modifying its practice as to be consistent with the preferential option for the poor?[11]

Since Elliott believes that this description of the psycho-spiritual dilemma of comfortable American Christians also applies to the ruling elites of the Church of England, he goes on to draw its implications for global economic justice by asking, 'Is international competitive capital capable of accepting the reorganisation of international trade . . . ?' The answer, he says, is: 'Technically, yes; politically and practically, no.'[12]

It is hardly surprising that the same sort of criticism has been levelled against the Brandt Report – and its applicability to the legacy of corporatism in the calm reasonableness of Anglican pronouncements is readily apparent. As Brian Wren argues in a World Council of Churches-inspired study of policies and strategies leading to a just, participatory and sustainable society, 'The most tragic, though fully understandable, flaw in the Brandt Reports is its confused reliance on "mutual interests" and "moral imperatives."' Thus

it does not consider the possibility that the real mutual interests might be between the elites of the North and South against the poor in both, or of 'capital' against 'labour' . . . or of other possible expressions of structural conflict. . . .
In other words, the Brandt Report's strand of thinking avoids basic questions about power.[13]

Leech, who served on the staff of the BSR for several years, also attacks its policy-focused incrementalism because it seldom penetrates below the surface so that it can direct attention to causes instead of symptoms. In concentrating on specific proposals and policies, says Leech, the Church is failing to perform its more important task of attacking the basic presuppositions of Thatcherism, and it remains therefore 'Constantinian.' Another prominent member of the BSR's inner circle of scholarly advisers echoes the lament reported at the beginning of Chapter 5 concerning the lack of *vision* in the thinking of Church House functionaries: in his view, they lack sophistication in both theology and social science, and they would be well advised to spend more time in study and reflection instead of scurrying around trying to find something to say on every issue under the sun.[14] As the author of *The New Dissenters* puts it:

On the one hand, we have a government whose leaders seem to be effectively ignorant of the entire tradition of Christian social thought and action . . . and whose view of what constitutes the essence of Christianity does not coincide with the theology or spirituality of any mainstream Christian church. On the other, we have a church which is so lacking in confidence that it has to defend, in the most genteel and apologetic way, positions which are so moderate and reformist that they would have caused not a flicker in a less reactionary period.[15]

To be blunt, we may summarize the criticism of the Christian radicals by saying that in their view the social action leadership of the Church of England is unrealistic (through *naïveté*, disingenuousness or dishonesty), shallow and, ultimately, *not serious* in its presumed commitment to authenticity and social justice.

Sorting Out the Criticisms

We must now attempt to evaluate the charges advanced by commentators on both ends of the political spectrum. The comments which follow will be grouped under two main headings: 'Replies to the Critics on the Right' and 'The Path Ahead.' In sorting out the wheat from the chaff in the criticisms from the Right and the Left, I speak partly in defence of the Church of England and partly in agreement with its critics. In summarizing my own convictions, I try to spell out the implications of the 'modest proposal' regarding church social witness presented in Chapter 2.[16]

Reply to the Critics on the Right

If the New Right theory of 'trickle down' were correct, its position on a variety of policy issues might be deserving of respect. But as Ronald Reagan's budget director revealed in an uncharacteristically candid moment, not even neoconservative ideologues *really* believe that the average citizen is going to benefit substantially and quickly from the handouts to the already affluent and privileged – from, that is, the 'private welfare state' – which are one of the most scandalous features of conservative capitalism.[17] So it is patently unconscionable, in my view, to endorse the irrationalities and the iniquities of Thatcherite economic policies. If one remembers social Christianity's refutation of nineteenth-century political economy and social Darwinism, and if one considers the catalogue of the cardinal tenets of the New Right summarized in Chapter 2, the disastrous implications of following this school of thought are abundantly clear.

But two of the major moral/philosophical themes voiced by religious New Right spokespersons require an answer. One has to do with the mainstream Church of England's apparent lack of emphasis on 'strength of character' and 'old-fashioned morality' as represented in the bourgeois virtues of honesty, conscientiousness, hard work, reliability, sobriety, etc. The other has to do with allegedly disingenuous reinterpretation of historic Christian doctrine.

The former is a lot easier to answer than the latter. It is not difficult to see why mainstream leaders are somewhat reluctant to come forth with a resounding reaffirmation of traditional notions of character and virtue, for despite their awareness of the tragic aspects of the dependency culture, they know that such affirmations are likely to be seized upon by simple-minded right-wingers and used to flog what they see as the lazy, irresponsible and insolent behaviour of welfare cheaters and other parasites on the body politic who have made a convenient racket out of dependence on the welfare state. When this misapplication of familiar pieties takes place, it is only one short step to the most odious rationalizations in support of the arrogant callousness of acquisitive individualism, for if poverty is really the fault of the poor, then the affluent need share nothing with them, and can indulge a high consumption life-style without having anything other than contempt and derision for the shiftless scoundrels who deliberately choose not to be self-reliant.

Very well. One must avoid saying anything which is subject to serious misinterpretation in matters of this kind. But why would it not be possible to make it *absolutely* clear that one will not be tricked by the sophistries of the New Right regarding blaming the victims *while at the same time* making it equally clear that the so-called bourgeois virtues are indeed vital to the health of any commonwealth? To put it in the language of the founding fathers of the United States:

> In a monarchy, . . . 'respect and obedience' were derived 'only from the passion of fear.' But in a republic, . . . order, if there was to be any, must come from below. . . . In a free government the laws, as the American clergy never tired of repeating, had to be obeyed by the people for conscience's sake, not for wrath's. . . . The eighteenth century mind was thoroughly convinced that a popularly based government 'cannot be supported without *Virtue*.' Only with a public-spirited, self-sacrificing people could the authority of a popularly elected ruler be obeyed, but 'more by the virtue of the people than by the terror of his power.'[18]

It must be possible to count on citizens not only to respect the laws, but also to accept the expectation that *everyone will do the best that he or she can* to make a contribution of labour to the common good. To be compassionate is *not* necessarily to be lenient in one's attitude to those who aspire to be free-loaders. To affirm the importance of *effort* is not to condone the self-serving simplifications of New Right ideologues who *fallaciously* contend that everyone who wants to can find a job, and that all who are unemployed are sluggards. The Church can ridicule the ideological nonsense of the New Right while at the same time affirming the *rightness* of the old-fashioned notion that every able-bodied person *does* have an obligation to be engaged in socially useful activity.[19] And in so doing it can reaffirm traditional teachings about both character and fellowship which are a vital part of English ethical socialism as well as Christianity.

The question of a disingenuous reinterpretation of doctrine is much more complicated. It is unfortunately true that traditional doctrine is otherworldly, and that the social gospel which emphasizes justice and humaneness in this fallen veil of tears represents a departure from the eschatological beliefs of Jesus and the early Church. But it is equally true that 'new occasions teach new duties; time makes ancient good uncouth': and the religious New Right spokespersons who accuse the mainstream leadership of a sell-out to secularism are guilty of disingenuous distortions of their own. For if (to use Tillichian language) Jesus is to be acknowledged as the Christ in the twentieth century, he must be seen as something other (and more) than the Lamb of God who atones for the sins of the world in the eyes of a patriarchal deity whose vanity requires a bloody sacrifice.

The trouble is, progressive theologians find it extremely difficult to say this forthrightly. They have to *seem* to ascribe to traditional doctrine even as they endeavour to pour the new wine of the social gospel into the old wineskins of primitive soteriology. Thus they are unable to explain their reinterpretation of Christian doctrine to the masses – and because of this they are vulnerable to the charge that they are betraying the faith by engaging in a dishonest secularization.

This dilemma admits no easy resolution. On the one hand, I am prepared admit that the *only* way in which an honest contemporary Christian can adhere to the faith is by means of a radical reinterpretation. On the other hand, though, I am cognizant of the fact that the average churchgoer may not be capable of comprehending, let alone endorsing, such a reinterpretation. What this means, of course, is that one must stress the *positive* aspects of the Christian tradition (i.e., its prophetic content) while maintaining that its primitive elements are nonessential – but this will not satisfy everyone.

Reply to Christian Radicals

There are two crucial questions which have to be addressed in coming to grips with the critique of radical Christians. The first pertains to the charge of *naïveté*, and raises the issue of the presumed power of social location as a determinant of perception, decision, action and (even) intentionality. The second pertains to the charges of shallowness and comparative triviality, and forces us to consider the latent dysfunctions of an incrementalist approach to social reform.

Social Location

The radicals' indictment of the *naïveté* of mainstream Anglican social reformers is very troublesome. It suggests that the reasonableness and the cautious moderation of the social action leadership are absolutely predictable, and that they may, in fact, be a respectable cover for a cowardly lack of any *real* or *thoroughgoing* desire to fight on behalf of the dispossessed.

I am of the opinion that it is always *interesting* to speculate on the power of psychological and sociological conditioning as determinants of one's point of view on substantive issues. Thus an examination of the social location of a speaker has *potential* value as a *partial* explanation of what he has to say on moral and political questions. But (as explained in Chapter 4) I believe that speculations of this kind should be taken with a large grain of salt: they *prove* nothing, and reliance on them may be an indication of the critic's lack of hard evidence.[20]

Be that as it may, the well-demonstrated pressures of social location have to be acknowledged as an ever-present reality and, therefore, as at least an occasional influence. At its worst, it may be an incapacitating false consciousness that makes us incapable of perceiving how limited our vision is and how lukewarm our commitment – indeed, 'false consciousness' itself is a kind of antiseptic euphemism, for lack of effectiveness may be less due to blindness than to half-heartedness or just plain hardness of heart. Consider, for example, these troubling realities:

1. A persistent classism seems to be manifested in the absence of working-class persons and working-class views in the counsels of the BSR and the General Synod. Commendable efforts are being made to overcome gender discrimination, and some strides have been made towards at least acknowledging the almost untouched problems of racism in the Church – but despite efforts to involve union leaders in some task forces and boards, classism endures (in part, perhaps, because of the familiar lip service given to transcending it).

2. There is something very troubling about the dearth of funding which vitiates the impact of so many of the excellent publications of the BSR and the often laudable public statements of church leaders. Reform activities – especially the kind of lobbying that has a chance to influence laws, administrative procedures, appropriations, negotiations and specific areas of social policy *right now!* – are essential. The radicals who pooh-pooh the incrementalism of mainstream do-gooders are wrong to suggest that lobbying for particular policy reforms is futile. This defence assumes, of course, that these incremental reform activities are cleverly planned and effectively executed; otherwise, they *are* of very little value. Although it may be true that 'putting down markers' has a latent impact which proves to be quite significant when events (and the passage of time) bring about the *kairos* of a particular social reform, the social action leadership must never be satisfied with *exclusive* reliance on this approach. If funds and personnel are drastically limited, it is better to sacrifice coverage of some issues so that all pronouncements are

accompanied by a carefully planned and adequately funded follow-up programme
that shows the Church *means business* when it speaks out. This *must* be done, for it
is essential to make the hard choices involved in prioritizing, even if this means dis-
appointing particular interest groups and constituents and their notions of what is
'politically correct.' Lacking this, the Church is always vulnerable to the suspicion
that its social witness is nothing but an innocuous 'for the record' tokenism (and –
worse! – that it really is not *intended* to be anything more).

To be sure, a 'for the record' posture is capable of moving beyond directions to
directives, but it seems nevertheless to fall short of determined *commitment to effective action* on behalf of rather particular stances and policy positions on specific
issues. Many of the pamphlets and reports issued by the BSR since 1975, and some
of the documents produced by Industrial Mission sources (including religious think-
tanks such as the William Temple Foundation) can be assigned to this category. To
be sure, they commend themselves to the attention of Christian people, and sometimes they are specifically targeted for debate in the General Synod and/or dissemination through the Anglican network of diocesan Social Responsibility Officers
or a local network of concerned citizens, religious or secular – but the lack of
systematic follow-up action, and the lack of funding *for* systematic follow-up action,
are fatal. This is especially true in a bureaucratic setting where all ecclesiastical
agencies have to compete for limited funds, and for the not unlimited attention of
administrative officers (e.g., bishops) to get 'time on the agenda' and other signals
of certification. Lack of funding and other kinds of symbolic certification encourage
staff personnel to feel they have done their jobs in a satisfactory way once the publications have been issued, 'commended for prayerful study' by the General Synod
and, in short, put on the record as the Church's 'official' social witness.

Latent Dysfunctions

The second crucial question posed by the radicals, of course, is a question about the
latent dysfunctions of reasonable ends and incrementalist means. Now, it is obvious
that much of what was said about dubious intentionality under the heading of 'Social
Location' is pertinent to the charge that the Church's social witness is superficial and
'not really serious.' But even if one chooses to discount these arguments as unduly
reductionistic, the fact remains that an unbiased observer (even one who has the
utmost respect for the intelligence and the integrity of Church House staff) may none
the less deplore the unintended consequences of official pronouncements and actions.

Yet we should begin this discussion of latent dysfunctions by acknowledging that
the incrementalism of the BSR may in fact constitute a 'creeping subversion' which
is as close to *effective* revolution as the churches will ever get! The source of this
comment is Kenneth Leech, who observed that many Conservatives regarded Giles
Ecclestone as the wiliest and most successful revolutionary on the scene, for they
thought that his work as General Secretary of the BSR showed the formidable
shrewdness of a man whose years in the civil service made it possible for him to
gauge with consistent accuracy just how far he could successfully go with his sometimes decidedly non-Establishment ideas and programmes. The thrust of the remark
is clearly in accord with Michael Atkinson's reminder that it is precisely the experienced bureaucrats who are in the best position to appraise 'the art of the possible,'
and with Ecclestone's doubts concerning what he dismissed as Leech's 'unworkable
doctrine of permanent revolution.' This line of thought recognizes that the incremental reforms won by oft-despised staff personnel are a half loaf which is *clearly* better
than none at all – whereas the 'blue sky' palaver of idealists often leads nowhere.

We must also recognize the need for role-differentiation, and its corollary, the validity of devoting substantial resources to pastoral activities.[21] The *Faith in the City* follow-up agenda should probably not be attacked because of its emphasis on mobilizing the Anglican constituency, so long as two caveats are observed: first, 'church renewal' cannot be complete or faithful to the gospel unless it mobilizes Christians for non-paternalistic mission; second, the money and effort allocated to the improvement of church structures and to an essentially pastoral ministry to the poor of the inner city must be matched by the allocation of resources to prophetic reform of the principalities and powers which govern secular life.

But the danger of goal-displacement is ever present, and this is particularly true of investments in internal improvement. The leaders of the *Faith in the City* enterprise are constantly warning against the tendency, for example, to think of the Church Urban Fund as a means to restore crumbling edifices, or simply to install a much-needed new furnace in an aging Sunday school building. Avoiding this pitfall requires constant vigilance and a firm administrative hand, because dozens of vestries throughout the land would love to divert funds intended for UPAs to their own purposes. And this tendency is aggravated by the aforementioned *localism* of the Church of England, which R. H. Preston pinpoints as one of its gravest organizational and administrative difficulties.[22] So - all success to those who are giving themselves to the current campaign for a kind of church renewal which has a built-in societal reform component. But let them be ever resolute in directing the energies they command towards the ultimate-consummatory goals of Christian mission, not simply the internal-instrumental goals of the ecclesiastical institution.[23]

Essentially the same sort of thing must be said about the primarily pastoral work of the Church. The plight of the dispossessed is too desperate for them to be ignored, so it will always be good to have a certain portion of the Church's ministers (ordained or lay) absorbed in binding up wounds and comforting the scorned and afflicted. But in the long run - as no less a figure than Martin Luther King used to be fond of saying - it is more important to build a 'Jericho Road Improvement Association' which can afford systematic protection to travellers than it is to rely on Good Samaritans to come to the rescue of a predictably large and ceaseless aggregation of victims.[24]

One particular qualm often voiced by the incrementalists themselves has to do with the danger of further undermining the welfare state by co-operating too unquestioningly or too extensively with the government's increased emphasis on the voluntary sector. It is astonishingly ideological (and perhaps hypocritical) for Thatcherites to pretend that private charity can take care of the shortfall which has been created by decreases in public appropriations for welfare purposes; moreover, it is only a drop in the bucket compared to the huge windfall profits handed out to the already affluent by the burgeoning of the *'private* welfare state' - i.e., subsidies, social overhead capital and tax breaks which benefit the *haves*. As the author of *The New Dissenters* avers:

> Certainly the rich have plenty to bestow. Their incomes have risen faster than anyone else's in the Eighties as the gap between the rich and the rest has widened. . . . [But] there is no evidence to suggest that the rich have given more than a fraction of their income to charity.[25]

The fact is - and the welfare state is an acknowledgment of it, private charity cannot be counted on to provide for the poor, and *ought* not be depended on to do so. The Sheffield Synod of the Methodist Church gave voice to this conviction as follows:

We are in danger of returning to a Victorian system of charity for the poor which we do not believe is right. We want the needy in our society to be properly helped and supported. The churches have an important role to play, but we cannot possibly bear the burden, and nor should we, as this is clearly the responsibility of society as a whole.[26]

In addition, voluntary sector agencies, including churches, are now being asked to help pay for infrastructure needs and large quantities of basic equipment demanded by various service providers:

Ten years ago the voluntary sector initiated things and central or local government took them up. [Today,] the pump priming role of trusts is . . . less accepted. Doctors needing new machines are approaching us for money; we're starting to get it from schools as well. What should we do? Should we be funding the basic tools of the trade?[27]

The Path Ahead

What can this study teach us about faithful and effective church social witness? Every reader will have his or her own opinions on this score, and a complete answer to that question would require another book. I will conclude by stressing the two most important kinds of suggestions which have asserted themselves in my mind as I have reached the end of a task I began five years ago. What emerges most clearly, I believe, is the need for a somewhat bolder vision of the Good Society in the content of church pronouncements on economic issues, and the need for a more sharply focused social change strategy in the implementation activities undertaken.

A Bolder Vision

The Church's apparent cautious moderation, and its commitment to putting down markers and pragmatic incrementalism, have many advantages and much appeal. Yet these characteristics of social witness lend credence to the complaint of the Christian radicals regarding its shallowness. Recent leadership appears to have preferred that its pronouncements should not be directed towards the elaboration of a fundamental vision of the Good Society or the theological rationale therefor. Instead, it has opted for a reiteration of rather familiar theological norms on the apparent assumption that its audience will accept these familiar verities without much debate, and it has assumed the desirability of a mixed economy welfare state as either good or (for the nonce) inevitable and therefore *given*. Judging from the writings and the interviews which form the basis for this study, the leaders are confident that they can rely on an already existing consensus on the nature of a healthy commonwealth. They apparently feel that it is sufficient merely to reiterate certain fundamental theological principles and ethical norms in the confidence that assent and commitment will be forthcoming. It is just this assumption which Raymond Plant feels called upon to challenge when he warns church leaders that they cannot appeal to familiar Christian notions such as justice and compassion when addressing the drastically new mind-set encouraged by the New Right. It is just this assumption which Kenneth Leech and other Christian radicals attack when they deplore the Church's reluctance to address power discrepancies more vigorously. One hears many impassioned pleas for the articulation of a more thoroughly developed restatement of Anglican social thought – but so far it has not yet occurred.[28]

Still I believe that the stance taken on most issues is sound, and that the *content* of the Church's social witness is less in need of improvement than its *dissemination and follow-up* phase. As noted above, I am sometimes troubled by what strikes me as excessive 'balance' and lack of precision or depth in the documents, but I understand the trade-offs which are at stake in the decision to produce documents which are in some sense representative of a range of church opinion, and which are accessible to unsophisticated readers. Perhaps this problem can be to some extent handled by carrying out the aforementioned staff suggestion that the BSR should put out two versions of each report. What is most important is a greater investment in, and a better plan for, dissemination, discussion and follow-up action regarding the studies that are conducted.

There are, however, three hitherto neglected topics which I would urge the social action leadership to examine in the coming decade. The first has to do with the qualitative aspects of wealth creation (see Chapter 4); the other two have to do with the fundamental ethical distinction between wants and needs, and the attainment of a much greater measure of economic democracy.

Wants and Needs

The needed stress on the qualitative aspects of wealth creation is inextricably related to the need for a more penetrating explanation of the difference between *wants* and *needs* – that is, the distinction between what every human being requires for a healthy biological existence and for decency as understood in the society where he or she lives and, on the other hand, those desires for non-essential commodities and experiences which are present in varying ways in the minds of different individuals. If notions such as human solidarity or 'the family of humankind' mean anything, and if the obligations of mutual caring and support we derive from such concepts are to have any potency, then surely we must be able to declare that the needs of all take priority over the wants of any. And if we can do this, then we have a valid moral basis for progressive tax policies and the socially provided welfare benefits which are rightly regarded today as the hallmark of a civilized nation.

Establishing a clear distinction between needs and wants is crucial for at least two extremely important reasons:

(1) The concept of needs will in large measure define the objectives of a welfare system: what nutritional levels are required for good health and normal development, what kind of housing, what sort of medical and dental care, etc. (even, although this is much more difficult, what sort of education is to be offered to every person).

(2) Such definitions can then be translated into the concept of *rights* ('rights of recipience,' as one contemporary philosopher has called them[29]) which can be paired with recognized obligations on the part of society (which is to say, the obligations of citizens acting through appropriate social institutions). This part of the moral justification of welfare benefits is crucial, for without it there may always be some kind of stigma attached to the status of beneficiary, and those who are fortunate enough to be benefactors will not provide *enough* aid for the needy, nor will they be *consistent* in providing it.

The distinction between wants and needs is not difficult to grasp, but articulating a convincing ethical argument concerning its implications will be a formidable challenge. The fundamental theory was stated long ago by the economist A. C. Piguo, who wrote:

It is evident that any transference of income from a relatively rich man to a relatively poor man of similar temperament, since it enables more intense wants [higher marginal utility] to be satisfied at the expense of less intense wants [lower marginal utility], must increase the aggregate sum of satisfactions.[30]

Persuading prosperous citizens to accept this proposition and its policy ramifications will not be an easy task. But this is surely a *sine qua non* of a new vision of Christian social witness for the modern age, and the Church of England ought to be able to carry out the undertaking with relative ease in view of the fact that one of its chief intellectual allies, Raymond Plant, has already done so much excellent scholarly work on this very theme.[31] I would like to urge the leadership of the Church to address this specific project immediately, for I believe that many of its worthy programmes would suddenly encounter far less opposition, and much of its theological, political and economic theorizing would suddenly flourish with a new clarity and intensity if this one comparatively simple intellectual/moral piece of work could be promptly taken care of.

Economic Democracy

More should be said, too, about the desirability of moving towards *economic democracy* (which requires a redistribution of wealth as well as the sharing of decision-making power with workers) and *community* (which cannot flourish unless something approximating the 'relative equality' demanded by recent papal documents is achieved[32]). Discussion of these possibilities – rather, I would insist, these *necessary goals* of a truly just, participatory and sustainable society – is often dismissed as utopian, but two decisive answers to that objection can readily be given. First, if specific legal, institutional and administrative measures are considered fairly, point by point, it is easy to see how any mixed economy *can* realistically move towards economic democracy because it is easy to cite features of one or more European or North American nation where such have measures have been tried and have proved successful.[33] Second, if intelligent role-differentiation in devising an overall social change strategy in modern life makes it a special responsibility of religious institutions to formulate long-range visions of the Good Life and the Good Society, then certainly the social witness of the churches should not be hamstrung by an excessively narrow understanding of 'political realism.'

The second answer is especially important for this study. It *is* the primary responsibility of the Church to speak the truth. Judgments about when and where the truth may be spoken with optimal effectiveness are complicated, so it is always problematic to assume a doctrinaire position on such questions. But if the *truth* of the matter is that humankind needs an economic system which is significantly different from world capitalism in its present form, then this is a conviction which *must* in some form, sooner or later, be proclaimed. Furthermore, it is important to take a long-range point of view. In Rosemary Ruether's words:

What we seek is not only a society that dismantles class hierarchies, founded on decentralized cooperative counterinstitutions, that dismantles racist and sexist hierarchies and promotes mutually supportive relationships between human and nonhuman ecological systems. Because this project is so complex and daunting, especially at a time when even the word 'liberal' has become an epithet, it is crucial at all times to maintain a sense of historical perspective. . . . [As Michael Harrington said,] 'To struggle for economic democracy [in North America today] is to commit yourself to a cause you will never see fulfilled in your own country.'[34]

A More Sharply Focused Social Change Strategy

According to sociologists such as Moyser and Medhurst, the most realistic goal for church social witness is the shaping of the moral ethos of the constituency and of the nation, and ethicists such as Ramsey and Gustafson agree this is theologically appropriate. They may be right – and if they are, then putting down markers is exactly the kind of activity to be stressed. I merely want to urge that this vital activity should be made more effective, and supplemented, by more extensive efforts to mobilize cadres and coalitions which are engaged in carefully planned attempts to influence specific policies of major institutions in the worlds of government, business and culture. I want to argue for a type of policy-focused incrementalism which is far more realistic and pragmatic than the radicals' 'permanent revolution,' but which generates support for *directives* instead of merely pointing out *directions* and urging individual Christians to take it from there.

It is gratifying to pose as a prophet of revolution, but an optimally effective strategy of social change cannot put all of its eggs in the revolutionary basket. When I am under the spell of an eloquent polemic penned by a true believer of the Christian left, I want to raise the same kind of question that a group of Presbyterian scholars in the USA recently asked regarding nuclear war and foreign policy issues: 'Are we now called to resistance?'[35] I want to join the radicals in proclaiming that conservative capitalism, and the demonic ideology of privilege associated with it, has become a Great Beast which authentic Christians ought to fight with all of the resources at our disposal. And even in more sober moments I do believe we must at least raise the really difficult questions about shared power and the truly threatening questions about meaningful solidarity with the poor in quest of a human community far more benign than anything our class-stratified society has known. We are not likely to get even tolerable justice, much less community, without a radical redistribution of power. We may be called, as Duchrow argues, to 'throw a spanner in the works.'[36] For it just may be the case that acquisitive individualism as it exists in Britain and America today constitutes a deadly menace which demands a new Barmen Declaration. Some of the best church leaders in England are pondering that question and considering that option, and no doubt North American Christians should do the same.

Unfortunately, however, there is something desperate, and desperately unsatisfactory about this course of action, for protest without a plan is seldom effective; indeed, it may be nothing more than a left-wing version of pseudo-transformationism. To imagine that a dramatic act by a militant dissident (or a handful of dissidents) can bring about significant social change is usually an illusion, an illusion which cloaks the deeper motives of the person concerned, i.e., to ventilate his feelings (or attest to the purity of his soul) without serious concern about the consequences *for those whom the rebel ostensibly wants to help.*[37]

So I am convinced that it would be a terrible mistake to jettison the current Church House bureaucracy and the activities its staff and committee people are now working so hard to organize. But I fear that their efforts are being undercut by a theory of social witness which partakes of many of the errors which are present in the excessive individualism which Durkheim called 'the great sickness of our time.' I submit that the Church of England's work on behalf of social justice is vitiated by this sickness, particularly in so far as it continues to operate in accordance with the assumptions of William Temple, whose belief in the sanctity of personality merged with his Platonism to give rise to his mighty conviction that Christian social action must be decided upon and carried out, finally, by individual Christians. But as an insightful critic of William Temple has declared, restricting the Church's social witness to directions (to the exclusion of directives) tends to emasculate church attempts to influence policy: in insisting that Christians 'should be concerned with principles rather than with policies, [Temple] ensured that nothing they said, as such, would be likely to have much immediate effect.'[38] This approach may elicit assent, but it does not inspire (or, we might add, *mobilize and enable*) action.

What is ironic here is that the social action leadership's practice is really better than its theory. For despite a theoretical legacy which urges church activists not to go beyond principles, 'directions' and middle axioms, the social witness of the past fifteen years has in fact dared to call for support of particular policy and programme 'directives,' and the modest successes of its lobbying attest to the fact that the Church can affect policy, *now*, not simply influence the general moral atmosphere and thus bring about change indirectly at some point in the future. Many of the policy recommendations in *Faith in the City* (particularly the one on mortgage tax relief), the reports on the National Health Service, and the documents on global economic justice are admirably specific, and much good might have been accomplished if these recommendations had been *forcefully* brought to the attention of Anglicans and Britons alike.

There are even some signs that the *theory* is also changing. The passages from *Living Faith in the City* and from Hinchliff cited in the last section of Chapter 2 echo Denys Munby's belief that the Church *can* effectively contribute a special dimension to policy deliberations, and it may well be that the time is ripe for the social action leadership to *proclaim* as well as follow a more audacious model of social witness.

But in order to do this the leadership will also have to convince a critical mass of its parishioners that Christian discipleship requires *active commitment to and involvement in the struggle for social justice*. The conventional wisdom assumes that all members of the Church of Jesus Christ recognize this requirement, but the fact is that the plausibility structures of the culture give a different message, i.e., you do not really have to *do* anything to certify your presumed social concern. William Temple's theory about leaving *action* up to the conscience of individual Christians does not work, because the reality of experience in our culture assures us that 'lip service' will suffice. That is why putting down markers which have been stated in a beautifully balanced fashion by study groups observing cautious moderation is not good enough unless some attention is also given to the task of organizing cadres of social change agents who will work strenuously and pointedly towards implementation of the stance that has been taken in the documents.

I propose a different conception of church membership as well as a different strategic approach. It involves the recognition that Christian discipleship logically leads to commitment to *some* important social reform goal, and to participation in a cadre of energetic social reform agents who are constantly working towards that goal.[39] It involves the further (more debatable, but less problematic) reorganization of the Church's implementation of social witness: it suggests that BSR staff and the SRO network ought to set up a division of labour in which (for, say, a five-year experimental period) some agents would devote themselves to the cultivation of vision and the articulation of long-range ends, and others would focus consistently on immediate pragmatic incremental changes.[40]

Of course, acting on such a daring proposal may be unrealistic or unwise. It must be admitted that there is something profound (and profoundly beguiling!) in the conventional wisdom's emphasis upon individual conscience and individual action. It is a lovely reflection of Temple's Platonism and, in a broader sense, of the whole humanistic tradition in its emphasis upon the soul. How noble! How inspiring as an affirmation of the doctrine of the *imago dei*: all, *all* depends upon this person's insight, then will, then courage, then virtuosity in seeing what needs to be done and mustering his resources to do his part in getting it done.

But there is a fatal flaw here. This model results in futility, because individuals hardly ever see their duty in the same way and mobilize themselves adequately to do it. It is actually a pseudotransformationist model – only this time you do not even have lots of individuals lighting candles; you have them doing a variety of uncoordinated activities, not all of which produce light, so that the cumulative outcome is continuing darkness.

Unfortunately, this excessively individualistic approach has also been adopted not only by churches but also by most programmes in business and professional ethics, with similarly self-defeating results. As William Frederick, an American business ethics practitioner, has astutely observed, it is hopelessly unrealistic to think 'that business itself is the institutional shell into which alternative values could be infused, as new, young leaders whose own personal values are more compatible with social demands occupy positions of power and influence in the corporate system.'[41] In Frederick's view, 'this hope is a vain one, for the contest between established organizational values and contrary personal values is always uneven, and normally reaches a foreordained conclusion: Goliath wins.'[42]

Does this mean the social change agent who specializes in business and professional ethics – or in church social witness – should simply give up? Not necessarily. The best alternative for applied ethicists may also be the best way forward for social activists in the Church, namely, to put more emphasis on what Frederick calls 'policy-focused coalitions.' He paints a gloomy picture of short-term prospects:

> Voluntary social responsibilities, which by themselves have never significantly addressed society's major social problems, may be expected to remain at present levels; mandated social responsibilities, which have produced the greatest social gains, will be weakened as government relaxes its regulatory purview. To put the matter plainly, the business community seems to favour a government policy whose effect is to exacerbate – rather than ameliorate – social problems and pressures. Under these conditions, there is every prospect that social tensions will increase, public criticism of business will mount, and the agenda of unresolved social issues will grow longer.[43]

Frederick goes on to say, however, that the long-term prospects are good for a 'new institutional system' which promotes 'cooperation, collaboration and coordination among organizations whose goals, purposes and values may vary greatly':

> For want of a better term, it will be useful to call these associations social partnerships or social coalitions. Neither capitalist nor socialist, such partnership would be more than pluralism but less than social cartels. Government, business, labor, church groups, trade associations, neighborhood community groups, ethnic groups, professional organizations, and other organizational units constitute the raw material for these social coalitions.[44]

To be sure, much of the work now going on under the banner of the BSR, Industrial Mission and *Faith in the City* could be described as an effort to build and act through policy-focused coalitions. My argument would be that more of the scarce resources of the Church of England should be devoted to efforts of this kind, and less to the more nebulous and often less fruitful endeavour of putting down markers.

Notes

1 'Open Acrimony': The Established Church vs Thatcherism

1 Personal conversation with Paul Abrecht, 15 November 1985.
2 Giles Ecclestone, 'Church Influence on Public Policy Today,' *Modern Churchman* 28.1 (1985), p. 47.
3 Jonathan Raban, *God, Man and Mrs Thatcher* (Chatto & Windus, 1989), p. 21.
4 This perception was intensified by the enthusiasm with which the popular press greeted massive cuts in social provision in the 1920s and 1930s. As Duncan Forrester observes in *Christianity and the Future of Welfare* (Epworth Press, 1985), p. 11:

> 'Much irreparable damage has been done,' pontificated the *Daily Telegraph* when welcoming a reduction in out-relief, 'in breaking down the old attitudes of independence. So long as out-relief is made easy there will be ever lengthening queues of persons lining up to receive it and grumbling at the inconvenience of having to wait their turn.' The poor and the unemployed were blamed for their own predicament.

5 Forrester, *ibid.*, p. 12.
6 *ibid.*, p. 13.
7 *ibid.*, p. 14.
8 Nicholas Deakin, *The Politics of Welfare* (Methuen, 1987), pp. 40–1.
9 *ibid.*, p. 45.
10 *ibid.*, p. 44.
11 P. Thane, *The Foundations of the Welfare State* (Longman, 1982), p. 253.
12 Peter Jenkins, *Mrs Thatcher's Revolution* (Jonathan Cape, 1987), pp. 31, 32 and chaps. 2–4, 6–7.
13 *ibid.*, p. 32.
14 Geoffery Gilbertson, *Power-Sharing in Industry: A Pattern for the Future* (BSR, 1975), p. 4.
15 Martin J. Wiener, *English Culture and the Decline of the Industrial Spirit 1850–1980* (Cambridge University Press, 1981).
16 Corelli Barnett, *The Audit of War* (Macmillan, 1986), chaps. 2–4 and 6–7.
17 *ibid.*, p. 13. Wiener reinforces this point by citing historian Neil McKendrick's 'instructive contrast' between the adulation showered upon Henry Ford and the disdain accorded to his British counterpart, William Morris (1877–1963), the founder of Morris Motors, the ancestor of British Leyland. Whereas Ford is a folk hero, 'Morris has received largely uninformed and unenthusiastic acceptance'; indeed, 'despite leaving one of the most popular cars in the world to bear his name, William Morris is completely

overshadowed by his Victorian namesake in the mental map of most educated men and women.' See Wiener, *English Culture and the Decline of the Industrial Spirit, 1850–1980*, p. 131.

18   Bob Jessop, Kevin Barnett, Simon Bromley and Tom Ling (eds.), *Thatcherism* (Polity Press, 1988), pp. 68–108.

19   Among the many sources which might be cited here, the most helpful are Kenneth Hoover and Raymond Plant, *Conservative Capitalism in Britain and the United States* (Routledge, 1989), Mostyn Davies, 'The New Right' (mimeographed occasional paper available through BSR, 1988) and Stuart Hall and Martin Jacques (eds.), *The Politics of Thatcherism* (Lawrence & Wishart, 1983). The Social Policy Unit, under the influence of New Right leader Digby Anderson, has produced a number of publications which articulate a theological version of neoconservatism. Especially interesting in this connection is an attack on (as the subtitle has it) 'the churches' simplistic response to complex social issues' entitled *The Kindness That Kills* (SPCK, 1984).

20   Hugo Young, *One of Us*, Part Two; cf. p. 530. The support suggested by opinion polls exists in defiance of the fact that the cost of the present welfare state is enormous. The state spent two-thirds of GDP by 1974, and by 1985 the social security system alone was costing one-third of total public expenditure and 11% of GDP ('equivalent to 650 pounds per head of the population'). 'Since the war the cost of this system had increased at a rate five times faster than prices.'

21   These actions were in accordance with the strategy outlined in a planning document composed by Thatcher aides which asserted: 'The one precondition for success will be a complete change in the role of the trades union movement.' See Young, *op. cit.*, p. 115.

22   David Blunkett and Keith Jackson, *Democracy in Crisis: The Town Halls Respond* (Hogarth Press, 1987), pp. 36-7.

23   This measure looks especially ominous in light of the fact that

> In 1981 the Social Services Secretary Mr. Patrick Jenkin attempted to suppress Sir Douglas Black's report on inequalities in health, publication being held up for two years. Only 273 copies of this public document were printed and only in cyclostyled form, . . . [and] its author was refused permission to hold a press conference.
>
> [Again, in 1987] Sir Brian Bailey, government appointee as chair of the new Health Education Authority . . . took the same step of banning a press conference by the Health Education Council to launch its report, 'The Health Divide,' because it was 'political dynamite' in an election year. (*ibid.*, p. 37)

24   *ibid.*, chap. 7.

25   *ibid.*, p. 158.

26   Deakin, *op. cit.*, p. 156.

27   Harold Macmillan spoke for the Christian patrician heritage when he said, in 1946, that the Fair Wages Resolution was absolutely necessary as a bulwark against some economy drive in government, as in fact 'the great protector of the standard of life of the mass of the wage earning classes.' See Fred Twine, *The Distribution of Wealth and Income* (Centre for Theology and Public Issues, 1988), pp. 17–18.

28   David Coates and F. H. Hilliard, *What Went Wrong?* (Russell Press, 1979), p. 336.

29   Interview #2, 4 June 1988.

30   Young, *op. cit.*, p. 115.

31   Jenkins, *op. cit.*, p. 70.

32   *ibid.*, p. 77.

33   Young, *op. cit.*, p. 418.

34   *ibid*, p. 419.

35   Jenkins, *op. cit.*, pp. 66–7 (italics as in the original).

36   *ibid.*

37   Raban, *op. cit.*, p. 21.

38   *ibid.*, p. 68.

39   Young, *op. cit.*, p. 418.

40   *ibid.*, p. 425.

41   As Young points out (*ibid.*, pp. 423–4), it may not be terribly significant, but it is rather a cause for ribald amusement, that Mrs Thatcher's chief religious supporter in the days after the publication of *Faith in the City* was the Chief Rabbi of Britain, Immanuel Jakobovits. Reducing Judaism to little more than a pre-Calvin gospel of the Puritan work ethic, Jakobovits deplored the emphasis on the welfare state in *Faith in the City*, and urged British blacks to emulate the Jewish immigrants of America who (in his view) achieved economic self-sufficiency on their own, without the soul-softening seductions of either the dole-dispensing bureaucrats or organized labour (which in present-day Britain is denounced as even *worse*, if that be possible, than the state).

42   Edward R. Norman, *Church and Society in England, 1770–1970* (Clarendon Press, 1976).

43   David Martin, 'The Church of England: From Established Church to Secular Lobby,' in Anderson, *op. cit.*, pp. 134–42.

44   Gareth Bennett, 'Preface' to *Crockford's Directory* (Church House Publishing, 1987), pp. 68–75. It should be noted, incidentally, that something very similar has happened in the United States in the past two decades. As Wade Clark Roof and William McKinney argue in *American Mainline Religion* (Rutgers University Press, 1987), the well-established, 'respectable' religious institutions are losing many of their followers and much of their cultural legitimacy as a result of the rise of religious bodies which emphasize simplistic beliefs and highly individualistic notions of social well-being. (This point is developed more fully in Chapter 7 of the present study.)

45   *ibid.*, p. 68.

46   In American usage, the term 'social justice' is used in a rather broad sense to include ethically satisfactory arrangements in almost all areas of institutional life, especially politics and economics. In a book which concerns itself primarily with matters of economic justice, it should be understood that 'social witness' or 'social justice' will sometimes be used to refer only or mainly to economic issues without the sometimes awkward necessity always to add the adjective or the adjectival phrase. If the main focus of the analysis shifts, as it occasionally does, to culture or politics, that will be made explicit – otherwise, though, we may occasionally speak simply of 'social witness' or 'social justice' when it is clear that we are speaking of justice or well-being in regard to economic matters.

47   Anthony Dyson, 'The Bishop of Durham and All That,' *The Modern Churchman* 27 (1985), pp. 1–2.

48   Paul Avis, 'The Church's One Foundation,' *Theology* 89 (1986), p. 259.
49   Gerald Parsons, 'The Rise of Religious Pluralism in the Church of England,' in Paul Badham (ed.), *Religion, State and Society in Modern Britain* (Edwin Mellen Press, 1989), p. 6.
50   Since the Anglican communion does not hold a monopoly on Industrial Mission, it might be contended that we are blurring the focus of this study by including an element which cannot be identified exclusively with the Church of England. We have chosen to include it for two reasons: (1) in Britain, the origins and the dominant *weight* of the movement (both qualitatively and quantitatively) are located in the Church of England, as will be documented in the discussion of Industrial Mission which follows; (2) to omit it would be to leave out a school of thought and a group of persons and activities which are especially important in regard to questions concerning economic justice. (See the opening section of Chapter 5.)

2 The Conviction Politics of the Church

1   Norman Dennis and A. H. Halsey, *English Ethical Socialism* (Clarendon Press, 1988), p. 33.
2   From this he concluded that wealth not 'under the rational control of the possessor . . . ceased to be wealth and became "illth,"' and that 'private opulence corrupted life and destroyed the simplicity of men and women from cottage to castle' (*ibid.*, p. 62).
3   *ibid.*, p. 214.
4   *ibid.*, p. 162.
5   *ibid.*, p. 215.
6   *ibid.*, p. 202.
7   M. B. Reckitt, *Maurice to Temple* (Faber & Faber, 1947), p. 104.
8   *ibid.*, p. 105.
9   Hastings contends that the driving idea at the heart of the movement was a specifically Anglo-Catholic notion of the incarnation which saw the poor as latter-day personifications of Christ, and which prompted the nineteenth-century Christian socialists to exclaim:

> You cannot claim to worship Jesus in the Tabernacle, if you do not pity Jesus in the slum. . . . It is folly – it is madness – to suppose that you can worship Jesus in the Sacraments and Jesus on the throne of glory when you are sweating him in the souls and bodies of his children.

(These words were uttered by the Bishop of Zanzibar at an Anglo-Catholic Congress of 1923 – but according to Hastings they are in fact a perfect description of the incarnational view of the poor which had been articulated several decades before.) See Adrian Hastings, *A History of English Christianity* (Cambridge University Press, 1987), p. 183; cf. Gary J. Dorrien, *The Democratic Socialist Vision* (Rowman & Littlefield, 1986), p. 21.
10   E. M. Howse, *Saints in Politics* (University of Toronto Press, 1952), p. 180.
11   Ronald H. Preston, 'The Legacy of the Christian Socialist Movement in England,' in Walter Block and Irving Hexham (eds.), *Religion, Economics and Social Thought* (The Fraser Institute, 1986), pp. 182ff.

12   Dorrien argues that the 'socialism' of the Guild of St Matthew (the most
      important organization espousing the Christian socialism of the late nineteenth
      and early twentieth centuries) was little more than a touching belief in the
      teachings of Jesus about feeding his lambs; moreover, 'what stalled the Guild
      and the church's other socialist organizations was their failure to organize
      within the working class.' Instead, they 'saw their primary task to be the
      reinterpretation of the church's theological doctrines,' and 'politics only inter-
      ested them insofar as the gospel pushed them into political involvement to
      serve "the least of these my brethren"' (Dorrien, *loc. cit.*).

13   *ibid.*

14   Preston, *loc. cit.*

15   Duncan Forrester, *Christianity and the Future of Welfare* (Epworth Press,
      1985), p. 27.

16   Hastings, *loc. cit.*

17   R. H. Tawney, as quoted in J. M. Winter and D. M. Joslin, *R. H. Tawney's
      Commonplace Book* (Cambridge University Press, 1972), p. 67.

18   *ibid.*, p. 105.

19   Dorrien, *op. cit.*, p. 32.

20   William Temple, *Nature, Man and God* (Macmillan, 1934), p. 396.

21   Alan M. Suggate, *William Temple and Christian Social Ethics Today* (T. & T.
      Clark, 1987), p. 159.

22   *ibid.*, p. 160.

23   *ibid.*

24   *ibid.*

25   The subsequent importance of the legacy provided by Temple's work as an
      organizational entrepreneur and administrator is explored in Chaptèr 3.

26   I am aware of the fact that 'corporatism' is a word which has several different
      meanings in the literature of the social sciences, and 'club government' may
      refer somewhat too specifically to a particular relationship between Parliament
      and the Crown. The essential point, in any case, is the one made by David
      Marquand in *The Unprincipled Society* when he speaks of the loss in the sec-
      ond half of the twentieth century of widely shared assumptions about the good
      life and the good society on which virtually all well-educated members of the
      governing classes had agreed: up until then, political leaders from both major
      parties could appeal to broadly held values in negotiating the details of policy,
      and 'muddling through' along these lines was a plausible course of action to
      take. Thus I shall occasionally use the term 'corporatism,' not at all in the
      sense of the right-wing Italian concept, but simply to refer to the assumption
      that social policy is best arrived at through a consultation involving crucial
      elites in government, industry, education, and the Church (especially the
      Church of England itself). See David Marquand, *The Unprincipled Society*
      (Fontana Press, 1988), pp. 178ff.

27   David Nicholls, 'William Temple and the Welfare State,' *Crucible* (1984),
      p. 167.

28   *ibid.*, p. 164.

29   Some commentators maintain that William Temple has a much better claim to
      be called a Christian socialist than several of those whose names are associated
      with that school of thought. Gary J. Dorrien contends that Temple was very
      much ahead of his time in capturing the vision of the sort of revisionist
      socialism known in some circles today as 'economic democracy.' In *The Hope
      of a New World* (1941), says Dorrien, Temple looks forward to a set of

arrangements very much like those found in Sweden's Meidner Plan. The 'overriding importance' of Temple's vision of economic democracy is that it embodies 'the essence of modern democratic socialism' as portrayed in these words:

> It offers a way beyond the welfare state, by expanding the base of economic power, while saving the social and political gains of liberalism. In Sweden, the move towards economic democracy has to some extent replaced the previous emphasis upon continually expanding the welfare state. The fact that the Social Democrats [in Sweden] have recently reduced the top marginal tax rate from 72 to 55 percent should be seen against this background.

See Gary J. Dorrien, 'Economic Democracy: Common Goals for Liberation Movements?,' *Christianity and Crisis*, 10 September 1990, p. 272.

30   Denys Munby, *God and the Rich Society* (Oxford University Press, 1961), p. 160.

31   *ibid.*, p. 167. In fact, says Munby, 'I would be extremely surprised if more than two or three bishops could be found who in the last fifteen years had read two books on economic matters.'

32   *ibid.*, p. 166.

33   *ibid.*, p. 169.

34   Michael Atkinson, 'A Sort of Episcopal Fly on the Walls of British Industry,' in Gordon Hewitt (ed.), *Strategist of the Spirit* (Becket Publications, 1985), p. 159.

35   David L. Edwards, *Priests and Workers* (SCM Press, 1961); cf. John Rowe, *Priests and Workers: A Rejoinder*.

36   This appraisal was given to me with the understanding that its source would not be revealed.

37   Edward R. Norman, *Christianity and World Order* (Oxford University Press, 1979), p. 78.

38   *ibid.*, p. 80.

39   Hugh Montefiore, *Christianity and Politics* (Macmillan, 1990), pp. 65–6.

40   Alexander Grey, 'Establishing Church and State Ethics,' *Crucible* (1982), pp. 52ff. He also cites Temple as an advocate of this approach in *Christianity and the Social Order*.

41   *ibid.*, p. 59.

42   Giles Ecclestone, *The Church of England and Politics* (BSR, 1981), p. 47.

43   *ibid.*, p. 48.

44   Montefiore, *op. cit.*, p. 26.

45   Simon Lee and Peter Stanford, *Believing Bishops* (Faber & Faber, 1990), p. 28. Some exponents of this view even object to a call 'for a Lenten day of prayer and fasting for justice in public expenditure': when the social responsibility spokespersons of several denominations (including the Roman Catholic Church) made this proposal in 1981, a disgruntled Jesuit wrote a letter to the editor of *The Times* in which he blustered, 'I hasten to dissociate myself from what must be classified as an outrageous example of partisan politics, excusable only in terms of what appears to be the invincible ignorance of its promoters.' See Peter Hinchliff, *Holiness and Politics* (Eerdmans, 1982), p. 11.

Gummer himself, while Chairman of the Conservative Party, opined that 'bishops can no more pontificate on economics than the Pope could correct Galileo on physics.' See the *Guardian*, 29 April 1985, as cited in Duncan Forrester, *Beliefs, Values and Policies* (Oxford University Press, 1989), p. 51.

46   Paul Ramsey, *Who Speaks for the Church?* (Abingdon, 1967), p. 149. Ramsey's opinion on this point is founded on the venerable assumption that God has ordained a harmonious relationship between natural and positive law which is mirrored in the proper role-responsibilities of ecclesiastical leaders and political leaders (i.e., the 'magistrates'). Each has an appropriate sphere of operation, and the boundaries should not be confused or crossed.

47   *ibid.*, p. 152.

48   Moreover, says Ramsey, Ralph Potter is naive (or in any case mistaken) to believe that some Christians can become sufficiently expert in one area of social policy to be trusted by all who are experts in some other area, and that together all these policy specialists can be trusted to tell church people what to do (*ibid.*, p. 139).

49   *ibid.*

50   *ibid.*, p. 140.

51   It is certainly far, *far* better, he would claim, than weekend get-togethers such as the National Inter-Religious Conference on Peace held in Washington in 1966, which formulated policy statements on the war in Vietnam in a matter of hours (*ibid.*, p. 141).

52   *ibid.*

53   *ibid.*, as quoted in *Peacemaking in a Nuclear Age* (BSR, 1988), p. 164. The authors of *Peacemaking* continue:

> The Biblical tradition, in not allowing the separation of morality and public policy, faith and theology, compellingly establishes foundations for political choice. Christian witness is therefore more than individual moral rectitude. It requires a forthright proclamation of religious values and their relevance to the political, social and economic conditions that shape our lives.

54   *ibid.*

55   *ibid.*, p. 165.

56   Ulrich Duchrow, *Global Economy* (World Council of Churches, 1988).

57   Suggate, *op. cit.*, p. 48.

58   R. H. Preston, *Towards Transnational Social Ethics?* (BSR, 1981), pp. 10–11.

59   Montefiore, *op. cit.*, p. 29.

60   James M. Gustafson, 'An Analysis of Church and Society Social Ethical Writings,' in *The Ecumenical Review* 40.2 (April 1988), p. 269.

61   John A. Williams, 'A Bishop Should Speak Out – But What Can He Say?,' *Crucible* (January 1985), pp. 15ff. See below, pp. 98–9, for a discussion of the significance of 'secular Anglicanism.'

62   *ibid.*, p. 18.

63   *ibid.*, pp. 22–3.

64   Belief in a rigorous separation between religion and politics is sometimes justified by a belief in what analysts of the devotional literature of twentieth-century America term 'pseudotransformationism.' It is based on the stoutly held (but pathetically naive) assumption that society will automatically be tranformed if the churches concentrate on promoting the redemption of individu-

als, and it often includes the further assumption that only redeemed individuals can accomplish anything lasting and worthwhile by way of the transformation of society. It may be true, as pseudotransformationists aver, that 'it is better to light one candle than to curse the darkness' – but lasting illumination requires collective effort in institutional structures which can bring about the installation of a dynamo and an adequate network of incandescent lights which do not flicker out, one by one, with the passage of time or the advent of a lively breeze. See Sanford Dornbusch and Leo Schneider, *Popular Religion* (University of Chicago Press, 1957).

65   *ibid.*, p. 3.
66   Lee and Stanford, *op. cit.*, p. 21. It should be noted (in charity) that the concern which drives some observers to this position is the legitimate fear of contaminating either religion or politics by intermixing it with its opposite. Hinchliff seems to worry more about the deleterious impact of religion on politics than he does about the latter's effects upon the former (!); nevertheless, he does seek to reassure those who are especially worried about the corruption of religion by stating that the empirical sociological entity which enters into the political fray (e.g., the Church of England in 1985) is not the Body of Christ postulated by theology – and thus cannot defile it. See Hinchliff, *op. cit.*, pp. 124ff.
67   George Moyser and Kenneth Medhurst, *Church and Politics in a Secular Age* (Clarendon Press, 1988), p. 274.
68   Montefiore, *op. cit.*, pp. 77f.
69   Hinchliff, *op. cit.*, p. 6.
70   Forrester, *op. cit.*, pp. 34, 33.
71   Hinchliff, *op. cit.*, pp. 140, 7. He also adds a proviso which would gladden the hearts of many New Right Christians: he suggests that every policy recommendation advanced by a church should be accompanied by a statement regarding 'where it [the church] thinks the cost of what it is asking for should fall; increased taxation or whatever may be the case' (*ibid.*, p. 140).
72   *ibid.*
73   Gustafson, *op. cit.*, p. 270.
74   I call my own point of view 'Niebuhrian' because that is the dominant school of thought in Christian ethics in America, and I am certainly a product of an era when Reinhold Niebuhr was looked to as a most important mentor for everyone going into this discipline. The term is pertinent here because it highlights certain assumptions about collective sin, pragmatism, and the need to use power which I see as necessary correctives to the excessive faith in reason and individualism in British ethical theory.
75   Duncan Forrester, in Michael H. Taylor (ed.), *Christians and the Future of Social Democracy* (G. W. & A. Heskith, 1981), pp. 35–6.
76   *ibid.*, p. 37.
77   See above, pp. 24–8.
78   *Living Faith in the City* (BSR, 1990), p. 89.
79   *ibid.*, p. 146.
80   *ibid.*, p. 88.
81   *ibid.*.
82   *ibid.*, p. xi.
83   Anwar Barkat and James Mutambirwa (eds.), *Challenge to the Church: A Theological Comment on the Political Crisis in South Africa* (World Council of Churches, 1985), p. 19.

84   Montefiore, *op. cit.*, pp. 6–7.

3 The Church of England's Stance on Economic Issues

1   The bibliography at the end of this book has a separate section listing all of the publications on Christian ethics and economic life which have been printed by Church House Publications during the period under consideration. To be sure, many of these items are short pamphlets, but many are very substantial publications representing the research findings and reflections of internationally recognized scholars in religion and the social sciences. The accusations of ignorance and neglect levelled against the Church of England as late as the early 1960s by an altogether friendly critic such as Denys Munby would hardly be justified today.

2   See Part III of *Faith in the City*, especially pp. 194f., 227f., 262ff., 290ff., 323f., and 354f.

3   E. R. Wickham, *Growth and Inflation* (BSR, 1975), pp. 2–3.

4   *ibid.*, pp. 4, 6.

5   *ibid.*, p. 12.

6   *ibid.*, p. 13.

7   Geoffrey Gilbertson, *Power-Sharing in Industry* (BSR, 1975), p. 3.

8   *ibid.*, p. 1.

9   *ibid.*, p. 3.

10   Kenneth Adams, *Ethical Choice and Business Responsibilities* (BSR, 1975), p. 6.

11   David Edwards, *The State of the Nation* (BSR, 1976), p. 21.

12   *ibid.*, p. 22.

13   *Industry Matters* (May 1987), p. 8. Making the underlying beliefs and principles explicit does a number of things: it lets recruits know the sort of company which invites them to join it; it tells customers whether the company believes in giving them priority; it helps people already in the organization to know what should guide them and their practices. All these are matters of information which help to make the market work.

14   See below, Chapter Six, p. 105.

15   Richard Harris, 'Morality and Markets' (IC/16/86), p. 4.

16   *ibid.*, p. 5.

17   *ibid.*, pp. 8, 10.

18   *ibid.*, p. 4.

19   John Atherton, 'Can a Christian Legitimately Support a Social Market Economy?' (BSR, 1986), p. 3 (IC/16/86).

20   *ibid.*, pp. 5–9.

21   *ibid.*, p. 14.

22   *ibid.*, pp. 9–10.

23   Margaret Thatcher, Speech to the General Assembly of the Church of Scotland, 23 May 1988.

24   *The Times*, 27 May 1988. Ecumenical Protestant thought since the third decade of the twentieth century has tried to avoid both of the totalitarian extremes represented by communism and Nazism, and it has also tried to steer a middle course between pure *laissez faire* and a collectivized economy. It is not surprising, then, that recent Anglican pronouncements assume the validity of a mixed economy in which the strengths of free enterprise are appreciated and reaffirmed. It may be instructive to point out the extent to which the

Church of England's endorsement of the social market economy parallels the posture adopted in the widely heralded American Catholic Bishops' pastoral letter on the US economy.

Economic Justice for All, the American document, announces a bold intent in asserting that the time has come to establish economic rights in a way that is analogous to the establishment of political rights in the founding of the republic; indeed, the first draft of the pastoral letter used the term 'economic democracy' to make this point. Yet the specific policy recommendations advanced do not include any ventures into public enterprise such as those proposed by full-fledged advocates of economic democracy. On the contrary, everything the bishops propose seems to take for granted the existence of the many diverse centres of economic initiative which exponents of the market claim as one of its key advantages, and they also exhibit corporatist assumptions in their exhortations to co-operation as the crucial path to constructive change.

To some American critics, this degree of acceptance of the market is not enough, for they are accused of having a 'flawed moral vision' in which not enough attention is given to freedom and the 'negative rights' which citizens are entitled to. To others, however – as we shall see, the middle path taken by the bishops does not go far enough. And the criticisms made by those who espouse this view would apply equally to the Church of England's position on the social market economy.

25　I am thinking here of the aforementioned *Power-Sharing in Industry* (1975), *Ethical Choice and Business Responsibility* (1975), and *The State of the Nation* (1976). But qualifications must be entered, for *The State of the Nation* at least takes note of class stratification in Britain and observes that community requires greater understanding and interaction among people from different classes, and *Growth and Inflation* (1975) calls for a new social contract which would feature a solid incomes policy and price and wage controls.

26　*Not Just for the Poor: Christian Perspectives on the Welfare State* (BSR, 1986), p. 82 (GS 756).

27　*ibid.*, pp. 55–6.

28　*ibid.*, pp. 79ff.

29　*ibid.*, pp. 73ff., 112ff.

30　*ibid.*, p. 82.

31　*ibid.*, pp. 119ff. The concluding section of the book seems to dismiss the first as inadequate, the second as never having been seriously sought and – perhaps – impossible as a realistic option any time soon, and the third as positively *destroyed* by the resentments engendered in the present system.

32　*ibid.*, pp. 116, 118–19.

33　'Reform of Social Security' (BSR, 1985).

34　'The Social Fund' (BSR, 1988), p. 5.

35　'A Briefing on Housing' (BSR, 1983), p. 1. This unpublished BSR file document contains a useful summary of the Church of England's early role in promoting housing associations and private benefactions in housing.

36　*Housing and Homelessness*, p. 6.

37　*ibid.*, p. 9.

38　*Faith in the City*, p. 263.

39　*Housing and Homelessness*, pp. 13–14.

40　*Faith in the City*, pp. 262–3.

41　'Briefing for a Debate in the House of Lords' (BSR, 11 April 1983).

42   'Briefing for a Debate in the House of Lords' (BSR, 8 February 1984).
43   White and green papers are the means by which the government in power des-
      cribes proposed legislation (at two different stages) and invites a reply from
      appropriate interest groups.
44   'Working for Patients' (BSR, 1989), p. 17 (GS 887).
45   *ibid.*, p. 18.
46   *ibid.*
47   *ibid.*, p. 19.
48   *ibid.*, pp. 19–20.
49   *ibid.*, p. 20.
50   *ibid.*, pp. 20–1. The BSR report applauds the White Paper's provision for 'a
      system of strengthened and adequately resourced Community Health Councils'
      as a healthy countervailing influence.
51   *ibid.*, pp. 22–4.
52   *ibid.*, pp. 25–6.
53   *Proceedings of the General Synod* (1990), p. 885.
54   In addition, the Church of England is also in good company internationally,
      because once again it has adopted a stance which parallels that of the Roman
      Catholic bishops of the USA.
         Like the leadership of the Church of England, the American Catholic
      bishops are 'mixed economy men' who have been attacked from the right for
      insufficient appreciation of the market, and from the left for a lack of moral
      imagination about far-reaching *structural* reforms. Their recent pastoral letter
      on *Economic Justice for All* called for a variety of promising 'economic alter-
      natives' which have already proven effective 'in other industrialized countries
      [with] increasing numbers of people and institutions committed to promotion
      of alternatives.' The progressive Catholic Center for Concern in Washington,
      DC, applauds their willingness to 'recognize the defects of the welfare role of
      the government' in the United States, but it also praises them for 'acknowledg-
      ing the substantial benefits of the system,' and comments that 'the bishops may
      be the strongest champions of the welfare system [in the USA] at this time.'
      See Claire Gilbert, 'The U. S. Catholic Bishops' Pastoral Letter on the U. S.
      Economy' (1990), p. 9. (Unpublished paper prepared for a conference at St
      George's, Windsor, April 1990.)
55   The generalizations adduced below have been distilled from *Faith in the City*
      and the following BSR publications: *Power-Sharing in Industry* (1975); *Work
      or What: A Christian Examination of the Employment Crisis* (1977);
      Understanding Closed Shops (1977); *Work and the Future* (1979); *Winters of
      Discontent* (1981); *Perspectives on Economics* (1984); *Growth, Justice and
      Work* (1985); *And All That is Unseen* (1986).
56   *And All That is Unseen* (BSR, 1986), pp. 55–6.
57   *ibid.*, p. 13.
58   *Man in his Living Environment* (BSR, 1970), p. 61.
59   *ibid.*, p. 61.
60   *ibid.*, p. 62.
61   *ibid.*, p. 61.
62   *ibid.*
63   *ibid.*, p. 63.
64   *Our Responsibility for the Living Environment* (BSR, 1986), pp. 29–33 (GS
      718).
65   *Transnational Corporations: Confronting the Issues* (BSR, 1982), p. 25.

66   *ibid.*, p. 34.
67   *ibid.*, p. 38.
68   *ibid.*, p. 40.
69   *ibid.*, pp. 40–1.
70   *ibid.*, p. 42.
71   *ibid.*, p. 56.
72   *ibid.*, pp. 54–7.
73   *ibid.*, p. 67.
74   *ibid.*, pp. 4–5.
75   *The Common Agricultural Policy and World Hunger* (BSR Briefing No. 6, 1982), p. 19.
76   *Let Justice Flow: A Contribution to the Debate About Development* (BSR, 1986), p. 8.
77   *ibid.*, p.13. In textiles, for example, the 1972 Multifibre Arrangement (MFA) has been so altered by industry pressure that it is now 'extremely difficult' – some would say impossible – for a new textile-producing country or firm to break into the market at all.
78   *ibid.*, pp. 13–14.
79   *Reflections on Brandt* (BSR, 1980), p. 25.
80   *Let Justice Flow*, p. 39.
81   *ibid.*, p. 40.
82   Charles Elliott, *Comfortable Compassion* (Hodder & Stoughton, 1987). This book has no official connection with the BSR, but it nonetheless deserves to be included in the sources highlighted here by virtue of the fact that Elliott is such an important adviser to the International Affairs Committee of the BSR.
83   'Sunday Trading' (BSR, 1989), para. 90. (Unpublished file document designated BSR (89) 10.)
84   *ibid.*, para. 28.
85   *ibid.*, para. 105.
86   *ibid.*
87   A third miscellaneous publication is difficult to classify. *Mainstream and Marginal* is an account of a trip to the USA made by Chris Beales, the BSR staff person who works most closely with, and is responsible for, the activities of the Industrial and Economic Activities Committee. It is fairly described, I believe, as a British observer's exploration of business ethics and other Industrial Mission-type projects in America.
88   James Siddons, *The Eurotunnel and the Churches* (Churches' Consortium on Industrial Mission/BSR, 1988), p. 3.
89   *The Single European Act* (Brussels: European Ecumenical Commission for Church and Society, 1988), p. 9.

4 Why the Church Took this Stance

1   'Voluntary simplicity' is a term which originated in the United States with a study of that movement conducted by the Stanford Research Institute in the mid-1970s. But its notion of social goals and priorities is shared by all exponents of what the World Council of Churches literature refers to as a 'just, sustainable and participatory society.' Since the life-style of voluntary simplicity involves such things as 'eating lower on the food chain,' less consumption of nonrenewable energy resources, recycling, conservation, and less pollution, environmentalists are inclined to regard it as a cultural adaptation

which all sensible people ought to embrace. And since a simpler life-style is usually associated with lowered competitiveness and acquisitiveness as well as greater sensitivity to the rights of nature, posterity and the poor, those who rate distributive justice at the top of the Church's moral agenda tend to see voluntary simplicity as a way of resisting what they view as the appalling selfishness and arrogance of the cultural atmosphere created and/or reinforced by Thatcherism.

2   The official mandate which is often quoted at the beginning of a BSR Annual Report is 'to promote and co-ordinate the thought and action of the Church in matters affecting the lives of men and women in society.' The more instructive formulation quoted here comes from John Sleeman, 'The Church and Economic Policy,' in George Moyser (ed.), *Church and Politics Today* (T. & T. Clark, 1985), p. 166.

3   It might be instructive to point out the extent to which the recent social witness of the Church of England parallels the position taken in the widely heralded American Catholic Bishops' pastoral letter on the US economy.

Economic Justice for All, the American document, announces a bold intent in asserting that the time has come to establish economic rights in a way that is analogous to the establishment of political rights in the founding of the republic; indeed, the first draft of the pastoral letter used the term 'economic democracy' to make this point. Yet the specific policy recommendations advanced do not include any ventures into public enterprise such as those proposed by full-fledged advocates of economic democracy. On the contrary, everything the bishops propose seems to take for granted the existence of the many diverse centres of economic initiative which exponents of the market claim as one of its key advantages, and they also exhibit corporatist assumptions in their exhortations to co-operation as the crucial path to constructive change.

To some American critics, this degree of acceptance of the market is not enough, for the bishops are accused of having a 'flawed moral vision' in which not enough attention is given to freedom and the 'negative rights' which citizens are entitled to. To others, however – as we shall see, the middle path taken by the bishops does not go far enough. And the criticisms made by those who espouse this view would apply equally to the Church of England's position on the social market economy.

See Claire Gilbert, 'The U. S. Catholic Bishops' Pastoral Letter on the U. S. Economy' (1990), p. 9. Unpublished paper prepared for a conference at St George's, Windsor, April 1990.

4   See Chapter 3, p. 52.

5   Chapter 3, p. 56.

6   To its credit, the BSR has raised important questions about unproductive transactions of this kind, and it now charges the staff person in charge of the Industrial and Economic Affairs Committee with keeping an eye on the world of finance as well as that of industry. But I include this item in my list of objections to uncritical praise of 'wealth creation' because I do not think the BSR publication on *The Ethics of Acquisition* goes nearly far enough in condemning these oftentimes unproductive manipulations of paper and numbers.

7   'The Ethics of Wealth Creation,' a position paper produced by the Division of Social Responsibility of The Methodist Church [in Britain], 1990.

8   George Moyser, 'The 1980 General Synod: Patterns and Trends,' *Crucible* (1980), p. 75.

9   *ibid.*, p. 75. An instructive perspective on these data is given by an article on
     the 1975 General Synod by Kathleen Jones. She points out that when the Gen-
     eral Synod was formed there were two models for it held in the minds of vari-
     ous people. Model A said the General Synod should be a sort of Anglican
     Academy, made up of the smartest people in the Church, with expertise on all
     the significant issues contained in the membership. Model B said it should be a
     microcosm of the Church of England as a whole (51% female, e.g.).
     Jones declares that nobody seriously wants either A or B *pure*, declaring
     that the real question is, 'How are we to get an acceptable balance between
     expertise and representation?' She stresses two indisputable points:
     1. 'It is more like an Academy than a representative body, and when it
     deals with issues which concern the non-Establishmentarian realities of Great
     Britain, there are very few members of Synod who can provide more than
     parochial anecdote, and the burden on them is a heavy one.'
     2. 'The results of elections . . . are very uneven. In some dioceses, the
     election is clearly preceded by active campaigning, and much thought. In
     others, the results seem almost random, and the electorate very unclear on
     what it is doing.' See Kathleen Jones, 'The General Synod: 1975 Version,'
     Crucible (1979), p. 152.
     Confirmation of this last observation is found in T. Page's article on 'Mak-
     ing the Synod' (during 1981), which complains about apathy and inadequate
     press interpretation of the results of the election. See T. Page, 'Making the
     Synod, *Crucible* (1981), pp. 116ff.
10   G. Moyser and K. Medhurst (eds.), *Church and Politics in a Secular Age*
     (Clarendon Press, 1988), p. 274.
11   On this point, see John Habgood, *Church and Nation in a Secular Age*
     (Darton, Longman & Todd, 1983), chs. 2–4 and Robin Gill, *Prophecy and
     Praxis* (Marshall Morgan & Scott, 1981).
12   Moyser and Medhurst, *loc. cit.*
13   *ibid.*
14   Interview, 16 July 1988.
15   Moyser and Medhurst, *op. cit.*, p. 359.
16   *ibid.*, p. 295.
17   *ibid.*, p. 298.
18   *ibid.*, p. 296.
19   *ibid.*
20   This attempt to fathom psycho-cultural complexities is admittedly problematic
     (especially, perhaps, when the analyst is a foreigner, an outsider who has no
     way of perceiving, let alone comprehending, many of the subtleties). Even so,
     however, the attempt must be made – and if the speculations that follow are
     occasionally *wild* (in the sense that they are laughably off the mark), they may
     none the less be justified by one or two insights which only an outsider would
     have been likely to come up with.
21   This phrase from the American Declaration of Independence is highlighted in a
     highly esteemed book by John Courtney Murray on the Christian/
     Classical/Anglo-Saxon heritage in political philosophy which he regards as one
     of the greatest treasures ever bequeathed to human civilization. The point of
     the title – *We Hold These Truths* – is that unless the patrimony of humane
     moral ideas is 'held' by being constantly debated and reviewed in intelligent
     political discourse, it may wither and die.
22   Giles Ecclestone, *The Church of England and Politics* (BSR, 1981), p. 40.

23   *Changing Britain* (BSR, 1987), pp. 18, 18–19.
24   *ibid.*, p. 66.
25   *ibid.*, p. 67.
26   Gareth Bennett, 'Preface' to *Crockford's Clerical Directory* (Church House Publishing, 1987), p. 8.
27   Proceedings of the General Synod meeting of 12 November 1987, pp. 1093–6.
28   The phrase is often used by Industrial Mission personnel who have a high regard for the pioneer work of E. R. Wickham.

5 What Church Agencies Did

1   Interview #16, 18 June 1988.
2   It would be a serious error to concentrate *exclusively* on the outward thrust of the social witness of the Church of England, for such a concentration would neglect two kinds of activity which are relevant to our concerns: first, efforts to achieve 'church renewal' which are of great instrumental importance in mobilizing the Church's full potential for mission in the world; and second, those activities aimed at *rehabilitation* of the 'wounded' (e.g., training in new job skills for those who have been forced into unemployment as a result of dislocations in the economy) which fall somewhere between 'relief' and 'reform' on the standard typology in terms of which activists often conceptualize their endeavours. To point out that our analysis must include both church renewal and rehabilitation is to declare that we are not only interested in activities which are directly prophetic in the sense that they are explicitly intended to change social policy, but also in activities which are *indirectly* prophetic. Especially important in this connection are the area redevelopment programmes being carried out by Industrial Mission personnel; indeed, it will be argued below that these programmes deserve to be considered 'indirect reform' and are therefore a distinctive and important reform activity in their own right. (Cf. the discussion of IM later in this chapter.)
3   John Sleeman, 'The Church and Economic Policy,' in George Moyser (ed.), *Church and Politics Today* (T. & T. Clark, 1985), p. 266.
4   See, for example, Henry F. May, *Protestant Churches and Industrial America* (Harper & Row, 1949) and C. Howard Hopkins, *The Rise of the Social Gospel in American Protestantism* (Yale University Press, 1940).
5   Administrative implementation of this corollary received a decisive impetus during the time of William Temple, whose ability as an administrator may have been even greater than his creativity as a theologian. See Adrian Hastings, *A History of English Christianity* (Cambridge University Press, 1987), pp. 257ff.
       Among the earliest and most important fruits of the trend towards the inclusion of experts were the celebrated Fifth Report of 1919 and the 1924 COPEC conference, both of which owed a great deal to the work and influence of Temple. Hastings singles out the COPEC conference and the report on *Men Without Work* in 1938 for special (though not unqualified) praise:

>   COPEC's message was even at the time so widely acceptable only because of its extreme vagueness. Temple was always better on the broad sweep than on the hard particularities of contested bastions. Yet COPEC is not simply to be dismissed. Its immediate consequences were small. Its importance lay within a longer process of adult education whereby the leadership,

clerical and lay, of the Church was being weaned from high Tory attitudes to an acceptance of the Christian case for massive social reform and the development of a welfare state. In this it and its like were almost over-successful. (*ibid.*, p. 179)

As for *Men Without Work*, its importance

is not just the subject but the efficiency with which it is tackled. It has generally been recognized as 'the best social study of unemployment made in the thirties'. Its value is not questionable and its existence in an area of such major concern to national life is adequate response to people who still assert that social do-gooding of the Temple type is both ignorant and ineffectual. . . . Here, perhaps for the first time outside the field of educa-tion, [the Church] had moved from an amateur to a fully professional model in approaching a social problem. *Men Without Work* limited the fron-tiers of the subject and made a lasting contribution. . . . (*ibid.*, p. 258)

6   Richard Harries, 'How We Wrote *The Church and the Bomb*,' *Crucible* (1983), p. 177.
7   Information on sales of Church House Publications is available from the CHP Office at Church House in London.
8   The four-year IEAC Report does not list activities in chronological order, yet there is no indication that any sort of ranking or emphasis is intended by the order in which items are presented. Thus it is without any intent to suggest importance or priority that we follow the report in our discussion of it on the next several pages.
9   Cover letter sent out to selected recipients of *Industrial Mission: An Appraisal*, p. 1. The letter is designated BSR (89).
10   IEAC Report, p. 2.
11   *ibid.*, p. 3.
12   This consultation involved not only John Atherton but also Peter Sedgwick, another of the most important theological consultants in BSR circles, who is now working on a special research grant concerning the theology of wealth creation.
13 *ibid.*, p. 4.
14   First Annual Report of the Anglican Association for Social Responsibility (1987), p. 2.
15   It may be a mistake to generalize very much or very far on the basis of this sample, for the Chelmsford Council for Social Responsibility may be less typi-cal than *ideal* – but a glance at its programme will certainly give the reader a glimpse of what is possible when the diocesan agency has a staff of nine per-sons, a budget of close to three hundred thousand pounds and an exceptionally gifted Director. (He is Paul Brett, a former BSR staff man, who for several years served as secretary to the Industrial and Economic Affairs Committee of the BSR.)
16   Under 'Working with People at the Local Level' the report cites work with people afflicted by AIDS, drug addiction, homelessness, and racial harassment among other miscellaneous community services (such as driving people to hospitals).
17   The announced purpose of each group is to 'select specific topics within the general subject area,' 'to collect information about [these] topics, both national and local,' 'to be in touch with other groups . . . which are working on their

issues,' 'to work on appropriate projects in a way that complements what is being done by others,' to make representations in public on their issues,' and 'to find ways of bringing these matters more effectively into the parish and the corporate life of the Diocese.'

18   Simon Lee and Peter Stanford, *Believing Bishops* (Faber & Faber, 1990), p. 23.
19   *ibid.*
20   *ibid.*, p. 22.
21   *ibid.*, p. 21.
22   *Christian Action Journal* (Summer 1981).
23   *Christian Action Journal* (August 1983).
24   Almost everyone I interviewed – with the exception of New Right observers! – commented on this feature of the study process.
25   *Survey of Parish Audits* (Church House Publications, 21 November 1988).
26   Richard Farnell, 'Faith in the City and Local Politics' (1988).
27   Needless to say, different convictions about faithfulness and effectiveness in mission lead to in-house debate on a number of key issues. A survey of the main features of this debate and an evaluation of salient trends will be offered in subsequent chapters; suffice it to say here that *self-examination* is one of the most diligently pursued activities of IM personnel, and the presence of IM themes in the thinking and the *modi operandi* of BSR staff officers is evident to even the most casual observer. As a statement concerning the Theology Development Group (TDG) of IM asserts, 'Industrial Mission has always been a highly self-critical movement, for two reasons: . . . to ensure their own integrity, [and] to justify IM to the Church at large.' It follows, then, that:

> About a third of the full-time membership of the IMA have, at one time or another, been members of the TDG, and about 20 members at any one time. . . . Recently, . . . it has become common to invite guests and outside consultants, which has been found both to increase the range of discussion and to counteract the dangers of introversion.

See *Industrial Mission: An Appraisal* (BSR, 1988), p. 43.
28   A summary of this concentration of concern is found in the 'Introduction' of *Ministry and Mission Examined* (BSR, 1989), one of the IEAC's latest booklets:

> In 1988 the Church of England published a study of the contribution of IM to the Church's response to the changing industrial and economic order. This report, entitled *IM – An Appraisal*, was the beginning of a process. It was widely studied, within the churches at large as well as within IM, and some of the responses from around Britain have been published under the title *Dear Mr. Green*. A follow-up paper to the original report examines appropriate structures of management and employment within IM – responding not only to the changes within society as a whole but to the changes within the churches that are making such progress down the road of ecumenism. . . . *Church and Economy: Effective Industrial Mission for the 1990s* is, however, an essentially organisational report. . . . There should also be some theological reflection on the place of mission (and specifically Industrial Mission) among the new realities of contemporary life and IM's

own story of adapting and reappraising its role and activities should be told.
(pp. 1–2)

29   Shigecko Masumoto summarizes the characteristics of the first two generations
as follows:

Phase I	Phase II
good economic times	recession
theology of secularity	liberation theology
confidence	'siege mentality'
humanize structures without questioning basic givens of the system	challenge structures *per se*
inductive	deductive
pastoral	prophetic

According to Mostyn Davies, the second phase noted above must be viewed
as a crucial development, for once industrial chaplains began to be aware of
the conflicts of interest between governments, employers and workers (and
unions), they began to see ethical issues of great significance; moreover, they
were driven towards professionalism in order to cope with the complexities
they now encountered and had to deal with. Two particularly noteworthy milestones in the trend away from simple affirmation of industry to prophetic challenge are highlighted by Masumoto, who attributes special importance to the
1977 debate within IM circles on 'the Chaplaincy model' vs. the 'missions
model' (which led to a preference for 'issue-based mission' and 'prophetic
stance') and to a 1980 conference which gave explicit endorsement to the
World Council of Churches' proclaimed goal of 'a just, sustainable and
participatory society' (JPSS). See Shigeko Masumoto, *Industrial Mission in
Britain Today* (BSR, 1987), p. 14 and Mostyn Davies, 'Local Economy Based
Industrial Mission' (BSR, 1988).

30   The appeal of this kind of activity owes something to the psychological need
of IM personnel to be 'at last able to show concrete results and demonstrate
their competence in ways the wider church could understand and accept'
(Davies, *op. cit.*, p. 2).

The significance of the Church's attempts to do something concrete to
repair the damage caused by deindustrialization is described in Paul Brett's
paper on 'The British Churches' Response to the Problems of Unemployment.'
Under the heading 'Personal Responses,' which Brett sees as the first phase of
the British churches' activity on this problem since the early 1970s, he says:

As the unemployment figures climbed . . . , many people in the churches
quickly caught something of the general anxiety . . . [and] joined together
with others to help people to adapt to the new situation and to offer various
forms of practical, pastoral care. In particular, they sought to offer
psychological and financial advice . . . [and] set up practical schemes with
financial help from the Manpower Services Commission, a Government-
funded organisation established in the early 1970's to oversee training and

work experience schemes for the unemployed. . . . The Churches also set up mutual help groups and resource centres through which people could . . . support each other and try to find constructive ways of using their time. They also tried to encourage the starting of new small businesses. *Much of all this was pioneered by Industrial Chaplains at work in some 40 different areas of the country* [italics mine].

As Brett notes, a hundred of these programmes were 'described in some detail' in *Action on Unemployment*, a book published in 1984 by Church Action on Unemployment (CAWTU). (Brett's account is noteworthy in part because of the close link it perceives between this type of directly beneficial social witness and the Industrial Mission movement, and also because of its mention of CAWTU, which is certainly one of the most active church-inspired ginger groups in Britain.)

31   Davies, *op. cit.*, p. 3. The key elements in the Fourth Generation of IM are summarized as follows:

1. 'The erosion of so many key IM bases has a liberating aspect. Now . . . IM is free to rethink its work and reset its priorities for ministry and mission.'

2. 'IM's experience of third generation IM (MSC projects) has led it to see the value of making more broadly based alliances in the local community and in the church.'

3. 'Many chaplains . . . have greatly extended their management and planning skills.'

4. 'Principle and practice from earlier models of IM can often be carried forward by reapplying them to the local economic community rather than particular factories and projects.'

5. Above all, whatever IM does must exhibit 'purposeful tracking,' i.e., the careful design of 'a path of action leading through the local economic network so the person following it can achieve definite results.'

It should be obvious, then, that 'once IM looks on the whole economy as its field, it must become highly selective about what it actually does. This 'selection process' becomes the most important but also the most difficult corporate task for IM management groups' (Davies, *op. cit.*, pp. 4–5). Cf. the statement on 'Models and Hopes' set forth by the Theology Development Group of the Industrial Mission Association in *Industrial Mission: An Appraisal* (BSR, 1988), pp. 89–90.

32   Enthusiasm for this approach as a decisively important frontier for Christian social action – perhaps *the* frontier! – is evident in a remarkable BSR document entitled *Mainstream and Marginal*. The booklet, which is subtitled 'Creating Economic Change in Inner City Life,' is a record of Chris Beales' visit to the USA in the summer of 1990. It is a resounding affirmation of the importance of locally based incremental reform, and as such it is a reliable indication of the extent to which the BSR staff person who was for several years responsible for the Industrial and Economic Affairs Committee is a product of Industrial Mission and true to its sense of goals and priorities.

33   Bernd Fechner, 'Church and the Resurgence of Capitalism' (London, 1989), p. 11. Cf. *Royal Docks Development: New Directions?* (A Review and Discussion Document from the Newham Churches Docklands Group, 1988).

34   See 'Linking Up: An Interim Report to Sponsors' (BSR, 1989).

35   More than 50% of the community based credit unions in England are church based.

36   'Linking Up' Report (BSR, 1989).
37   It should be noted that Michael Atkinson sees *Understanding Closed Shops* as asserting an unequivocal affirmation of the need for and the legitimacy of this still (in Britain) controversial policy.
38   Lee and Stanford, *op. cit.*, p. 24.
39   *ibid.*
40   *ibid.*, p. 25.
41   *ibid.*, p. 140.
42   *ibid.*
43   It may conceivably make sense to use the term to describe bureaucratic leadership's efforts to obtain certain internal objectives, and since serious lobbyists often get into the habit of defining *everything* as 'political' (!) they may think of almost everything they say, to supporters and targets alike, as lobbying. But surely we have to agree on a less all-embracing definition of the term – and we get a clue on this from the fact that lobbyists themselves typically make a distinction between relatively general efforts to 'affect public opinion' and lobbying *per se*, which has precise targets and goals; moreover, they make a distinction between simply 'maintaining contact' with a target policy-maker and 'asking for something.' Many of the more or less routine meetings, exchanges of written materials or phone conversations which take place between lobbyists and the persons they want to influence are intended to do nothing more than 'keep the channels of communication open' or 'grease the wheels' for a some later contact which has a more specific and immediate purpose: to guide a vote on a proposed piece of legislation, to urge a particular administrative decision, etc. So the analysis of lobbying that follows will include references to the former type of interaction, but it will be focused primarily on the latter, and the term will not be used to refer to internal manoeuvring.
44   Giles Ecclestone, *The Church of England and Politics* (BSR, 1981), p. iv.
45   *ibid.*, p. 52.
46   *ibid.*, p. 40.
47   'Reform of Social Security' (BSR, 1985). This document registers the BSR's response to the government's Green Paper on proposed reform of the social security system.
48   'The Social Fund' (Social Policy Committee of the BSR, 1988). This is a nine-page briefing paper which was prepared by the Principal Social Workers group of the Church of England.
49   Interview, 14 December 1988.
50   Interview, 18 June 1990 (and IEAC file on Ambulance Strike).
51   Hilary Russell (ed.), *The Bird's Eye Debate* (Merseyside Churches' Urban Institute and Centre for Urban Studies of the University of Liverpool, 1990), p. 1.
52   *ibid.*, p. 3.
53   *ibid.*, p. 4.
54   *ibid.*, p. 5.
55   *ibid.*, p. 21.
56   *ibid.*, p. 22.
57   This statement is reported in an Industry Year 1986 press release which was issued at the time the programme was launched.
58   All of these statements are taken from the record of a conference at St George's House, Windsor Castle, 17–19 September 1984, entitled 'Attitudes to Industry in Britain.'

59   'Industry Matters' (1987), p. 2.
60   The specific list of objectives to be sought included the following items:
      - Ensuring [that] all secondary schools are linked with industry.
      - More company and trade union open days.
      - Extension of work-shadowing schemes.
      - Greater involvement of small businesses.
      - Development of company codes of practice.
      - Encouragement of 'positive purchasing' policies by companies.
      - More company links with primary schools.
      - Increased involvement of industrialists with teacher training.
      - Secondment of industrial managers to schools and colleges, and of
      teachers to industry.
      - Encouragement of positive industry/media links.
      - Greater involvement with industry of women and women's
      organizations.
      - Building on relationships between churches and industry. Among its
      salient achievements was a conference on 'The Business Relevance of Com-
      pany Codes,' held on 24 March 1987 under the auspices of The Institute of
      Business Ethics, an organization which was created at the end of 1986.

6 Impact Assessment

1   In the 1960s, I worked very diligently to mobilize Christian opinion in support
     of a variety of legislative proposals intended to advance the cause of racial jus-
     tice in America, I served for a time as Coordinator for Urban Affairs at the
     National Council of Churches. As a result of my work with American Indus-
     trial Mission - which was at the height of its influence in the USA, I wrote a
     book entitled *Ministries of Dialogue* on 'new forms of the Church' (especially
     IM). Since then, I have been a practitioner of business and professional ethics
     in university settings for more than twenty-five years. During all these years of
     service in ecclesiastical and academic settings, I have heard a great deal of lip
     service paid to the importance of research and evaluation, but I have seen very
     little time and money poured into the task.
2   See Graham Allison, *Essence of Decision* (Little, Brown & Co., 1971).
3   See Jacques Ellul, *The Technological Society* (Knopf, 1964).
4   George Moyser and Kenneth Medhurst, *Church and Politics in a Secular Age*
     (Clarendon Press, 1988), pp. 291-2; cf. Part II of George Moyser (ed.),
     Church and Politics Today (T. & T. Clark, 1985).
5   This memory of the *modus operandi* of the first General Secretary of the BSR
     is a part of the oral tradition among staff persons. Chris Beales was the first
     Church House worker who passed it along to me, but since then I have heard
     many other insiders confirm its perceived veracity.
6   Moyser and Medhurst, *op. cit.*, p. 310.
7   The loss of influence bemoaned by Moyser and Medhurst, and confirmed by
     Clarke, has a curious analogue in a perceptive criticism of the decline of
     Industrial Mission by one of its most experienced exponents. The complaint
     here is not simply that of Charles Elliott, i.e., that IM is too reformist, and too
     unimaginative even in that (to the point where its work often degenerates into
     nothing more than mere *relief*, when it really ought to be about revolution).
     One can easily discount this sort of criticism on the grounds that it is
     unsympathetic to the goals which the Industrial Mission movement has chosen

for itself; therefore, it may not be a fair assessment of the impact attained for its own goals on its own terms. But the thrust of the insider's complaint has to do with the 'watering down' of the movement as a result of the notoriety it achieved in its early days. (See the discussion of IM in Chapter 2.)

8   Moyser and Medhurst, *op. cit.*, pp. 349–50.

9   *ibid.*, pp. 332–3.

10   *ibid.*, p. 333.

11   *ibid.*, p. 346.

12   *ibid.*, pp. 2–3.

13   *ibid.*, p. 7.

14   Giles Ecclestone, *The Church of England and Politics* (BSR, 1981), p. 48.

15   Moyser and Medhurst, *op. cit.*, p. 317.

16   Peter A. Welby, *A History of the Church of England* (Oxford University Press, 1984), pp. 226–33. Cf. B. A. Pym, 'Pressure Groups on Moral Issues,' *Political Quarterly* 43 (1972), pp. 321f. To be sure, conservative Anglicans had occasion to chastise their leaders when the British divorce rate skyrocketed during the years immediately following the enactment of the liberalized law, and those who accuse the Church's current intellectual leadership of capitulating altogether too easily to secularism doubtless draw some of their passion from the 'successful' impact of this particular lobbying effort. But no one who understands the force of historical change can blame the bishops of the Church of England for *causing* the so-called (and inconclusive) 'sexual revolution' of the 1960s and 1970s – and only a legalist who values statistics more than persons can regret the logic or the wisdom which prompted church leaders to take a decisive hand in reforming the British divorce law.

17   Moyser and Medhurst, *op. cit.*, p. 317.

18   *ibid.*, p. 359. Cf. Robin Gill, *Prophecy and Praxis* (Marshall Morgan & Scott, 1981), ch. 3.

19   Moyser and Medhurst, *op. cit.*, p. 359.

20   *ibid.* Yet the social witness of the Church is dominated by the imperatives of prudence, and the impetus towards 'orderly amelioration' instead of 'drastic innovation' was certainly evident in the deliberations that produced and surrounded the publication of *The Church and the Bomb*. Concern about the Church's credibility created a penchant for 'discretion' and 'sensitivity to the complexities of existing realities prompt[ed] a somewhat pragmatic and incremental approach to change.' This meant that 'the prevailing style of Anglican political involvement was demonstrated in the rejection of even a carefully graduated approach to unilateral disarmament.' One decisive factor in leading to this formulation of the Church's final stance on the matter at this time was the Archbishop of Canterbury's argument that 'unilateralist gestures [tend to] hinder rather than facilitate the quest for disarmament.' Thus 'the ultimately prevailing view [was] that the way forward lay through a more urgent search for multilateral disarmament' (*ibid.*, p. 318).

21   It was crucial for the success of AGIN that Ann Dummett was an employee of one of the coalition organizations, and could spend 'most of [her] working time (though not all) on AGIN.' It depended mainly on 'voluntary and spare-time effort up to the end of 1978, followed by three years of funding from the Rowntree Social Service Trust, sufficient to cover overheads, travel expenses and a small proportion of printing costs.' Ann Dummett, 'Across Party Lines: The British Nationality Bill, the Lobbyists and the Churches,' *Modern Churchman* 25.1 (1982), p. 37.

22   *ibid.*
23   *ibid.*, p. 38. The tactics carried out by AGIN were boldly conceived and intelligently executed. 'At least one bishop was present at every debate in the House of Lords,' and AGIN representatives 'attended every debate during the ten months when the Bill was in Parliament.' The group was instrumental in seeing to it that people who would be especially affected by a given provision were present for the debate on that provision (e.g., representatives 'from the Hong Kong government office, from Gibraltar, from East Africa and so on'). 'The lobbyists were there not only to listen, but to talk to M.P.s in the corridors, to deliver written information, and to react to the way the debates were going by calling on groups they represented to produce relevant facts and arguments for the next stage.' Their most effective gambit was 'the provision of detailed and accurate information,' because 'facts [relevant to this legislation] speak for themselves, and if the Press, and backbench MPs pick them up, there is a chance of getting a case heard which otherwise might not have been adequately debated.'

Dummett sees an interesting evolution of thought and strategy here. Since 'the really big issues in political debate have not divided along party lines, . . . individuals and voluntary associations have attempted to promote new policies in particular fields, and directed their energies at influencing, if they can, all the political parties.' Moreover, 'The people who work in such groups are often people who would naturally have turned, twenty-five years ago, to trying to become Members of Parliament themselves, but who now take it for granted that an individual M.P. can do little.' Dummett stresses the fact that the religious groups co-operating in AGIN could not fairly be accused of partisanship, because the Roman Catholic Church had already issued a statement concerning the principles on which a new British nationality law ought to be based in 1979. Thus opposition to the 1980 White Paper could hardly be called partisan. Because the churches had already formulated their thinking on the matter, the Catholic Archbishops and the BSR were able to express their opposition 'just after [the White Paper] had been published and before the first debate in the Commons':

> The timing . . . was of crucial importance. The Government announced two major amendments to the Bill immediately after that [first] debate and before the Committee stage, and there can be little doubt that, without the public expression of the churches' views (backed up by private representatives) these would not have been made. There was a series of government concessions on points stressed by the churches during the next three months of Committee debate. (*ibid.*, p. 42)

The following remarks by a staunch supporter of the government illustrate the impact the churches had:

> I must admit that this is still not a very good Bill. . . . I, for one, cannot help being impressed by the attitude of the Churches. . . . If it has not been possible for the Government to satisfy opinion outside – opinion in the Churches and impartial opinion in many quarters . . . perhaps it must raise a doubt even in their minds. . . . If anything were to go wrong, and the Bill were not to pass into law in this session, it might be a blessing in disguise to the Government. (*ibid.*, p. 43)

24 Moyser and Medhurst, *op., cit.*, pp. 333f.; cf. the first 'impressionistic observation' reported at the beginning of this chapter.
25 *ibid.*, p. 338.
26 *ibid.*, p. 339.
27 *ibid.*
28 Cf. John Habgood, *Church and Nation in a Secular Age* (Darton, Longman &
Todd, 1983), chs. 2-4, and Gill, *Prophecy and Praxis, passim.*
29 Moyser and Medhurst, *op. cit.*, pp. 272-3.
30 *ibid.*, p. 273.
31 *ibid.*, p. 364.
32 *ibid.*, pp. 291-2; cf. Part II of George Moyser (ed.), *Church and Politics
Today.*
33 Michael Fogarty, *Policy Studies* 9.4 (Summer 1989), p. 47.
34 I would argue that impacts ought to be analysed in terms of the targets which
they are intended to affect. The notion of 'targets' is one which is embedded in
a general theory of strategic planning for social change which includes the following categories:
   – A *goal* is an outcome one hopes to see realized; e.g., the raising of
almost all of those who now have an income below the 'poverty line' to a level
that is considered 'adequate' in terms of their ability to obtain safe nutrition,
housing, medical care, etc.;
   – A *programme* (or a *policy*) is an institutional arrangement that contributes
significantly to a desired goal (e.g., a guaranteed annual income which is
available to all in need through a negative income tax or some similar device);
   – A *target* is a person, agency, organization or identifiable reference group
which must be persuaded, cajoled, manipulated, intimidated or in some sense
moved into doing something it has the power to do which helps to bring about
the achievement of a goal;
   – A *tactic* is an action taken with the intention of moving a target effectively;
   – An *agent* is a person, agency, group or organization which can carry out
an effective tactic in regard to some target and goal.
   These categories of analysis are employed in the speculative judgments
about impact in the final section of this chapter.
35 It is obvious, by the way, that one of the sub-groups within the church constituency which benefits most from social witness activities is the ecclesiastical
staff itself, which finds much reinforcement for its own sense of worth from
the excitement and sense of purpose generated by its own expenditure of
energy in 'doing the Lord's work.' This is by no means unimportant – but
since it has to do with the internal/instrumental goals of the Church instead of
the external/consummatory goals which are of most interest to us, we shall say
no more about this point.
36 Interview, 14 June 1990.
37 A prominent Church of England executive reportedly feels that personages
such as Bishop Jenkins play into this by making 'wild' statements that are
bound to be perceived as heresy or partisan political pleading.
38 *The Times*, 30 January 1990.
39 Simon Lee and Peter Stanford, *Believing Bishops* (Faber & Faber, 1990),
p. 28.
40 *ibid.*, pp. 28-9.

41 Interview, 23 June 1988. One of the colourful tactics used in 1980 was to dramatize the inadequacy of prevailing appropriations by having bishops walking around residential areas putting up posters announcing 'This house must last 450 years.'

42 *ibid.*, p. 30.

43 These opinions were expressed in my interviews with Richard O'Brien and Eric James.

44 Graham Bowpitt, 'The Church of England and Social Policy in the 1980s,' in Maria Brenton and Clare Ungeson, *Social Policy Review 1988–89* (Longmans, 1989).

45 Hilary Russell, *The Bird's Eye Debate* (Merseyside Churches' Urban Institute and Centre for Urban Studies of the University of Liverpool, 1990), p. 22.

46 Interview, 26 June 1988.

7 Evaluation

1 Interview #19, 12 July 1988. Cf. Digby Anderson, *The Church's Debate on Social Affairs* (Centre for the Study of Religion and Society, 1987), and Antony Flew, *The Philosophy of Poverty: Good Samaritans or Procrusteans?* (Social Affairs Unit, 1985).

2 David Martin, 'The Church of England: From Established Church to Secular Lobby,' in Digby Anderson (ed.), *The Kindness That Kills* (SPCK, 1984), p. 140.

3 *ibid.*

4 Roger Scruton, *The Meaning of Conservatism* (Pelican Books, 1980), pp. 171, 170; cited in Paul Weller, 'Thinking the Unthinkable and Saying the Unsayable,' in David Edgar, Kenneth Leech and Paul Weller (eds.), *The New Right and the Church* (The Jubilee Group, 1985), p. 43.

5 Interview #8 (with a very highly regarded scholar, the author of numerous books, and an Anglican of international stature who knows the inner councils of the Church very well).

6 Kenneth Leech, *Struggle in Babylon* (Darton, Longman & Todd, 1989), p. 147. The same point is made even more emphatically by Raymond Plant, who faults its authors for not realizing that its Pollyanna-ish assumptions about the prevailing culture ignore the extent to which large numbers of British citizens (especially, of course, those influenced by New Right ideology) are in *fundamental disagreement* with traditional Christian notions concerning social solidarity and the appropriate role of government in a welfare state:

> . . . To what extent is it morally right for government to use its coercive power, for example through the tax system, to make sure that . . . an equitable distribution of social resources [is actualized]? One traditional answer to this question is that government should seek to ensure social justice . . . [and] this traditional assumption is both mirrored in *Faith in the City* and challenged by the New Right, who regard the pursuit of social justice as a mirage. . . . So at the heart of the social theology of *Faith in the City* is an unmet challenge to one of its central assumptions, and one which goes to the centre of its presumed view about the nature and the role of government.

See Raymond Plant *et al*, 'Conservative Capitalism: Theological and Moral Challenges,' in Anthony Harvey (ed.), *Theology in the City* (SPCK, 1989), p. 71.

7   Walter Schwarz, *The New Dissenters* (Belford Square Press, 1989), p. 16. Rebuke of political *naïveté* is often exceedingly blunt. After defining the Right as 'the political tendency within capitalism which seeks to preserve (or where necessary to restore) the status quo and oppose change . . . [and] to conserve, preserve, defend and maintain the world-wide structures of capitalism,' Kenneth Leech goes on to assert that when things are well under control the ruling classes present a human face to the world – but 'when confronted by the possibility of its own destruction, [the Right] becomes brutal and cruel.' He quotes with approval an Irish rebel who declared, 'One great strength of the ruling class has ever been their willingness to kill in defense of their power and privileges.'

8   Edgar, *et al*, *op. cit.*, pp. 16–17.

9   John M. Krumm, *Letters from Lambeth* (Forward Movement Publications, 1988), p. 15.

10 Interview #104, 20 September 1989.

11 Charles Elliott, 'Preface to a Document,' in Kenneth Leech (ed.), *The Bishops and the Economy* (The Jubilee Group, 1985), p. 1.

12 *ibid.*, p. 2. According to Elliott, the Bishops would say that the purpose of their statement is to 'get Catholics to see that the politics and practicalities must be made subservient to the Gospel,' and this can be done, because 'It's not different in principle to labour law,' where we have come a long way (towards improvement) since 1919. He concludes:

> There's the rub: is reform of the international economic system . . . 'no different in principle' to reform of labour law? I believe it is utterly different, [for] the very nature of the accumulation process in international capital is such that a thorough-going address to the terms of trade problem is inconsistent with the survival of international capitalism. (*ibid.*)

He adds: 'And that is a hard message for Middle America – which could be one reason why the Pastoral, though long on the rhetoric . . . of the preferential option for the poor, finally fails to face the hard truths' (*ibid.*).

13 Brian Wren, 'Movements for Change – Issues in World Development Action,' in Dideri Mattijsen (ed.), *Church, Society and Change* (CIP-gegevens Koninklijke Bibliotheek, 1985), pp. 106, 107.

14 Interview #12, 13 June 1988.

15 Schwarz, *op. cit.*, p. 17.

16 To presume to evaluate the efforts of a group of fellow Christian activists is always a perilous undertaking. On the one hand, one hardly feels entitled to criticize: they have probably done more than you ever have, and besides, there are so few people who are actively and consistently striving to make a better world that you hate to undermine their efforts by saying anything at all which may be construed as belittling their achievements. On the other hand, of course, it is incumbent upon the serious analyst to call 'em as he sees 'em, and the Cause is too important to forgo serving it by expressing your considered judgments.

17 Raymond Plant and Kenneth Hoover, *Conservative Capitalism in Britain and the United States* (Routledge, 1989).

18   Gordon S. Wood, *The Creation of the American Republic* (University of North
      Carolina Press, 1969), pp. 66, 68.
19   I realize that what I am urging here is rather tricky – that is, it must be done
      very adroitly, or it *will* be seized upon by the right and used for purposes
      which we do not wish to serve.

      Even so, I am in fundamental agreement with Krouse and McPherson's
      conviction that 'welfare policy, while fulfilling the right of the needy to
      assistance, can also justifiably impose constraints on recipients that discourage
      dependence and self-damaging or antisocial conduct.' They reinforce their
      argument by quoting an insightful comment from Christopher Jencks:

> Those who work should end up 'better off' than those who do not
> work. . . . Even if *nobody* quit work to go on welfare, a system that pro-
> vided indolent Phyllis [who does not make any attempt to find employment]
> with just as much money as diligent Sharon [who works] would be
> universally viewed as unjust. To say that such a system does not increase
> indolence – or doesn't increase it much – is beside the point. . . . We care
> about justice independent of its effects on behavior.

      See Richard Krouse and Michael McPherson, 'The Logic of Liberal Equality,'
      in J. Donald Moon (ed.), *Responsibility, Rights and Welfare* (Westview Press,
      1988), p. 89.
20   I am deeply sceptical of psychological or sociological *reductionism*, i.e., an
      attempt to offer factors associated with social location as a *complete* explana-
      tion for what someone says on substantive matters (as though one's stance
      were *nothing but* a function of class, childhood psychology, etc.). Recent
      events have provided some thought-provoking evidence on this point, for I
      find that persons who inhabit the same social location have an almost *infinite*
      variety of viewpoints concerning the war in the Persian Gulf. As I listen to
      them explain their stance on this particular issue, with all its complexities, it
      seems clear beyond question that whatever they say is a matter of *reasoned
      moral conviction*, not a function of their social status, their profession, their
      economic condition or anything else apart from *what they really believe is
      right.* They may be selective about the facts they consider, and their interpreta-
      tion of the facts may be problematic – but if such errors exist, it is not because
      their perceptions or interpretations are *predetermined* by their social location. I
      may not agree with their normative assumptions (their beliefs about right and
      wrong), and I may not be fully persuaded by the moral reasoning which leads
      them from assumptions to conclusions about what policies ought to be pursued
      – but in neither case is it a foregone conclusion that either of us will begin
      with certain first principles instead of others, use a given mode of moral logic,
      or reach whatever conclusions we do in fact arrive at.
21   Perhaps the best way to make this point is to reiterate the familiar (and com-
      forting) principle of the need for a variety of strategies and the legitimacy of
      various vocations. This principle is certainly true and valuable, not only as a
      warning against self-righteousness and contention within the ranks of the
      would-be prophets, but also as an absolutely essential recognition of the need
      to have many different agents fighting against many different targets by using
      all kinds of tactics on several fronts. To say this is to endorse an overall
      strategy which calls for societal reformers to have some of their forces
      engaged primarily in providing relief to the downtrodden through pastoral

work, some using government and corporation money to rehabilitate the unemployed, some pursuing incremental change through policy innovations in secular institutions, and some devoting their lives to revolutionary transformation of social structures and/or theological ideas – and we certainly need to have all parties maintaining respect for the integrity of the vocations of allies involved on other fronts, so that arguments about priorities and in-fighting for funds do not result in destructive factionalism.

22   See above, p. 64. As Preston observes, localism consistently makes it difficult for denominational officers to get the entire national membership to do *any-thing*, especially carry out a plan which is frankly intended to redistribute finances, personnel, and status or power to hitherto neglected fellow Anglicans and fellow citizens.

23   The jargon may be annoying, but the point is extremely important: one should never confuse successful completion of organizational tasks (the money is raised, the programmes are smoothly run and well attended) with the achievement of the goals for which all this organizational bustling about is presumably done and towards which it is directed. There is no automatic correlation between the two, and functionaries who *assume* this correlation and fix their attention on programmatic success have succumbed to the grievous sin of goal-displacement.

24   King's audiences (many of whom were very conservative religiously, and previously steeped in the notion that the Church should concentrate on works of mercy and piety while avoiding the contamination of politics) would have recognized the allusion to the 'Montgomery [Alabama] Improvement Association,' which King founded to support the bus boycott in 1955 which in effect began the American civil rights movement of the next decade and a half.

25   Schwarz, *op. cit.*, p. 58.

26   *ibid.*, p. 57.

27   *ibid.*, p. 57. Cf. Tony Addy and Duncan Scott, *Fatal Impacts: The MSC and Voluntary Action* (The William Temple Foundation, 1988).

28   I do not believe, however, that Paul Ramsey's attack on America's social action leadership for not giving sufficient attention to *deliberation* is applicable to the Church of England in any serious way or to any alarming degree. It may be true that a long deliberative process – with much attendant publicity – captures public attention and therefore ensures greater impact; indeed, that advantage is a feature of *Faith in the City* as well as of Vatican II and the two pastoral letters issued recently by the American Roman Catholic bishops. But the study-group process followed by the BSR almost always has *enough* expertise and takes *enough* time to obviate Ramsey's criticism. What a conservative neoscholastic such as Ramsey *really* disliked about the World Council of Churches' Geneva conference in 1966 was *what it said* (just as what the New Right most abhors is the position taken by the BSR on most issues).

29   Peter Singer, 'Rights and the Market,' in John Arthur and William H. Shaw (eds.), *Justice and Economic Distribution* (Prentice-Hall, 1978), pp. 207–21.

30   Cited in Stanley L. Brue, 'Poverty and Income Inequality,' in John A. Schiller (ed.), *The American Poor* (Augsburg, 1989) p. 85.

31   See Raymond Plant, *et al*, *Political Philosophy and Social Welfare* (Routledge & Kegan Paul, 1980).

32   See Drew Christiansen, 'Americanizing Catholic Social Teaching: The United States Bishops' Economic Pastoral and Recent Roman Teaching,' *Quarterly Review* 7.4 (Winter 1987), pp. 15–32.

33   See, *inter alia*, Martin Conroy and Derek Shearer, *Economic Democracy* (M.
      E. Sharpe, 1980).
34   Cited in Gary J. Dorrien, 'Economic Democracy,' *Christianity and Crisis*, 10
      September 1990, p. 274.
35   Ronald Stone and Dana Wilbanks, *Presbyterians and Peacemaking* (Advisory
      Council on Church and Society, 1985).
36   Ulrich Duchrow, *Global Economy* (World Council of Churches, 1987).
37   I am aware of the fact that I may be charged with culpable stupidity in failing
      to acknowledge that the time for desperation has come. What if, after all,
      incremental reform efforts are doomed to total futility? Perhaps I should state
      my reasons for believing that the two major objections to the very *possibility*
      of effective church social witness are finally less than compelling.
          The first of these objections would point to the overwhelming pressure of
      events, institutional inertia and a culture which glorifies and rewards self-
      seeking, and would conclude that the churches' pathetic attempt to speak up
      for a bit of altruism is altogether futile – and, because hopeless, not worth
      attempting. Or – less cynically and more in accord with tradition – a second
      line of attack might claim that an Established Church should not attempt to
      urge sectarian pieties upon a constituency and a culture which are more com-
      fortable with symbolic gestures towards compassion than with serious attempts
      to achieve compassionate outcomes through institutional policy.
          I believe that the first objection deserves to be taken more seriously than it
      sometimes is. For when one considers the enormous *momentum* developed by
      technological, economic and political variables which have elective affinities
      for one another – that is, which tend towards mutual reinforcement and
      acceleration, and thus give each other a decisive simultaneous boost – one is
      tempted to conclude that 'mere ideas,' especially ideas about morality, do not
      have a ghost of a chance to be heard, let alone prevail. In *The Prize* (Simon &
      Schuster, 1991), Daniel Yergin makes a rather persuasive case for the proposi-
      tion that 'hydrocarbon man' has an *addiction* to petroleum which will be
      extremely hard to break. Once it became clear that petroleum could be used to
      fuel the productive engine of industrial civilization in ways which produced
      both stupendous profits and colossal power for the corporations and nations
      which invested in and used it for economic, political and military purposes,
      what ideas would have had sufficient power to prevent or constrain the initial
      surge in that direction? And what ideas about ecology or long-term human
      welfare have the power even today to motivate the technologically developed
      nations to shift *promptly* to other energy sources?
          But moralists have always refused – rightly, I believe – to submit to the
      presumed futility of speaking the truth and striving for good. There are two
      reasons for this, either of which is compelling in itself to anyone who believes
      in the reality of the human soul and the abiding consequences of spiritual com-
      mitments. In the first place, there is always *some segment* of humanity which
      benefits *to some degree* from protests against injustice or exhortations to
      humane behaviour: it may be no more than 6% of a nation's population which
      is only 12% better off in some particular respect, but that represents several
      thousand people whose lives are decisively better off in such-and-such a way,
      and that in itself, although it is truly no more than a drop in a bottomless
      bucket, is exceedingly significant. Although the rock which Sisyphus rolls to
      the top of the hill always rolls back down, it may be that with each heroic
      effort there is a small bit of turf which is no longer subjected to the crushing

weight of the stone – and those yards or feet (or inches!) may mean the difference between life and death for some forms of life in the path of the relentless forces of degradation and destruction.

Moreover, as a greatly undervalued theologian of our time maintained, there is some sort of intrinsic worth in the very fact that these poor forked creatures who are made, however dimly, in the image of God, refuse to capitulate entirely in the face of evil. The very struggle against evil, although it can never succeed completely within history, is in itself a triumph of God in history: it does not have to succeed completely in order to be of enduring importance. (See Daniel Day Williams, 'Niebuhr and Liberalism,' in Charles Kegley and William Bretall (eds.), *Reinhold Niebuhr: Theological, Ethical and Political Thought* (Macmillan, 1956), pp. 206ff.)

But this point of view can only be a 'fallback position': it is too defeatist to suffice in itself, and it might serve to undercut maximum effort if it seemed to say that 'putting down markers' is all that one really can do, and therefore all one must aspire to do. I would submit that it is not at all unrealistic to believe in the efficacy of unrelenting demands for a *moral* assessment of the consequences of all important institutional policies, and to labour diligently for policies which can very well approximate to what Reinhold Niebuhr called a 'rough' or 'tolerable' justice in the life of a given society.

Although it is true enough to say that a Church should try to be effective instead of 'pure,' and therefore must not be ignorant, foolish nor *stupidly* unrealistic or 'extreme' in its analyses of human nature or society, and the limited potential of each, it is also true that twentieth-century churches (including, even, the Church of England!) are *and ought to be* unremitting in their demand that certain ethical fundamentals of the faith must be honoured in nations whose values are informed by the best resources of the Christian tradition.

38 David Nicholls, 'William Temple and the Welfare State,' *Crucible* (1984), p. 164.

39 This understanding of church membership was proposed twenty-five years ago in Stephen Rose, 'The Grass Roots Church: Manifesto for a Renewal Movement,' *Renewal* (February 1966), pp. 3–5.

40 It may be cavalier to make a proposal of this kind without being able to suggest a realistic plan for its actualization. But that is a matter which can only be decided by those who are closer to the British situation than I am, and who therefore know more about the realistic possibilities than I do. Even so, I propose this course of action as something which would be highly desirable if it could be achieved.

41 William C. Frederick, 'Corporate Social Responsibility in the Reagan Era and Beyond,' *California Management Review* 25.3 (Spring 1983), p. 155.

42 *ibid.*

43 *ibid.*, p. 156.

44 *ibid.*

Bibliography

BOOKS

Adams, Richard, *Who Profits?* (Oxford: Lion Publishing, 1989).

Addy, Tony and Duncan Scott, *Fatal Impacts: The MSC and Voluntary Action* (Manchester: William Temple Foundation, 1988).

Advisory Council for the Church's Ministry, *Teaching Christian Ethics* (London: SCM Press, 1974).

Aganbegyan, Abel, *The Challenge: Economics of Perestroika* (London: Hutchinson, 1988).

Agenda for Social Democracy (London: Institute of Economic Affairs, 1983).

Allison, Graham, *Essence of Decision* (Boston: Little, Brown & Co., 1971).

Ambler, Rex and David Haslam (eds.), *Agenda for Prophets* (London: Bowerdean Press, 1980).

Anderson, Digby (ed.), *The Church's Debate on Social Affairs* (London: Centre for the Study of Religion and Society, 1987).

—, *The Kindness That Kills* (London: SPCK, 1984).

Anderson, Digby, June Lait and David Marsland, *Breaking the Spell of the Welfare State* (London: The Social Affairs Unit, 1981).

Arthur, John and William H. Shaw (eds.), *Justice and Economic Distribution* (Englewood Cliffs, N.J.: Prentice-Hall, 1978).

Atherton, John, *Faith in the Nation* (London: Mowbray, 1988).

Badham, Paul, *Religion, State and Society in Modern Britain* (Toronto: Edwin Mellen Press, 1989).

Barkat, Anwar M. and James Mutambirwa (eds.), *Challenge to the Church: A Theological Comment on the Political Crisis in South Africa* (Geneva: World Council of Churches, 1985).

Barker, Edwin and Ronald Preston, *Christians in Society* (London: SCM Press, 1939).

Barnett, Corelli, *The Audit of War* (London: Macmillan, 1986).

Bauer, P. T., *Western Guilt and Third World Poverty* (Washington, D.C.: Ethics and Public Policy Center, Georgetown University, 1976).

Beeson, Trevor, *Britain Today and Tomorrow* (London: Collins, 1978).

Bell, Daniel, *The End of Ideology* (New York: The Free Press, 1960).

Bellah, Robert, 'Religious Evolution,' in William Lessa and Evon Vogt (eds.), *Reader in Comparative Religion*, 2nd ed. (New York: Harper & Row, 1965), pp. 73–87.

Bennett, Gareth, 'Preface' to *Crockford's Clerical Directory* (London: Church House Publishing, 1987).

Block, Walter and Irving Hexham (eds.), *Religion, Economics and Social Thought* (Vancouver: The Fraser Institute, 1986).

Blunkett, David and Keith Jackson, *Democracy in Crisis: The Town Halls Respond* (London: Hogarth Press, 1987).

Booker, Christopher, *The Seventies* (London: Penguin Books, 1980).

Bowpitt, Graham, 'The Church of England and Social Policy in the 1980s,' in Maria Brenton and Clare Ungeson, *Social Policy Review 1988–89* (London: Longmans, 1989).

The Brandt Commission, *Common Crisis* (London: Pan Books, 1983).

—, *North–South: A Programme for Survival* (London: Pan Books, 1980).

Brownhill, Sue, *Developing London's Docklands: Another Planning Disaster* (London: Paul Chapman, 1990).

Business for People (London: Industrial Christian Fellowship, 1986).

Carnoy, Martin and Derek Shearer, *Economic Democracy* (Armonk, N.Y.: M.E. Sharpe, Inc., 1980).

Changing Industrial Mission: Models and Hopes (London: Industrial Mission Association Theology Development Group, n.d.)

Churches and the Transnational Corporations (Geneva: World Council of Churches, 1983).

Churches – Transnational Corporations: European Dialogue, 1975–1980 (Bruxelles: UNIAPAC, 1980).

Clark, Henry, *The Christian Case Against Poverty* (New York: Association Press, 1965).

Clarke, Roger, *Work in Crisis* (Edinburgh: St Andrew Press, 1982).

Coal, Church and Community (Durham: Theological Consultancy to the North-East Churches, 1986).

Coates, David and F. H. Hilliard, *What Went Wrong?* (Nottingham: Russell Press, 1979).

The Creation of Wealth (Manchester: The William Temple Foundation, 1984).

Davies, John D., *On Creating Wealth* (London: Industrial Christian Fellowship, 1987).

Davis, Howard and David Gosling, *Will the Future Work?* (Geneva: World Council of Churches, 1986).

Deakin, Nicholas, *The Politics of Welfare* (London: Methuen, 1987).

Dennis, Norman and A. H. Halsey, *English Ethical Socialism* (Oxford: Clarendon Press, 1988).

Dickinson, Richard D. N., *Poor, Yet Making Many Rich* (Geneva: World Council of Churches, 1982).

Diocese of Birmingham, *Faith in Birmingham* (Exeter: Paternoster Press, 1988).

Dorrien, Gary J., *The Democratic Socialist Vision* (London: Rowman & Littlefield, 1986).

Douglas, Mary and Aaron Wildavsky, *Risk and Culture* (Berkeley: University of California Press, 1982)

Douglass, R. Bruce (ed.), *The Deeper Meaning of Economic Life* (Washington: Georgetown University Press, 1986).

Duchrow, Ulrich, *Global Economy* (Geneva: World Council of Churches, 1987).

Duggan, Margaret, *Runcie: The Making of an Archbishop* (London: Hodder & Stoughton, 1983).

Edgar, David, Kenneth Leech and Paul Weller, *The New Right and the Church* (London: The Jubilee Group, 1985).

Edwards, David L. (ed.), *Priests and Workers* (London: SCM Press, 1961).

Eliot, T. S., *The Idea of a Christian Society* (London: Faber & Faber, 1939).

Elliott, Charles, *Comfortable Compassion* (London: Hodder & Stoughton, 1987).

Ellul, Jacques, *The Technological Society* (New York: Knopf, 1964).

Faith in the City: Theological and Moral Challenges (Winchester: The Diocese of Winchester, 1986).

Field, Frank, *Losing Out: The Emergence of Britain's Underclass* (Oxford: Basil Blackwell, 1989).

Flew, Anthony, *The Philosophy of Poverty* (London: The Social Affairs Unit, 1985).

Food, Work and Justice (Geneva: World Council of Churches, 1983).

Forrester, Duncan B., *Beliefs, Values and Policies* (Oxford: Clarendon Press, 1989).

—, *Christianity and the Future of Welfare* (London: Epworth Press, 1985).

— and Danus Skene, *Just Sharing* (London: Epworth, 1988).

Gannon, Thomas M., *The Catholic Challenge to the American Economy* (New York: Macmillan, 1987).

Gilbert, A. D., *The Making of Post-Christian Britain* (London: Longman, 1980).

—, *Religion and Society in Industrial England* (London: Longman, 1976).

Gill, Robin, *Prophecy and Praxis* (London: Marshall Morgan & Scott, 1981).

—, *Theology and Social Structure* (London: Mowbray, 1977).

Habgood, John, *Church and Nation in a Secular Age* (London: Darton, Longman & Todd, 1983).

Hall, Stuart and Martin Jacques (eds.), *The Politics of Thatcherism* (London: Lawrence & Wishart, 1983).

Harvey, Anthony (ed.), *Theology in the City* (London: SPCK, 1989).

Hastings, Adrian, *A History of English Christianity* (Cambridge: Cambridge University Press, 1987).

Hewitt, Gordon (ed.), *Strategist of the Spirit* (Oxford: Becket Publications, 1985).

Hexham, Irving, *The Bible, Justice and the Culture of Poverty* (London: The Social Affairs Unit, 1985).

Hinchliff, Peter, *Holiness and Politics* (Grand Rapids, Mich.: W. B. Eerdmans, 1982).

Hoggart, Richard, *The Uses of Literacy* (London: Penguin Books, 1957).

Hoover, Kenneth and Raymond Plant, *Conservative Capitalism in Britain and the United States* (London: Routledge, 1989).

Hopkins, C. Howard, *The Rise of the Social Gospel in American Protestantism, 1865-1915* (New Haven, Conn.: Yale University Press, 1940).

Houck, John W. and Oliver F. Williams, *Catholic Social Teaching and the U. S. Economy* (Washington: University Press of America, 1984).

Howse, E. M., *Saints in Politics* (Toronto: University of Toronto Press, 1952).

Illich, Ivan, *Medical Nemesis* (New York: Pantheon Books, 1976).

—, *Toward a History of Needs* (New York: Pantheon Books, 1977).

Jenkins, Peter, *Mrs Thatcher's Revolution* (London: Jonathan Cape, 1987).

Jenkins, Daniel, *The British: Their Identity and their Religion* (London: SCM Press, 1975).

Jessop, Bob, Kevin Bonnett, Simon Bromley and Tom Ling, *Thatcherism* (Oxford: Polity Press, 1988).

Jones, Peter d'A., *The Christian Socialist Revival 1877-1914* (Princeton, N.J.: Princeton University Press, 1968).

Knight, Derrick, *Beyond the Pale: The Christian Political Fringe* (Leigh, Lancaster: Caraf Publications, 1982).

Krumm, John M., *Letters from Lambeth* (Cincinnati: Forward Movement Publications, 1988).

Kuttner, Robert, *The Economic Illusion: False Choices Between Prosperity and Social Justice* (Boston: Houghton Mifflin Company, 1984).

Lee, Simon and Peter Stanford, *Believing Bishops* (London: Faber & Faber, 1990).

Leech, Kenneth (ed.), *The Bishops and the Economy* (London: The Jubilee Group, 1985).

— (ed.), *Christianity Reinterpreted?: A Critical Examination of the 1978 Reith Lectures* (London: Jubilee Publications, 1979).

— and Terry Drummond (eds.), *Letters From Seven Churches* (London: Jubilee Publications, 1984).

—, *Struggle in Babylon* (London: Darton, Longman & Todd, 1989).

— (ed.), *Till All Be Held in Common* (London: The Jubilee Group, 1981).

Lekachman, Robert, *The Age of Keynes* (New York: Random House, 1966).

Lessa, William and Evon Vogt (eds.), *Reader in Comparative Religion* (New York: Harper & Row, 1965).

MacIntyre, Alisdair, *After Virtue*, 2nd ed. (Notre Dame, Ind.: University of Notre Dame Press, 1984).

Marchant, Colin, *Signs of the City* (London: Hodder & Stoughton, 1985).

Marquand, David, *The Unprincipled Society* (London: Fontana Press, 1988).

Martin, Hugh (ed.), *Christian Social Reformers of the Nineteenth Century* (London: SCM Press, 1927).

Marwick, Arthur, *British Society Since 1945* (London: Penguin Books, 1982).

Masumoto, Shigeko, *Industrial Mission and the Church in Britain Today* (London: BSR, 1987).

Mattijsen, Dideri (ed.), *Church, Society and Change* (Den Haag: CIP-gegevens Koninklijke Bibliotheek, 1985).

May, Henry F., *Protestant Churches and Industrial America* (New York: Harper & Row, 1949).

Montefiore, Hugh, *Christianity and Politics* (London: Macmillan, 1989).

Moon, J. Donald, *Responsibility, Rights and Welfare: The Theory of the Welfare State* (Boulder, Colo.: Westview Press, 1988).

Moore, Peter, *The Synod of Westminster: Do We Need It?* (London: SPCK, 1986).

Moyser, George (ed.), *Church and Politics Today* (Edinburgh: T. & T. Clark, 1985).

— and Kenneth Medhurst (eds.), *Church and Politics in a Secular Age* (Oxford: Clarendon Press, 1988).

Munby, Denys, *Christianity and Economic Problems* (London: Macmillan, 1956).

—, *God and the Rich Society* (London: Oxford University Press, 1961).

Murchland, Bernard, *Humanism and Capitalism* (Washington: American Enterprise Institute, 1984).

Neuhaus, Richard John, *The Naked Public Square* (Grand Rapids, Mich.: W. B. Eerdmans, 1984).

Newbigin, Lesslie, *The Other Side of 1984* (Geneva: World Council of Churches, 1983).

Norman, Edward R., *Christianity and World Order* (Oxford: Oxford University Press, 1979).

—, *Church and Society in England, 1770-1970* (Oxford: Clarendon Press, 1976).

—, *The Victorian Socialists* (Cambridge: Cambridge University Press, 1987).

Orens, John R., *Politics and the Kingdom: The Legacy of the Anglican Left* (London: Jubilee Publications, 1981).

Paradise, Scott. I., *Detroit Industrial Mission* (New York: Harper & Row, 1968).

Perman, David, *Change and the Churches* (London: The Bodley Head, 1978).

Plant, Raymond *et al*, *Political Philosophy and Social Welfare* (London: Routledge & Kegan Paul, 1980).

—, *Responding to Faith in the City: Report from the Diocese of Winchester's Working Party on Faith in the City* (Winchester, 1986).

Poverty (London: British Council of Churches, 1982).

Preston, Ronald H., *Explorations in Theology 9* (London: SCM Press, 1981).

—, *The Future of Christian Ethics* (London: SCM Press, 1987).

Putting Theology to Work (Manchester: William Temple Foundation, 1983).

Raban, Jonathan, *God, Man and Mrs Thatcher* (London: Chatto & Windus, 1989).

Ramsey, Paul, *Who Speaks for the Church?* (Nashville and New York: Abingdon Press, 1967).

Randerson, Richard, *Christian Ethics and the New Zealand Economy* (Auckland: Diocese of Wellington, 1987).

Rasmussen, Douglas and James Sterba, *The Catholic Bishops and the Economy* (New Brunswick and London: Transaction Books, 1987).

Reckitt, M. B., *Maurice to Temple* (London: Faber & Faber, 1947).

Roof, Wade Clark and William McKinney *American Mainline Religion* (New Brunswick: Rutgers University Press, 1987).

Sacks, Jonathan, *Wealth and Poverty: A Jewish Analysis* (London: The Social Affairs Unit, 1985).

Sadowsky, James, *The Christian Response to Poverty: Working with God's Economic Laws* (London: The Social Affairs Unit, 1985).

Santa Ana, Julio, *Separation Without Hope* (Geneva: World Council of Churches, 1978).

Schiller, John A. (ed.), *The American Poor* (Minneapolis: Augsburg, 1982).

Schwarz, Walter, *The New Dissenters* (London: Belford Square Press, 1989).

Sedgwick, Peter, *Mission Impossible* (London: Collins, 1990).

Seger, Imogen, *Durkheim and His Critics on the Sociology of Religion* (New York: Columbia University Bureau of Applied Social Research, 1957).

Sheppard, David, *Bias to the Poor* (London: Hodder & Stoughton, 1983).

Singer, Peter, 'Rights and the Market,' in John Arthur and William H. Shaw (eds.), *Justice and Economic Distribution* (Englewood Cliffs, N.J.: Prentice-Hall, 1978), pp. 207-21.

The Single European Act (Brussels: European Ecumenical Commission for Church and Society, 1988),

Stain, Charles R. (ed.), *Prophetic Visions and Economic Realities* (Grand Rapids, Mich.: W. B. Eerdmans, 1989).

Stevenson, John, *British Society 1914-45* (London: Penguin Books, 1984).

Stone, Ronald and Dana Wilbanks, *Presbyterians and Peacemaking* (New York: Advisory Council on Church and Society, 1985).

Stout, Jeffrey, *Ethics After Babel* (Boston: Beacon Press, 1988).

Studdert-Kennedy, G. A., *Democracy and the Dog Collar* (London: Hodder & Stoughton, 1921).

Suggate, Alan, *William Temple and Christian Social Ethics Today* (Edinburgh: T. & T. Clark, 1987).

Tawney, R.H., *The Acquisitive Society* (London: Bell & Son, 1921).

—, *Equality* (London: Unwin, 1964).

—, *R. H. Tawney's Commonplace Book* (Cambridge: Cambridge University Press, 1972).

Taylor, Michael H. (ed.), *Christians and the Future of Social Democracy* (Ormskirk, Lancashire: G. W. & A. Heskith, 1981).

Temple, William, *Christianity and Social Order* (London: Penguin Books, 1942).
—, *Citizen and Churchman* (London: Eyre & Spottiswoode, 1941).
—, *The Church Looks Forward* (London: Macmillan, 1944).
—, *Nature, Man and God* (London: Macmillan, 1934).
Thane, P., *The Foundations of the Welfare State* (London: Longman, 1982).
Thatcher, Margaret, Speech to the General Assembly of the Church of Scotland, 23 May 1988. (Commonly referred to as 'The Sermon on the Mound.') Reprinted in Jonathan Raban, *God, Man and Mrs Thatcher* (London: Chatto & Windus, 1989).
Thompson, E. P., *The Making of the English Working Class* (New York: Alfred A. Knopf, 1966).
Timms, Noel and David Watson (eds.), *Talking About Welfare* (London: Routledge & Kegan Paul, 1976).
Vogel, David, *Lobbying the Corporation* (New York: Basic Books, 1978).
Welby, Peter A., *A History of the Church of England* (Oxford: Oxford University Press, 1984).
The Welfare State in the 1980s (Manchester: William Temple Foundation, 1982).
Welsby, Paul A., *A History of the Church of England* (Oxford: Oxford University Press, 1984).
—, *How the Church of England Works* (London: Church Information Office Publishing, 1985).
What Have You Done to Your Homeless Brother? (London: Catholic Truth Society, 1988).
Which Future for Scotland (Edinburgh: S. R. T. Home Board, Church of Scotland, 1979).
Wickham, E. R., *Church and People in an Industrial City* (London: Lutterworth Press, 1957).
Wiener, Martin J., *English Culture and the Decline of the Industrial Spirit, 1850–1980* (Cambridge: Cambridge University Press, 1981).
Williams, Daniel Day, 'Niebuhr and Liberalism,' in Charles Kegley and William Bretall (eds.), *Reinhold Niebuhr: Theological, Ethical and Political Thought* (New York: Macmillan, 1956).
Winner, Langdon, *Autonomous Technology* (Cambridge, Mass.: MIT Press, 1977).
Wogaman, J. Philip, *Christian Perspectives on Politics* (London: SCM Press, 1988).
—, *The Great Economic Debate* (Philadelphia: Westminster Press, 1977).
Wood, Gordon S., *The Creation of the American Republic* (Chapel Hill: University of North Carolina Press, 1969).
Work, Unemployment and the Churches (Manchester: William Temple Foundation, 1986).
Yergin, Daniel, *The Prize* (New York: Simon & Schuster, 1991).
Young, Hugo, *One of Us* (London: Macmillan/Pan, 1989).

BSR DOCUMENTS

The Church of England has its own publishing firm in London, and most of the studies produced by the BSR and all other official branches of the Church are published by this company, which is known as Church House Publishing. Since most of the sources used in the main text of this book are produced by the BSR, I use that designation in the Notes.

Adams, Kenneth, *Ethical Choice and Business Responsibilities* (1975).

Anglicans and Racism (1986).

Annual Report of the Anglican Association for Social Responsibility (1986)

Atherton, John, 'Can a Christian Legitimately Support a Social Market Economy?' (1986). (IC/16/86)

Beales, Chris, *Mainstream and Marginal* (1990).

Bennett, Ian, David Horn and Rob Morris, *Before You Leap: A Practical Guide for Ministers About Moving to an Inner City Parish* (Advisory Council for the Church's Ministry Occasional Paper No. 28, 1988).

'A Briefing on Housing' (11 April 1983).

Board for Social Responsibility Annual Report (1982-90; GS 564D, 617D, 723, 768, 815, 870 and 913).

Changing Britain (1987).

Christian Faith and Economic Policies and Priorities (1991).

Church and Economy (1989)

The Church of England and the World Council of Churches (1979).

The Common Agricultural Policy and World Hunger (BSR Briefing No. 6, 1982).

Cover letter sent out to selected recipients of *Industrial Mission: An Appraisal* in 1989. Letter is designated BSR (89).

'Dear Mr Green': Responses to IM – An Appraisal (1989).

Development Education (1983).

Dyson, Anthony (ed.), *Transnational Corporations; Confronting the Issues* (1983).

Ecclestone, Giles, *The Church of England and Politics* (1981).

Edwards, David, *The State of the Nation* (1976).

Facing the Facts: The United Kingdom and South Africa (GS 529, 1982).

Faith in the City (London: Church House Publishing, 1985).

Gilbertson, Geoffrey, *Power-Sharing in Industry: A Pattern for the Future* (1975).

Growth, Justice and Work (1985).

Harris, Richard, 'Morality and Markets' (1986). (IC/15/86)

Housing and Homelessness (GS 541, 1982).

I.M. – An Appraisal: The Church's Response to the Changing Industrial and Economic Order (1988).

Industrial Mission and the Church in Britain Today. A series of six papers commissioned by the Industrial and Economic Affairs Committee of the BSR (1987).

The International Year of Shelter for the Homeless (GS 783, 1987).

Leech, Kenneth, *The Fields of Charity and Sin: Reflections on Combating Racism in the Church of England* (1986).

— (ed.), *Theology and Racism: The Bible, Racism and Anti-Semitism* (1985).

Let Justice Flow: A Contribution to the Debate About Development (1986).

'Linking Up: An Interim Report to Sponsors' (1989).

Living Faith in the City (1990).

Man in His Living Environment (1970).

Mission and Ministry Examined (1989).

Not Just for the Poor: Christian Perspectives on the Welfare State (GS 756, 1986).

Our Responsibility for the Living Environment (GS 718, 1986).

Owers, Anne, *Sheep and Goats: British Nationality Law and its Effects* (1984).

—, *Families Divided: Immigration Control and Family Life* (1984).

Peacemaking in a Nuclear Age (1988).

Preston, R. H., 'Toward a Transnational Social Ethic' (1982)

Proceedings of the General Synod (published each year).

Reform of Social Security (1985).

Reflections on Brandt (1980).

Siddons, James, *The Eurotunnel and the Churches* (Churches' Consortium on Industrial Mission/BSR, 1988)

Survey of Parish Audits (21 November 1988).

The Social Fund (1988).

Theology and Social Concern (1986).

Theology in Practice (Advisory Council for the Church's Ministry Occasional Paper No. 29, 1988).

Transnational Corporations (1982).

Twenty Questions: Making Synod Documents Work (Resource Paper No. 2 of the Board of Education of the Church of England, 1990).

Working for Patients (GS 887, 1989).

Understanding Closed Shops (GS-Misc. 66, 1977).

Wickham, E. R., *Growth and Inflation* (1975).

Wilkinson, John, Renate Wilkinson and James H. Evans, Jr., *Inheritors Together: Black People in the Church of England* (1985).

Winters of Discontent (GS 481, 1981).

Work and the Future (GS 429, 1979).

Work or What? A Christian Examination of the Unemployment Crisis (1977).

Working for Patients (1989).

OCCASIONAL PAPERS AND ARTICLES

Annual Report of the Social Responsibility Office of the Diocese of Chelmsford, 1989.

Atherton, John, 'Feasible Alternatives to a Two-Nations Policy' (Oxford: Oxford Institute for Church and Society, 1985).

Atkinson, Michael, 'Morale and Motivation – Particularly in Church House' (1982).

—, 'Much Ado about Norman,' *Crucible* (1979), pp. 1–4.

— and Paul Brett (eds.), *Mission in Industrial Society* (Papers from the Industrial Mission Association in Britain for a Conference at the Selly Oak Colleges, Birmingham, 1978).

'Attitudes to Industry in Britain.' Proceedings of a conference at St. George's House, Windsor Castle, 17–19 September 1984.

Avis, Paul, 'The Church's One Foundation,' *Theology* 89 (1986).

Blewitt, Jane *et al*, 'Comments on the Second Draft of the NCCB Pastoral Letter on Catholic Teaching and the U. S. Economy' (Washington, D.C.: Center of Concern, 1985).

Bowpitt, Graham, 'The Church of England and Social Policy in the 1980s' (1988). Unpublished paper available through Alison Webster, BSR staff.

Brett, Paul, 'The British Churches' Response to the Problems of Unemployment' (1988).

Christian Action Journal, August 1983.

Christiansen, Drew, 'Americanizing Catholic Social Teaching: The United States Bishops' Economic Pastoral and Recent Roman Teaching,' *Quarterly Review* 7.4 (Winter 1987), pp. 15–32.

Davies, Mostyn, 'Local Economy Based Industrial Mission' (1988)

Dorrien, Gary J., 'Economic Democracy,' *Christianity and Crisis* (10 September 1990)

Dummett, Ann, 'Across Party Lines: The British Nationality Bill, the Lobbyists and the Churches,' *Modern Churchman* 25.1 (1982), pp. 36–43.

Dyson, Anthony, 'The Bishop of Durham and All That,' *Modern Churchman* 27 (1985).

Ecclestone, Giles, 'Church Influence on Public Policy Today, *Modern Churchman* 28.1 (1985), pp. 36–47.

—, 'The Conscience of the Nation' (Audenshaw Paper No. 110, 1986).

'The Ethics of Wealth Creation,' a position paper produced by the Division of Social Responsibility of the The Methodist Church [in Britain], 1990.

The Ecumenical Review 37.1 (January 1985); 40.2 and 40.3-4 (April 1988 and July–October 1988).

Farnell, Richard, 'Faith in the City and Local Politics' (1988). A mimeographed paper available from the Faith in the City Follow-Up Program Office at Church House in London.

Fechner, Bernd, 'Church and the Resurgence of Capitalism.' Mimeographed paper prepared and disseminated by the author (London, 1989).

Fogarty, Michael, *Policy Studies* 9.4 (Summer 1989), pp. 43–8.

Frederick, William C., 'Corporate Social Responsibility in the Reagan Era and Beyond,' *California Management Review* 25.3 (Spring 1983).

Gilbert, Claire, 'The Church of England and Public Policy' (1990).

—, 'The U. S. Catholic Bishops' Pastoral Letter on the U. S. Economy' (1990).

Grey, Alexander, 'Establishing Church and State Ethics,' *Crucible* (1982), pp. 51–9.

Gustafson, James M., 'An Analysis of Church and Society Social Ethical Writings,' *The Ecumenical Review* 40.2 (April 1988), pp. 267–78.

'Industry Matters' (1987). A follow-up newsletter produced by the Industry Year 1986 office.

Jones, Kathleen, 'The General Synod: 1975 Version,' *Crucible* (1979), pp. 152–8

Leonard, Graham, 'The Christian and Politics,' *Crucible* (1983), pp. 101–6.

Moyser, George, 'The 1980 General Synod: Patterns and Trends,' *Crucible* (1982), pp. 75–86.

—, 'Patterns of Representation in the Elections to the General Synod in 1975,' *Crucible* (1979), pp. 73–9.

National Conference of Catholic Bishops, 'Economic Justice For All: Catholic Social Teachings and the U. S. Economy (Third Draft)', *Origins* 16 (5 June 1986).

Nicholls, David, 'William Temple and the Welfare State,' *Crucible* (1984), pp. 161–8.

Page, Trevor, 'The Making of the Synod,' *Crucible* (1981), pp. 116–23.

Preston, Ronald H., 'Anglican and Ecumenical Styles in Social Ethics, *Crucible* (1978), pp. 117–26.

Pym, B. A., 'Pressure Groups on Moral Issues,' *Political Quarterly* 43 (1972), pp. 321f.

Roberts, Richard, 'Religion and the "Enterprise Culture": The British Experience in the Thatcher Era (1979–90).' A paper presented at a conference on 'Religion and the Resurgence of Capitalism' at Lancaster University, July 1991.

Russell, Hilary (ed.), *The Bird's Eye Debate* (Liverpool: Merseyside Churches' Urban Institute and Centre for Urban Studies of the University of Liverpool, 1990)

Sleeman, John, *The Economics of the Distribution of Income and Wealth* (Edinburgh: Centre for Theology and Public Issues, Occasional Paper No. 15, 1988).

The Social Fund: An Urgent Problem for the Churches. A document prepared by
The Division of Social Responsibility of The Methodist Church in association
with The British Council of Churches' Division of Community Affairs (1988).

Tiranti, Dexter, 'The Big Clampdown,' *The New Internationalist*, No. 133 (March
1984).

Tweedie, Jill, 'Why It Became a Matter of Pride to Bite the Hand that Feeds You'
(The *Guardian*, 10 October 1983).

Twine, Fred, 'The Distribution of Wealth and Income' (Edinburgh: Centre for
Theology and Public Issues, Occasional Paper No. 14, 1988).

Wickham, E. R., *The Task of the Church in Relation to Industry – 1986* (1986).

Williams, John A., 'A Bishop Should Speak Out – But What Can He Say?' in
Crucible (January 1985), pp. 14–21.

Yates, John and John Gladwin, Reply to Mrs Thatcher's Speech to the General
Assembly of the Church of Scotland. (An open letter, printed in *The Times*, 23
May 1988.)